IMAGES
of America

THE JEWISH COMMUNITIES OF GREATER STAMFORD

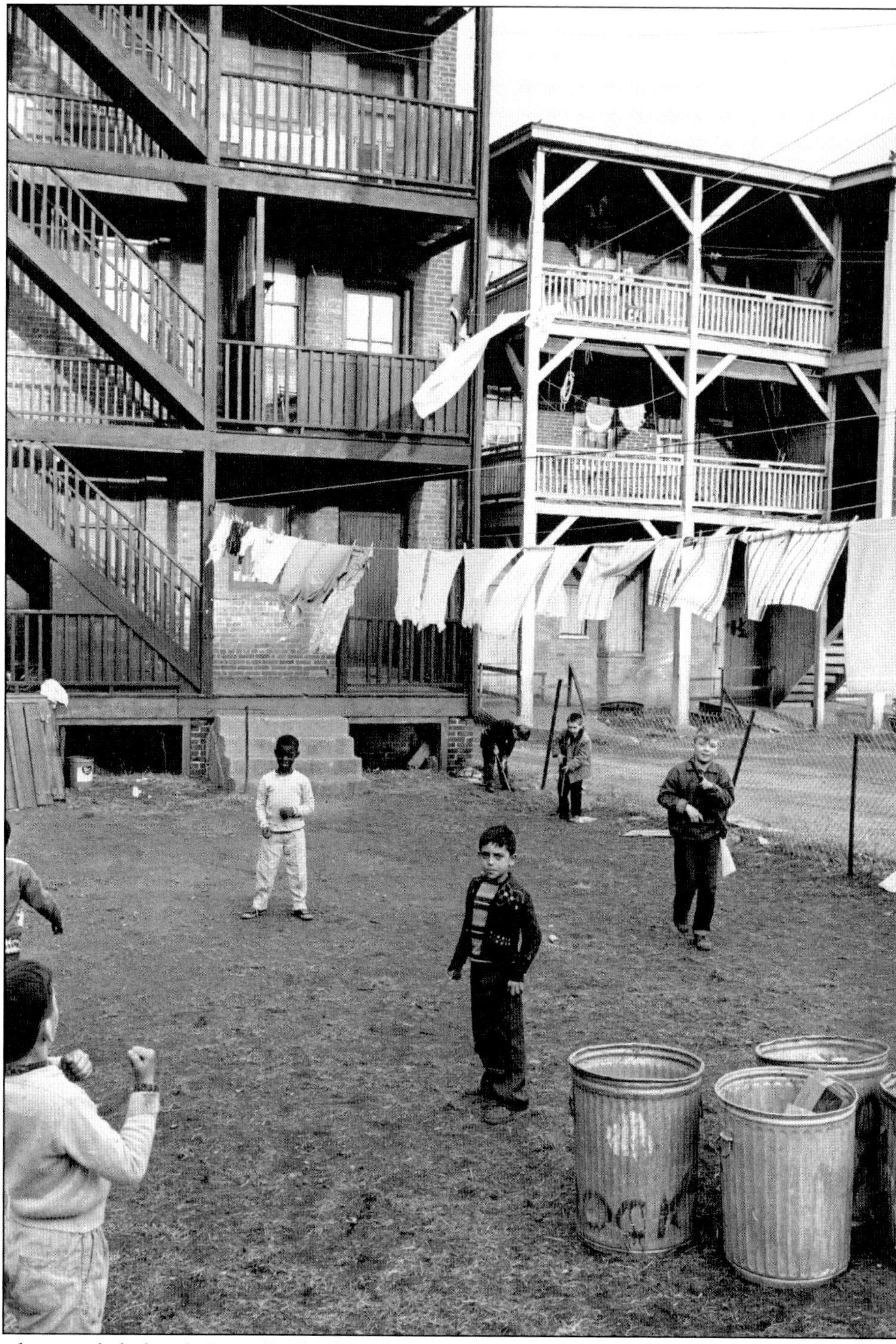

In the yard behind Brazel's kosher butcher store, neighborhood youngsters play an impromptu game. The Pacific Street tenements were home to many immigrant groups. In 1967, urban redevelopment replaced the entire area with the Stamford Town Center, a regional shopping mall.

IMAGES of America

THE JEWISH COMMUNITIES OF GREATER STAMFORD

Linda Baulsir and Irwin Miller

ARCADIA PUBLISHING

ISBN 978-0-7385-1144-3

Published by Arcadia Publishing
Charleston, South Carolina

Printed in the United States of America

Library of Congress Catalog Card Number: 2002111903

For all general information contact Arcadia Publishing at:
Telephone 843-853-2070
Fax 843-853-0044
E-mail sales@arcadiapublishing.com
For customer service and orders:
Toll-Free 1-888-313-2665

Visit us on the Internet at www.arcadiapublishing.com

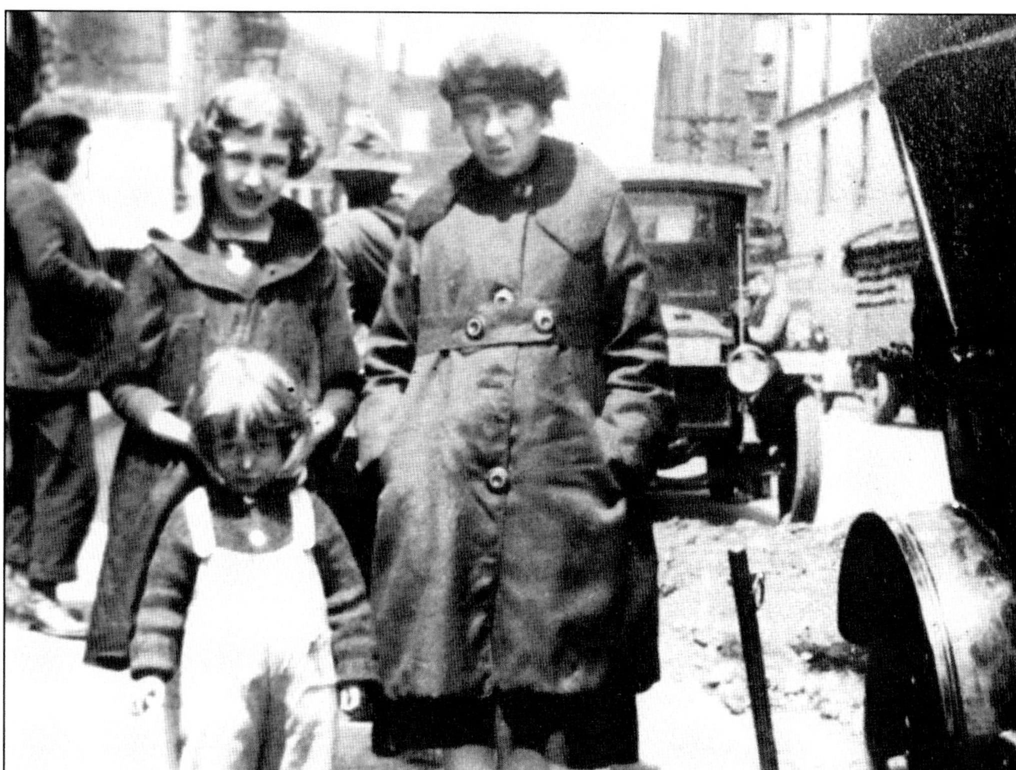

Shown on Pacific Street in 1922 are Rose Sherman (left), toddler Seymour Wattenberg, and Rose Sandhaus.

Contents

ACKNOWLEDGMENTS

We are most grateful to Vivian Miller, who tirelessly keeps the archives organized; Eileen Nemoitin, who was an invaluable right hand as we sorted through the archives; Ellie Scher, who taught us how to use a semicolon and reviewed and rereviewed the captions and narrative materials; and Arnold and Rob Yelin, who donated their professional expertise and services. In addition, for their efforts and commitment in making publication of the images of our Jewish community possible, we are indebted to Jeanette Fishkow, Evelyn Fowler, Maggie Levy, Evelyn Sutin, Gail G. Trell, and the individuals and organizations who donated their precious photographs and documents to the archives of the Jewish Historical Society of Greater Stamford. Thank you.

—Linda Baulsir and Irwin Miller

To Ed Baulsir, who couldn't have known what a roller coaster ride his life would be when he asked me to marry him in 1954.

To Vivian Miller, my wife of 55 years, I can only thank her for her patience and fortitude in being at my side whether it was scrambling through a pioneer Jewish gold rush cemetery in California or delving into old Stamford records at the vault at Government Center.

The adventures and love continue.

INTRODUCTION

Photographs and paper-based ephemera give a broad historical view of the people and activities that constitute the Jewish communities of Stamford, New Canaan, Greenwich, Darien, and Pound Ridge.

Moses Levy was the first Jew of record in Stamford. On June 23, 1698, he purchased a slave named Dinah from Mary Turney, mother of Samuel Hoyt who was the builder of Stamford's oldest existing structure the Hoyt Barnum House.

The pioneer Jewish settler in Greenwich was Abraham Hays, who arrived in 1728; he married Elizabeth Finch and became a prominent member of the community. Coming from Rye, New York, several years later, two of his brothers, Jacob and David Hays, purchased the original structure now known as the Bush-Holley House. Greenwich never developed—as did Stamford, Norwalk, and Stratford—into a seaport town, which discouraged young Jewish entrepreneurs from settling there in any numbers. Added to this was the dominance of the established Congregational Church in civic as well as religious matters, which further discouraged settlement of nonbelievers. It was not until the 1880s that the next Jewish family settled Greenwich.

Historic tax records in 1728 identify Jacob Hart as an early Jewish settler in Stamford. By January 1732, Hart had purchased a "mansion house" in the area that we now know as Columbus Park. In fact, in 1738, he was the fifth-largest taxpayer in the town. Hart married Esther Levy, daughter of Moses Levy, *c.* 1746. The family lived in Stamford for many years and their three children were the first Jewish babies born in town. Hart left Stamford in 1763 for Newport, Rhode Island, where one of his sons was a Bar Mitzvah in what is now known as the Touro Synagogue. Hart also had a Darien connection, leasing two mills and a house from John Clock in 1737. In 1761, he purchased property on the Post Road in Darien, but continued to live in Stamford.

In 1776, Manuel Myers and his wife, Miriam Pinto Myers, fled British-occupied New York for Stamford. With him came his brother-in law Isaac Pinto, editor of the first English language Jewish prayer books and High Holiday *mahzor*. In 1777, Joseph Pinto, another of Miriam's brothers and a silversmith, also came to Stamford with his wife, Jochebed Hays, and their young son. Rachel Pinto, the unmarried sister of Miriam, also came to town. Upon the death of Miriam Pinto Myers in 1781, her husband had to get permission from Gov. Jonathan Trumbull of Connecticut to cross into British occupied New York so that she could be buried in the Jewish cemetery at Chatham Square. It was Abraham Davenport who interceded and wrote to the governor attesting to Myers's patriotism and attachment to the American cause.

During the federal period, starting *c.* 1804, Moses Gomez (scion of a wealthy New York family) and his wife, Esther Lopez Gomez, arrived with their children and her brothers Joshua and Samuel Lopez. Moses Gomez was listed in the New York City directory as a chocolate maker. He officiated at the first recorded Jewish wedding, in Stamford on August 22, 1805, with a Minyan (10 men), according to the records of Congregation Shearith Israel in New York. The bride was Maria Lopez, Esther's sister and the daughter of the late merchant prince of Newport, Aaron Lopez. The groom was Jacob Levy Jr. of Wilmington, North Carolina.

Joseph B. Nones, advertised in the *Stamford Advocate* in 1847 that he had a commission from the governor of Connecticut to function as an attorney. Nones was the grandfather of Walter Marks Nones, who founded Norma-Hoffman Bearings Corporation, an internationally known ball-bearing company that had its manufacturing facility in the Glenbrook section of Stamford from 1915 through the 1980s. The Nones family was descended from Pvt. Benjamin Nones, who came to America from Bordeaux, France, to fight with Lafayette in the American Revolution. Joseph B. Nones, the attorney, was himself a midshipman in the War of 1812.

In 1856, Wolff Cohen, a new arrival in town, originally from Poland via New York City and Peekskill, New York, advertised ready-to-wear men's clothing from his shop at the Union House Hotel. By 1867, he was selling both custom and ready-to-wear clothing and had "five hands" working for him. Cohen's wife, Harriet Cohen, was listed as a milliner in 1850, residing and working on Bleeker Street. Wolff Cohen moved to 7 Park Row in 1874 as a merchant tailor. By 1880, he appeared to have retired and his daughter-in-law, Kitty Cohen, was operating as a milliner at the same address.

Two Cohen sons, Samuel and Byron, were the first resident Jewish attorneys and had offices on Atlantic Street. Samuel Cohen was appointed judge of the probate court when he was 25 years old in 1876; his term, however, only lasted six months.

In 1859, Jacob Fox, clothing merchant, came to town, paving the way for his extended family. Isaac Fox, his brother, arrived in 1870 to open a saloon on Main Street opposite West Park. By 1875, David Fox was listed as a clothing salesman, and Charles and Peter Fox opened a saloon on Gay Street in 1875 and later expanded to a second location in the Atlantic House Hotel. Louis Fox operated a bakery and ice-cream parlor on Main Street near Pacific Street *c.* 1885. In 1887, he moved his business to Springdale at the foot of Weed Hill Avenue. He moved back to Main Street in 1890. By 1912, the Fox family had moved to New York. The last Fox working in Stamford was Regina Fox, a milliner.

During the Civil War, A. Benas was a cigar maker on Main Street and Ralph Benjamin ran a billiard parlor. In 1870, Ellchana Carensky, a blacksmith, practiced his trade for a while. In 1885, brothers Charles, Daniel, and Gustave Frohman, New York theatrical managers, purchased an estate on Noroton Hill for use as a country home and residence for their parents, Henry and Barbara Frohman.

The earliest Jewish settler in New Canaan was Louis Drucker, a tailor who arrived from Hartford in 1869. Drucker was also a town constable and a member of the volunteer fire department. A few other Jewish families began to settle in New Canaan in the 1890s, such as the Kurianskys. Local lawyer Jeroll Silverberg recalled that his grandfather left Darien in the 1890s and moved to New Canaan because "there was more room." Darien had several Jewish families in the 1890s, including a Jewish Civil War veteran who lived at the Old Soldier's Home. Few Jews remained, however, as the town developed very slowly and real estate restrictions became the norm by World War I.

Restrictions were not uncommon throughout the nation after the start of the 20th century. The movement to these communities by largely wealthy families seeking to divorce themselves from the teeming immigrant populations pouring into the big cities, was a factor in limiting Jewish settlement in some of these towns.

Fortunately, those barriers are mostly a matter of the past. The New Canaan Jewish Group is a growing and vibrant organization active in community affairs. The once small Jewish community of Greenwich is now quite large, supporting two congregations, a Chabad, and the United Jewish Appeal Federation.

The once numerous Jewish merchants of the region have faded into history. However, their contribution to the progress of the communities was an important factor in contributing to prosperity, growth, and the quality of life that developed. Stamford, Darien, Greenwich, New Canaan, and Pound Ridge benefited greatly from the presence of Jewish men and women, the pioneers who paved the road for future generations.

One

Where We Shopped

Pacific Street was the center of Jewish commerce in lower Fairfield county. The shops along the street teemed with housewives buying kosher meat, produce, and dairy products and with families shopping for everything from shoes to hardware, paints, and furniture. A partial listing of Pacific Street Jewish merchants and manufacturers from 1895 to 1901 includes Mrs. Minnie Sissenwein, dry goods; Max C. Rosen, picture frames and glazier; Julius Sissenwein, bartender; Minna Cohn, greengrocer; Morris Levi, shoemaker and candy store; Henry Freed, liquor dealer; Sigismund Kronholtz, optical specialist and jeweler; Lewis Feuerstein, barber and chiropodist; Isidore Zax, locksmith; Leopold Cohn, fur factory; Louis Cohn and David Cohen, clothing; and Solomon Abrams and Jacob Rosenbloom, kosher butchers. In the late 1960s, urban renewal replaced this once vibrant hub with the Stamford Town Center, a regional shopping mall. This picture was taken in 1967, just before Pacific Street became a memory.

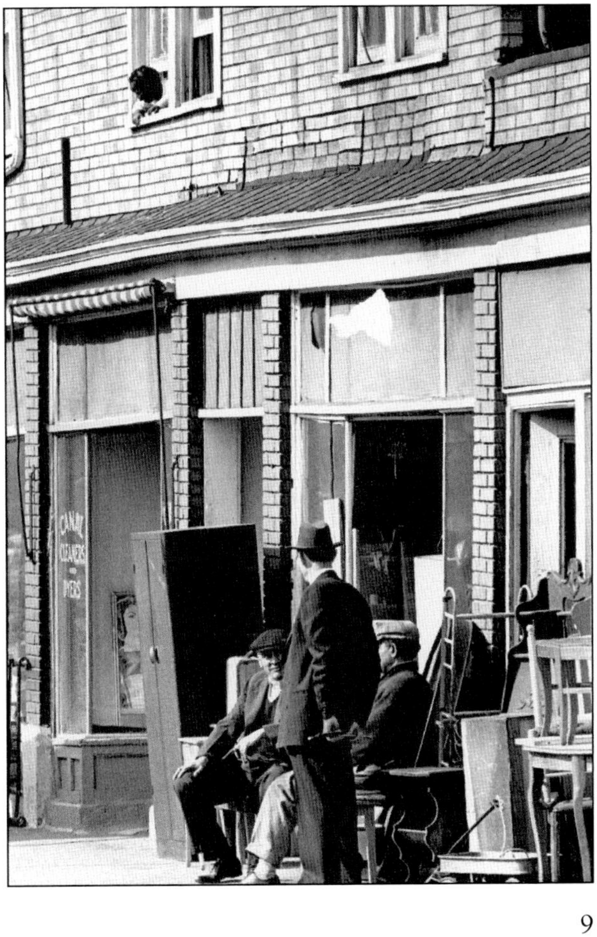

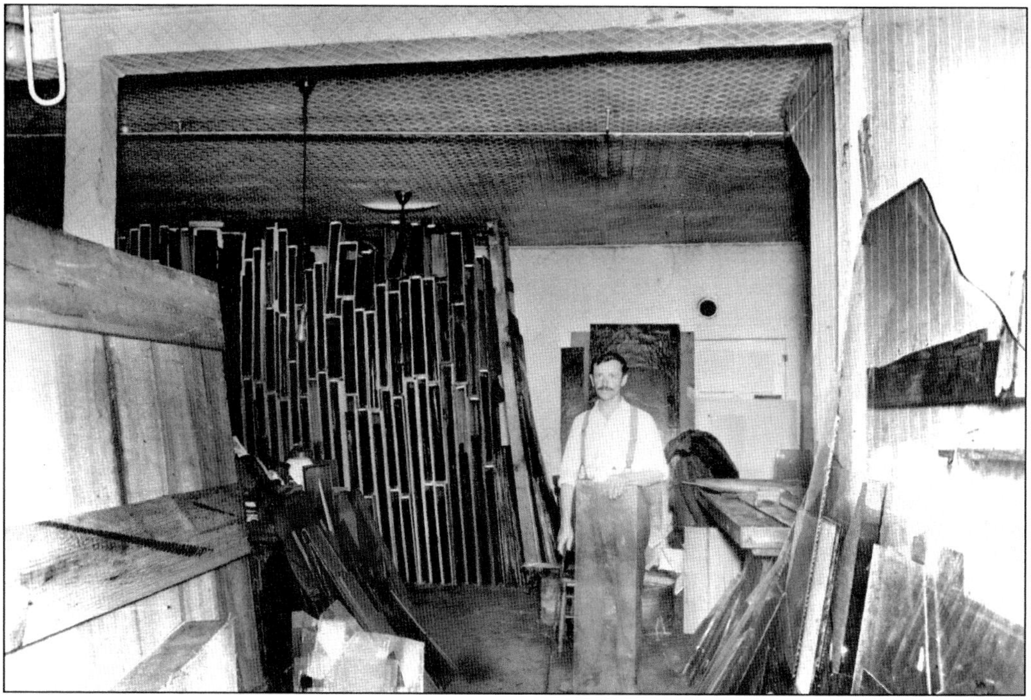

Connecticut Plate Glass Company, on Pacific Street, was owned by Isaac Sackman in 1910.

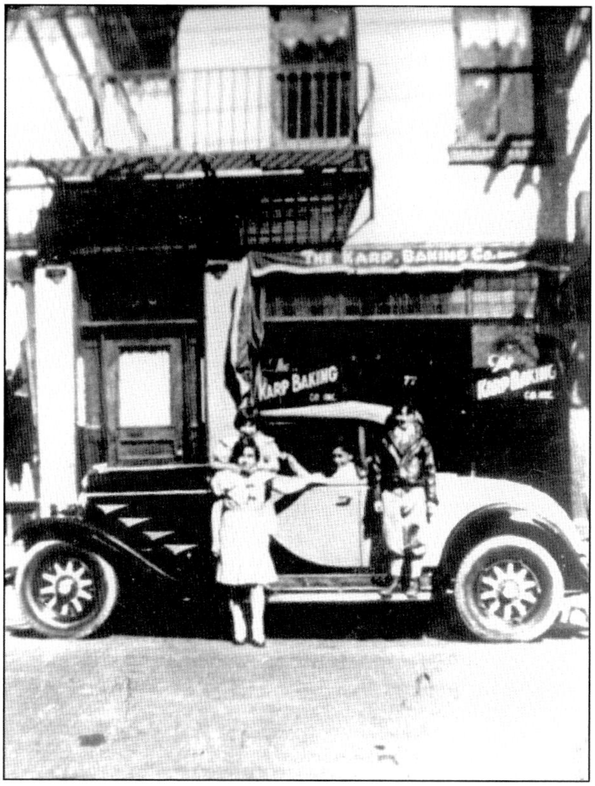

Shown is Karp's Bakery, at 77 Pacific Street, *c.* 1935.

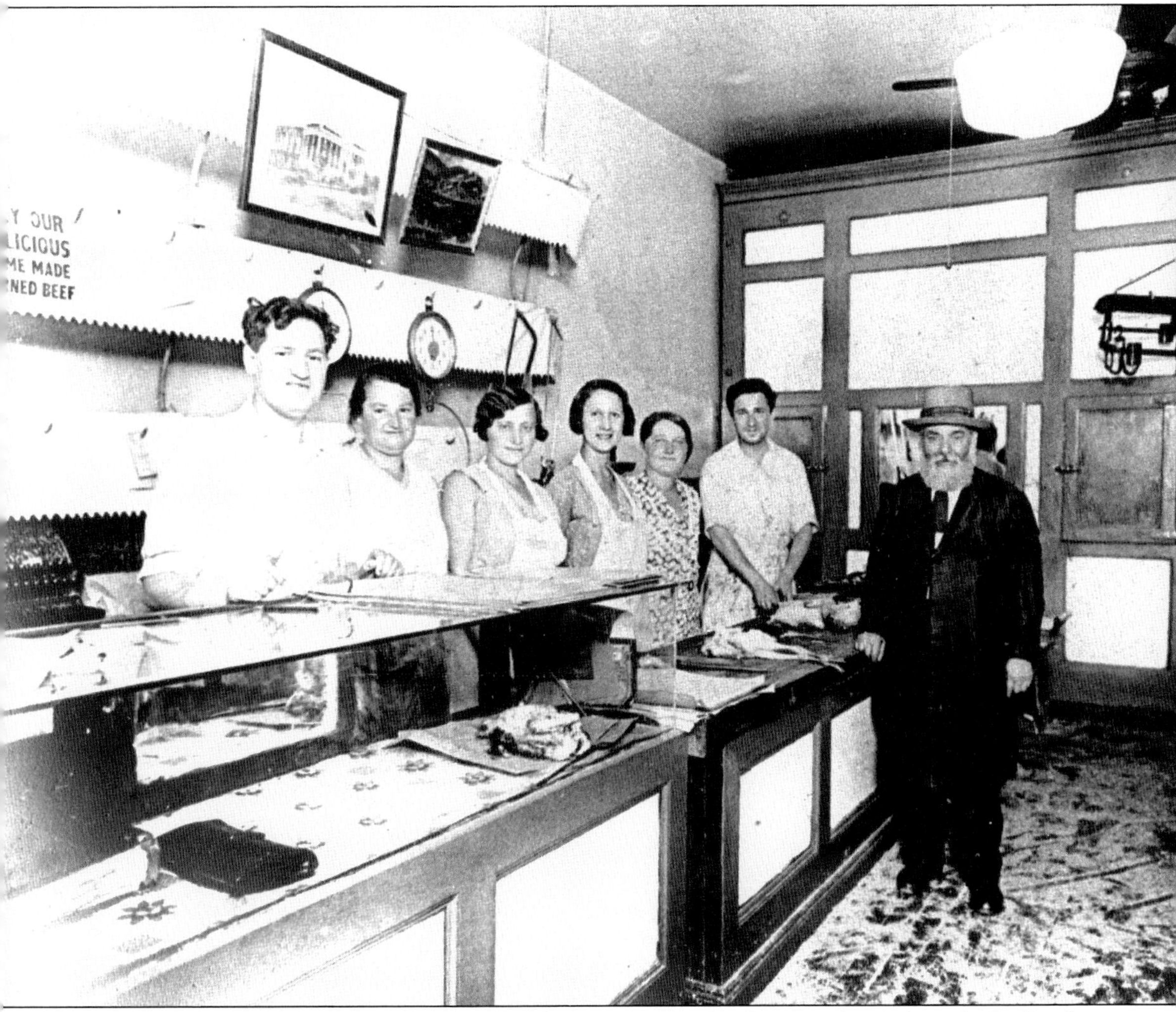

Everyone met at Brazel's kosher meat market at 69 Pacific Street, where the whole family served customers. Shown in this c. 1933 photograph are, from left to right, Hyman Brazel, Bertha Brazel, Bea Brazel (wife of Hyman), Frieda Brazel, Ida Frankel, Beryl Brazel, and S. Bernstein (the *schochet*, or ritual slaughterer). In the 1899 city directory, Bernstein was listed as "Jewish Rabbi."

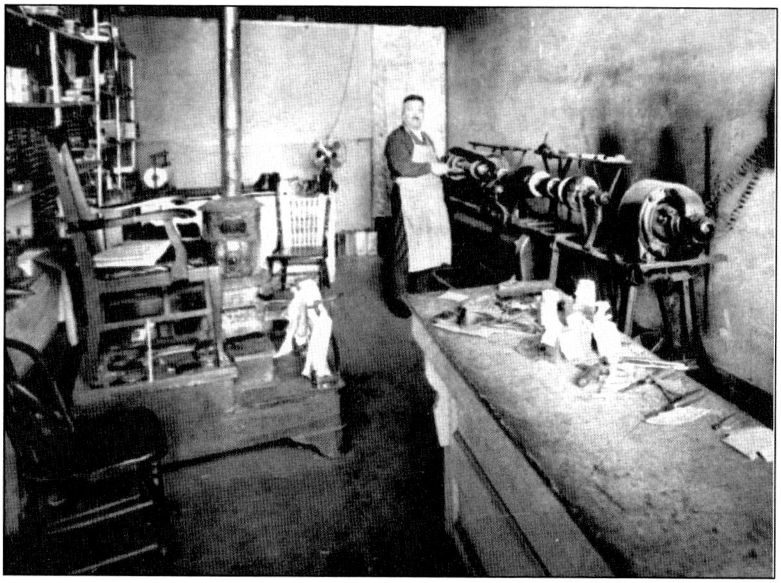

Weissman the shoemaker is pictured at his Canal Street store in 1927.

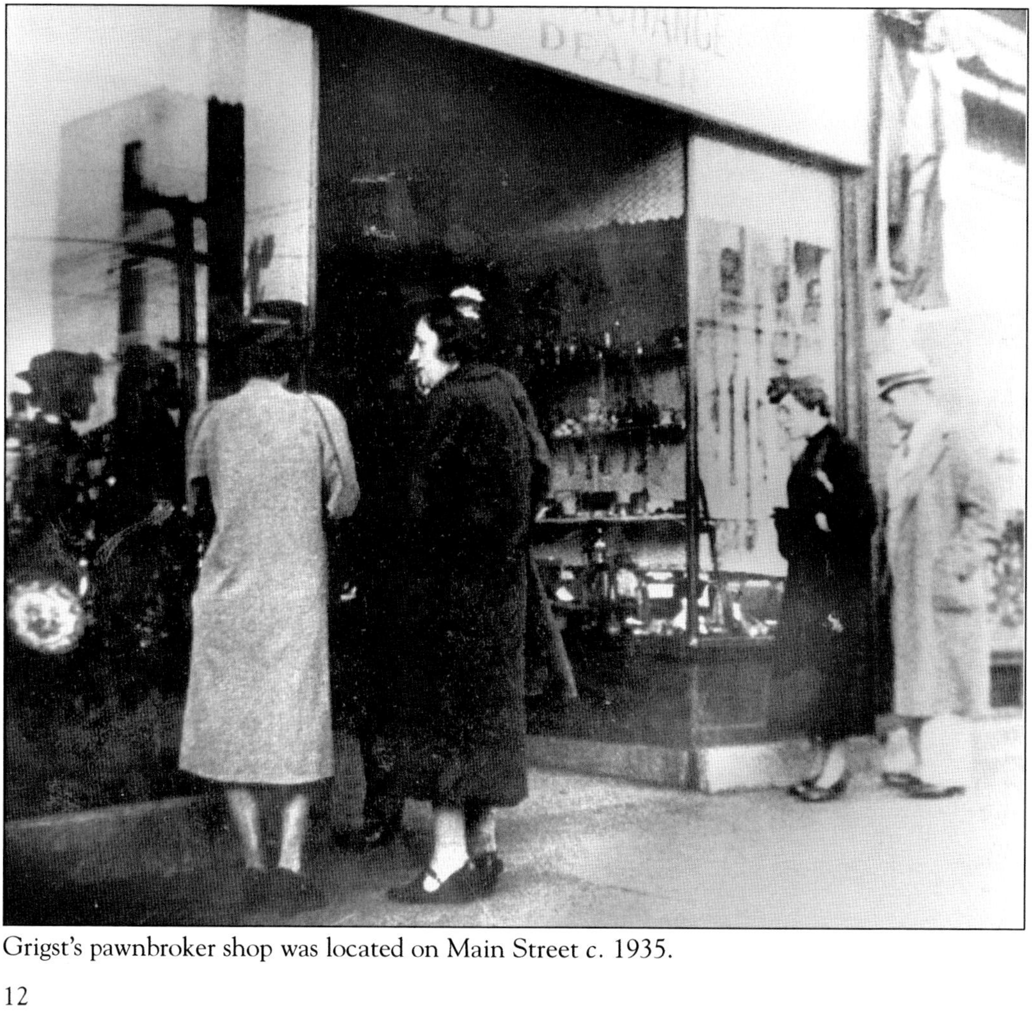

Grigst's pawnbroker shop was located on Main Street *c.* 1935.

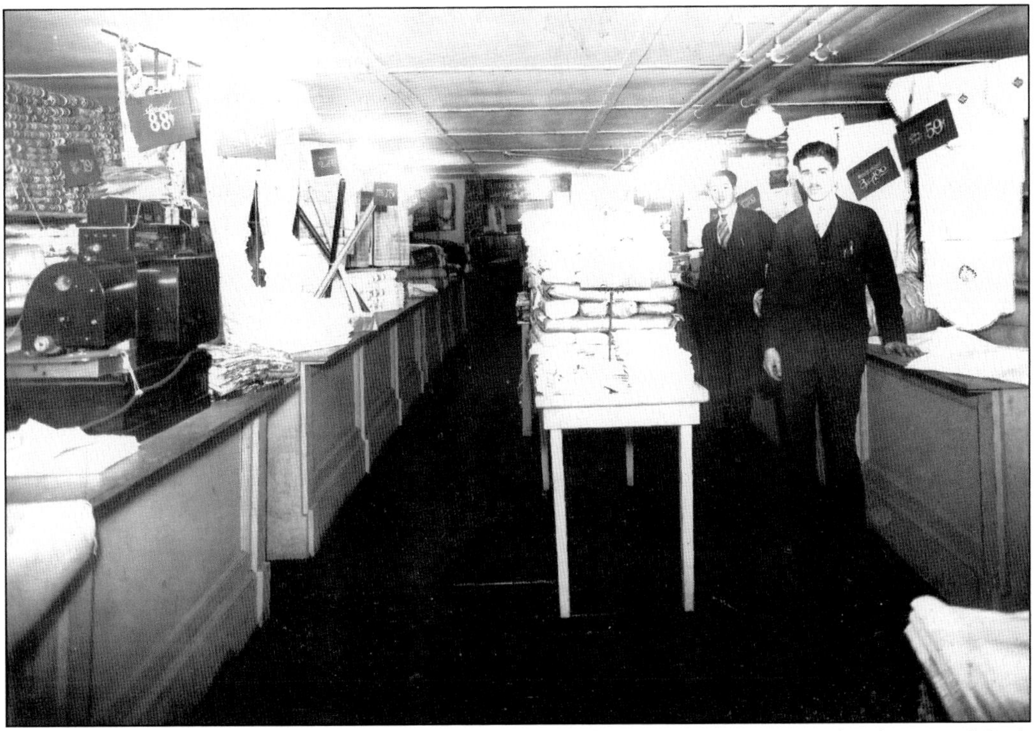

This was Roven's first store, on Atlantic Street, in 1933. Al Roven is in the front and Jack Schmukler is behind him.

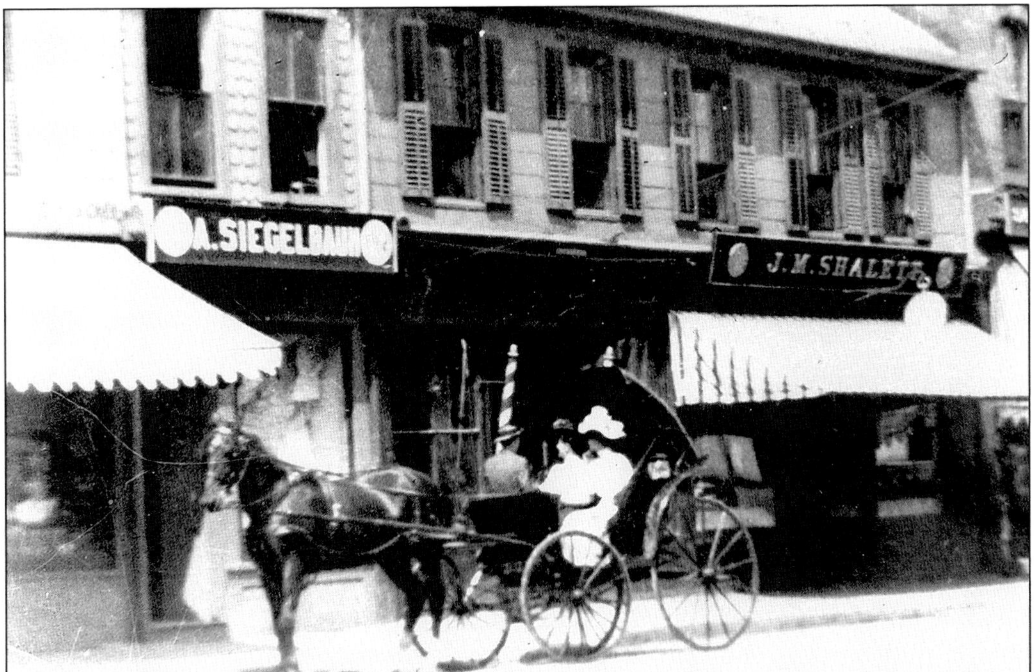

Siegelbaum Dry Goods and J. Shalett Jewelers and Opticians were located on Main Street in 1910.

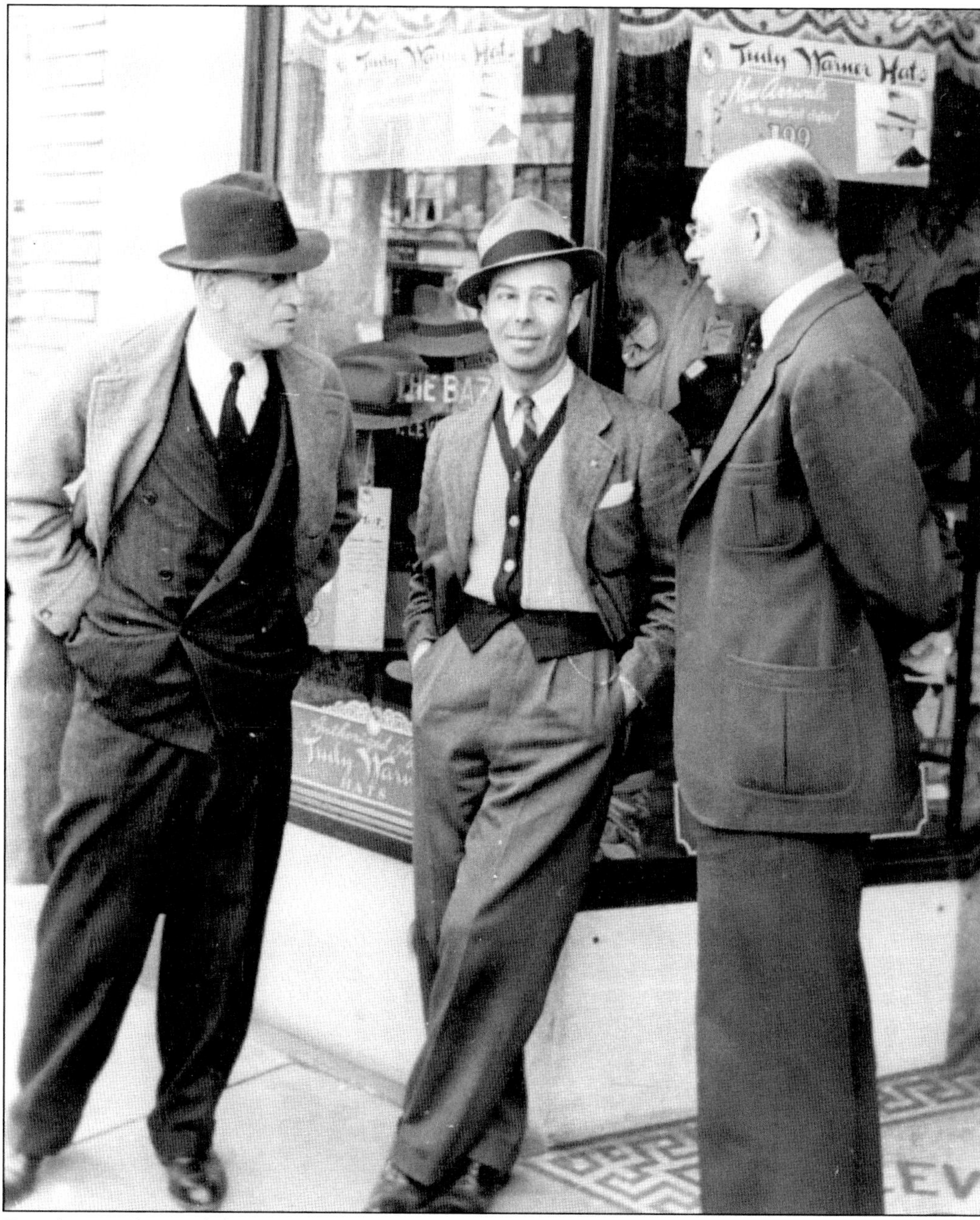

Standing in front of the Bazaar on Main Street *c.* 1930 are Abe Levenson (center) and Bernie Fine of Fine's Shoes (right).

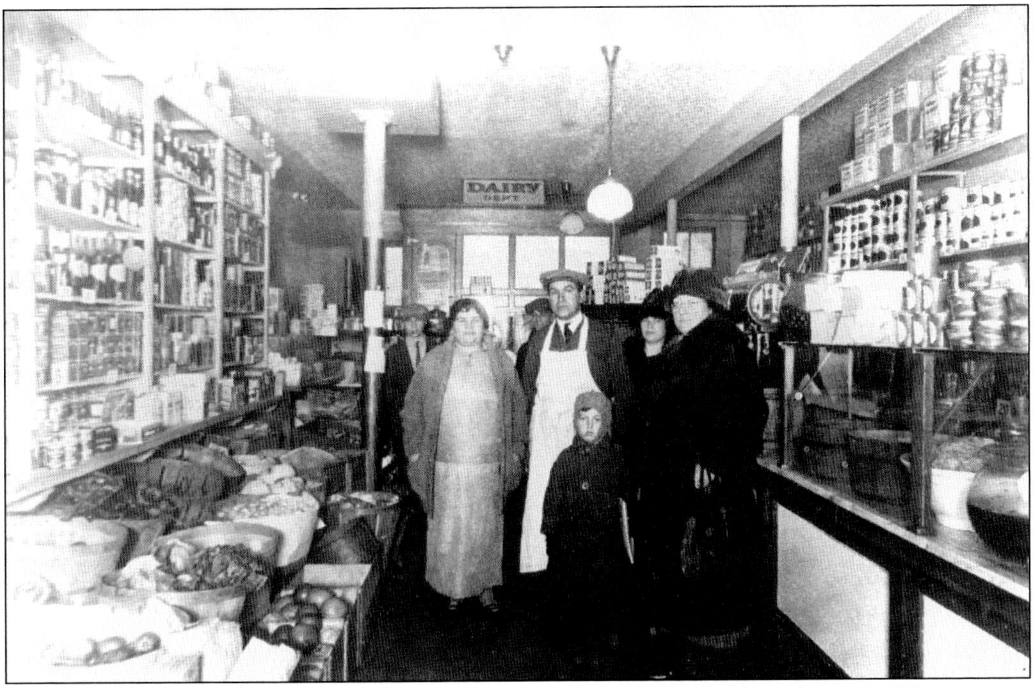

Harry Weinstein's grocery store was at 66 Pacific Street. The child in this *c.* 1929 picture is Morris Weinstein, who became a dentist.

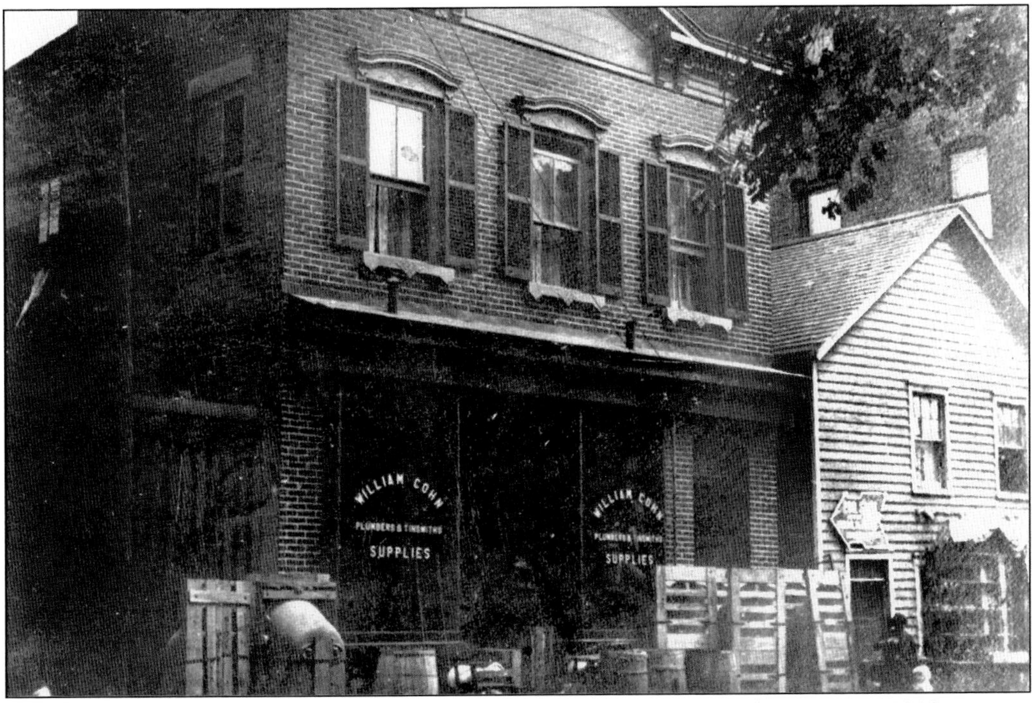

William Cohen's plumbing supply store was located at 104–106 Pacific Street in 1913.

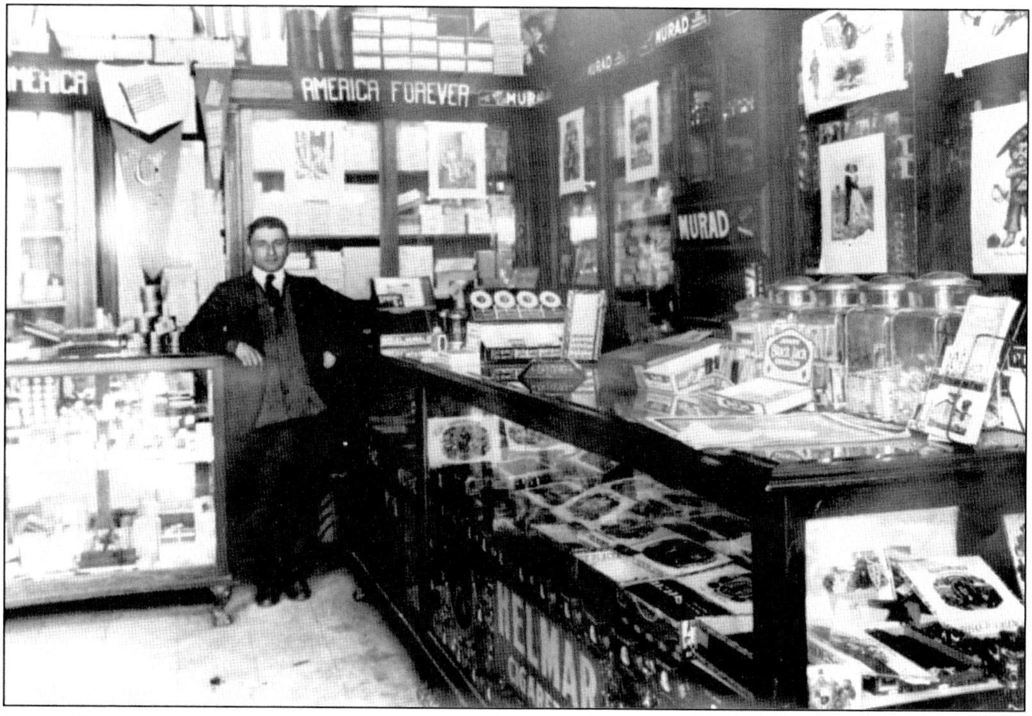

Harry Karp is pictured in his cigar store at 411 Main Street c. 1918.

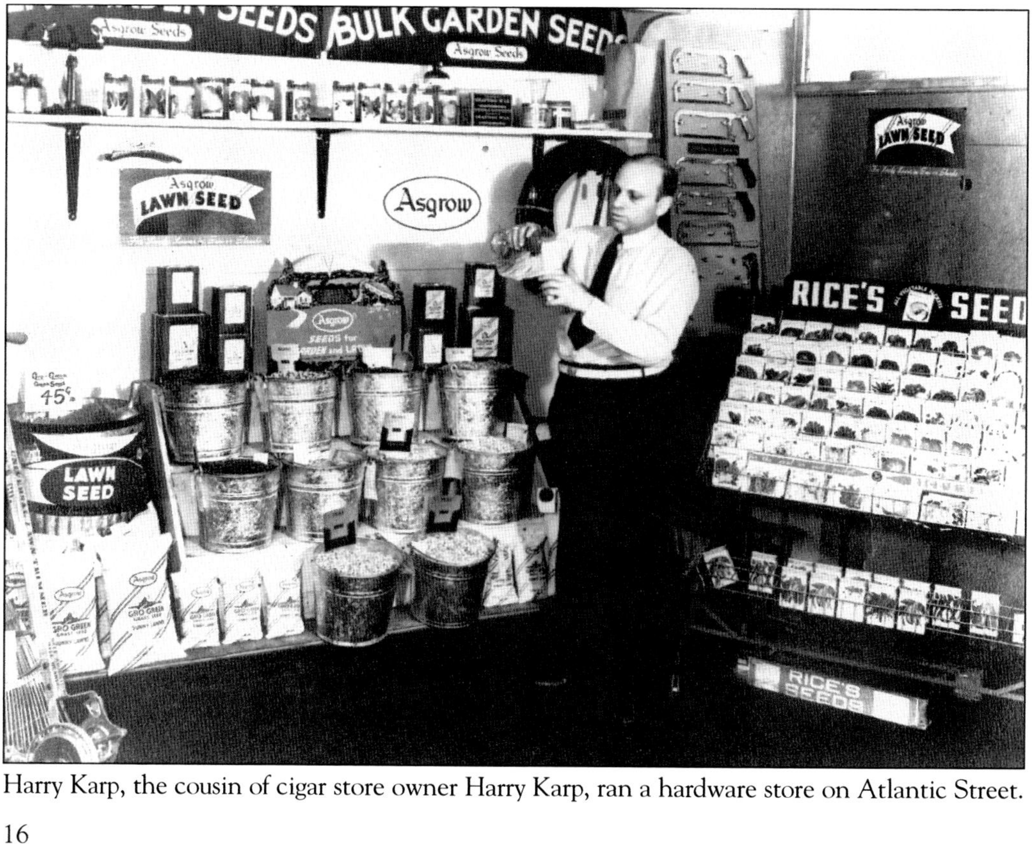

Harry Karp, the cousin of cigar store owner Harry Karp, ran a hardware store on Atlantic Street.

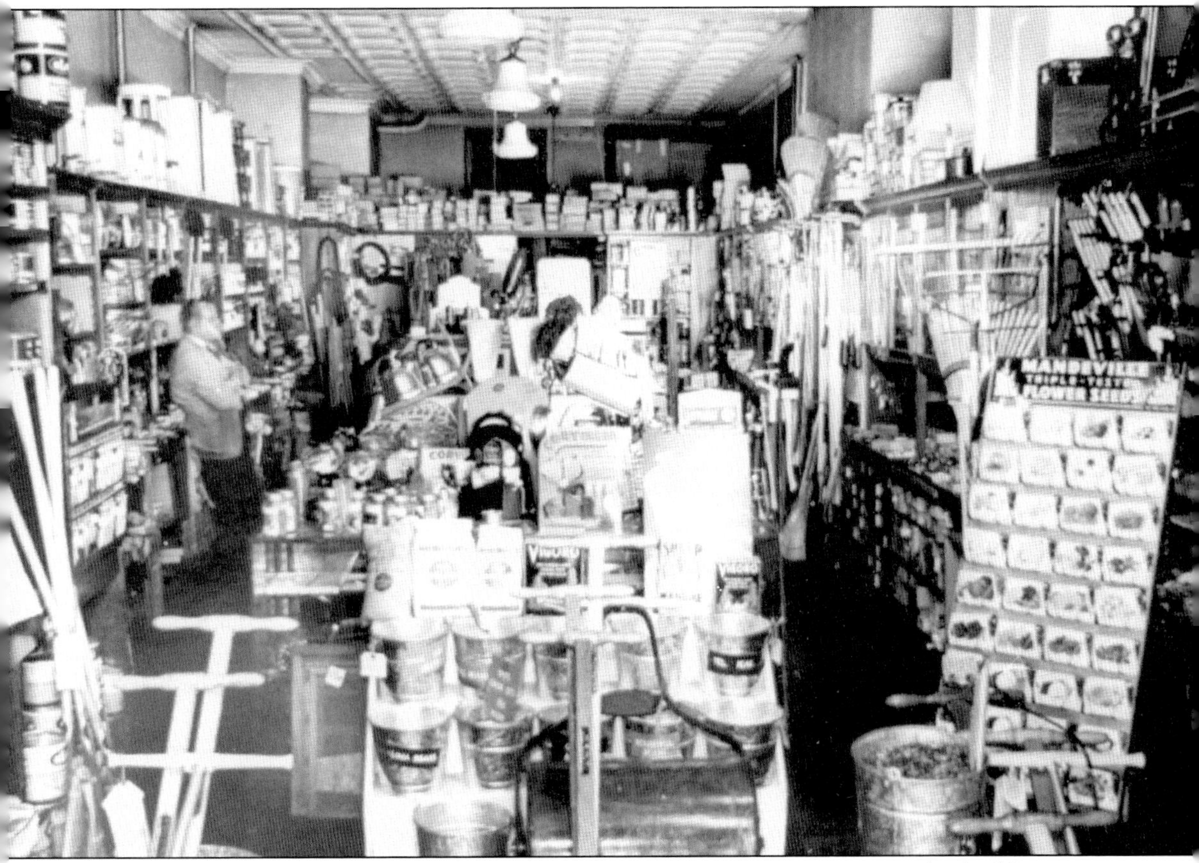

Karp's Hardware on Atlantic Street was opposite the post office in 1927. The building was demolished in 1977.

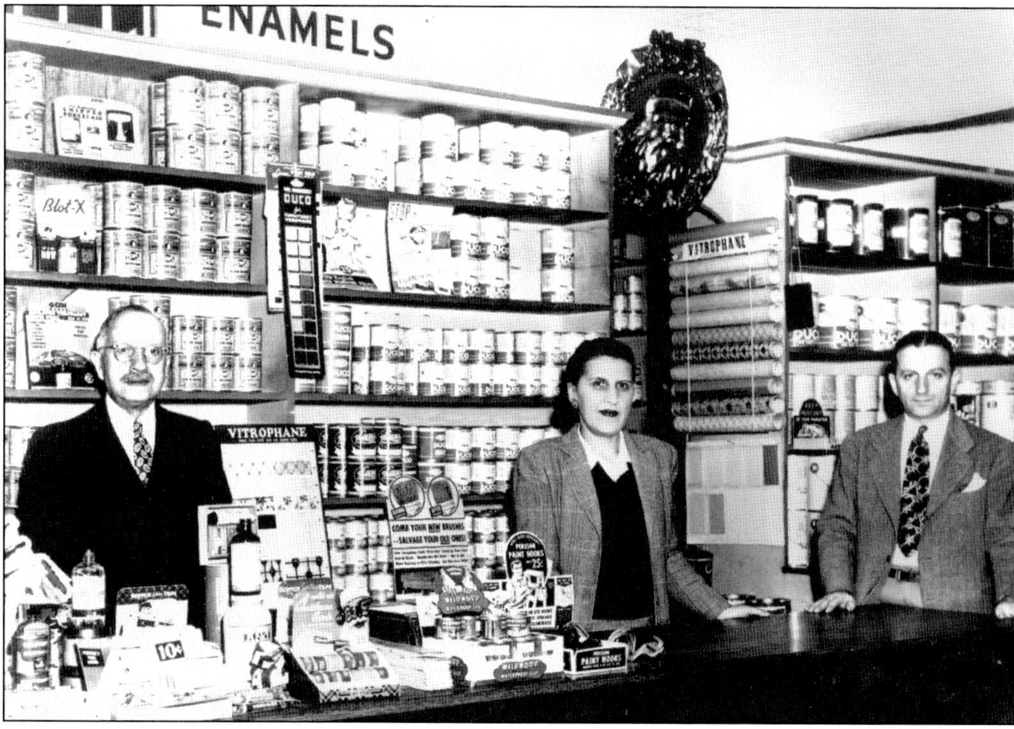

Shown at their paint store are, from left to right, Meyer Wise, Faye Wise Rind, and Sam Wise.

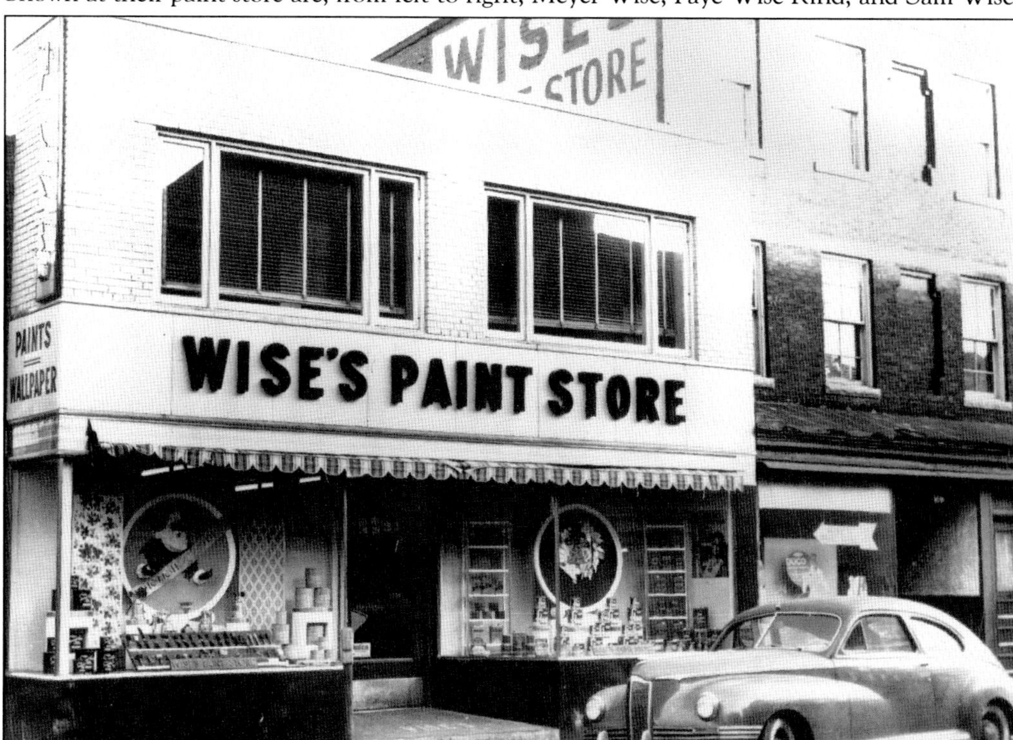

Wise's Paint Store was founded in 1907. Pictured is the store at 28 Pacific Street in 1923.

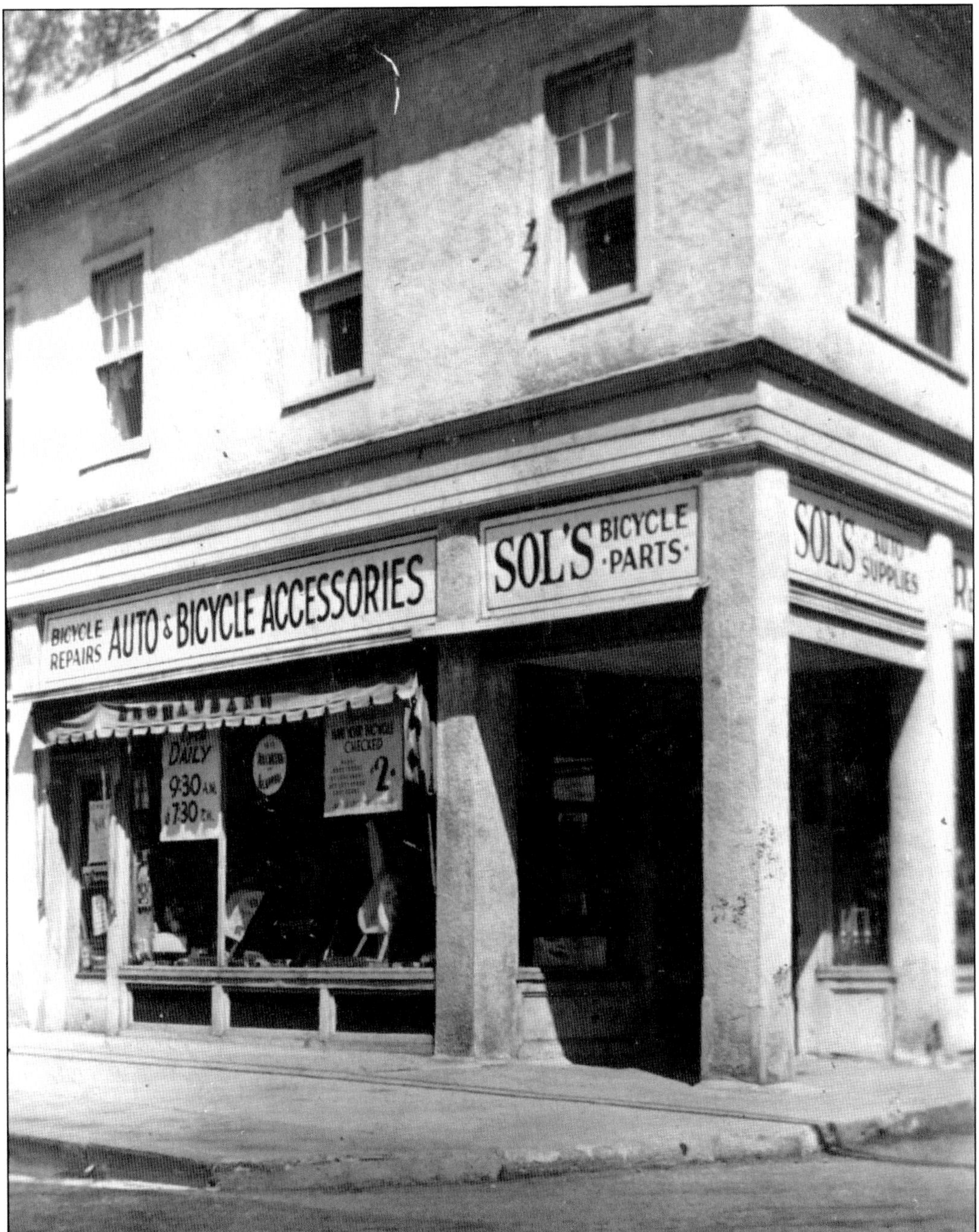

Sol's Bicycle Shop was at 1001 Hope Street on the corner of Cushing Street in 1943.

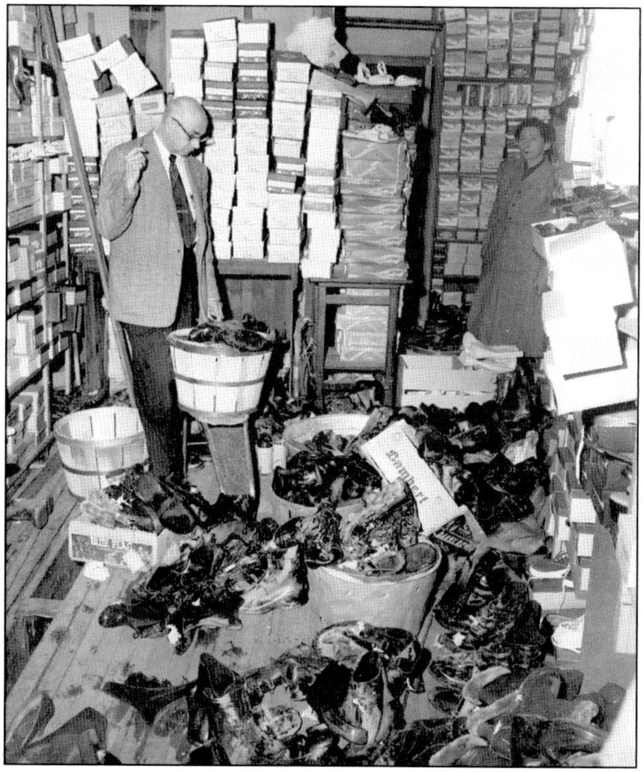

Bernie and Gert Fine survey the damage at Bernie Fine's shoe store after the flood in October 1955.

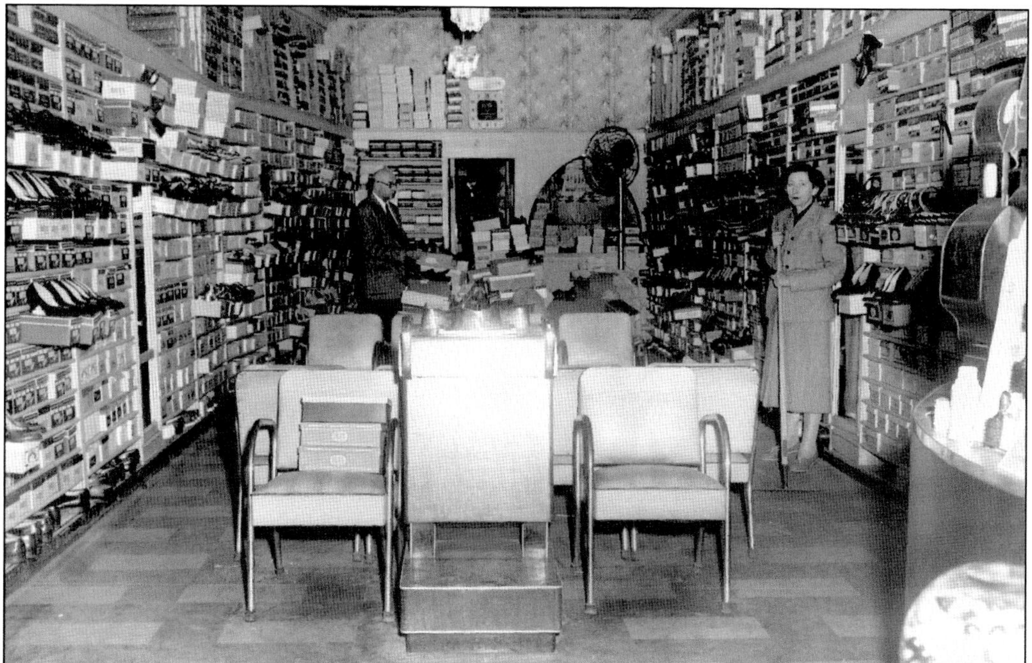

The Fines clean their store after the October 14 low-pressure storm, classified as a "baby hurricane," flooded the region.

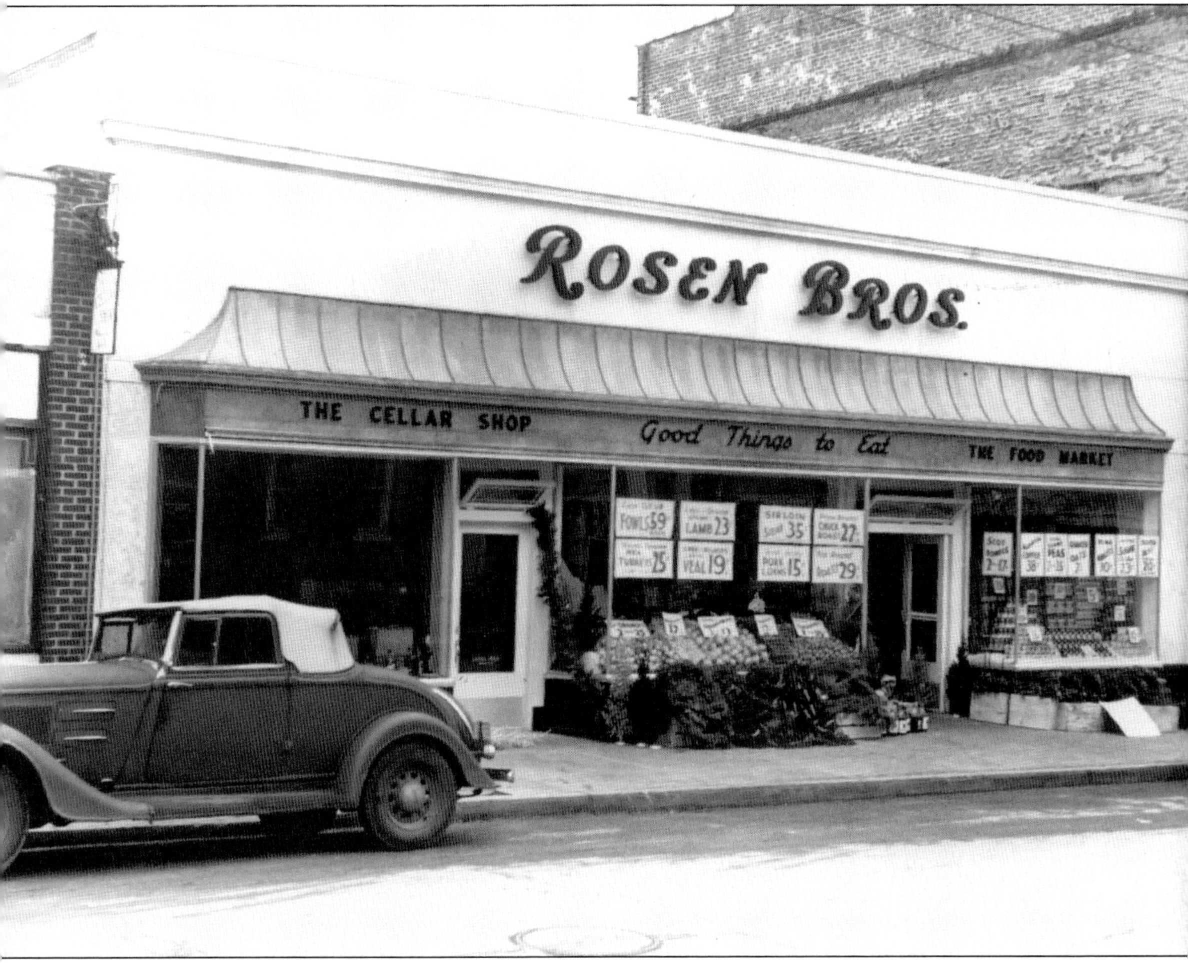

This is Rosen Brothers' Market in New Canaan *c.* 1940. The earliest Jewish settler of record was Louis Drucker, who came to New Canaan *c.* 1869. He lived and operated a tailor shop on East Avenue and Summer Street. He was also a town constable and an active member of the New Canaan Volunteer Fire Department. By the 1930s, a small community of Jewish merchants, professionals, and artists had been established. Among the most prominent were Judge Julius "Caesar" Groher, Dr. Leo Davidoff and his wife, Dr. Ida Davidoff, and Arthur Szyk.

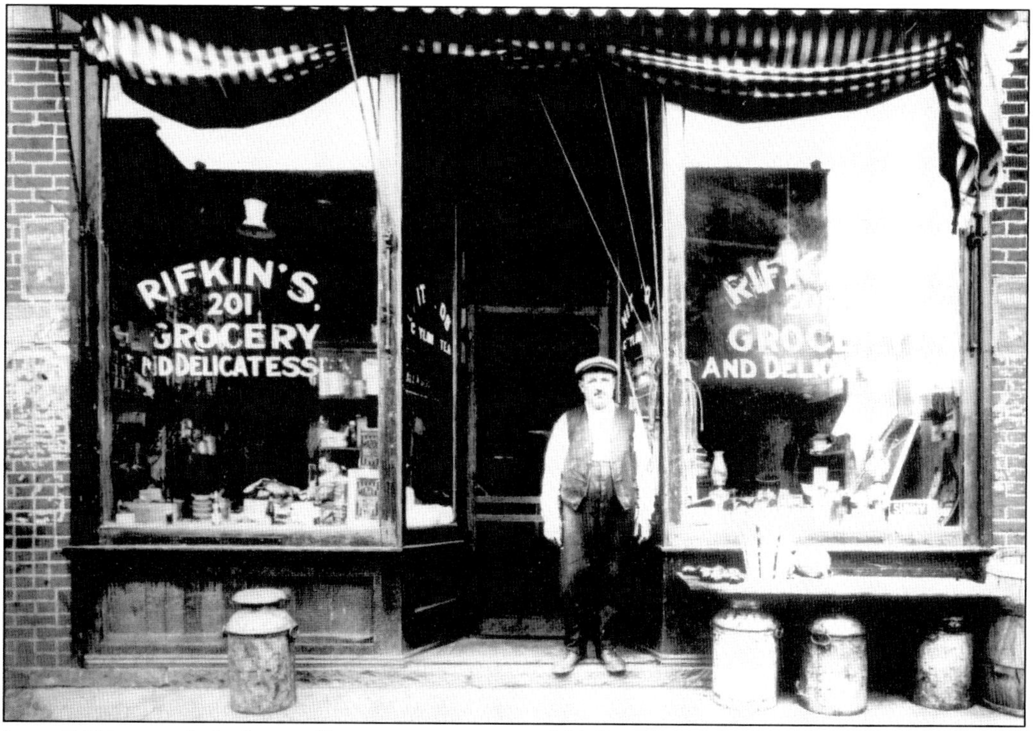

Isaac Rifkin stands in front of his grocery store, at 201 Pacific Street, *c.* 1919.

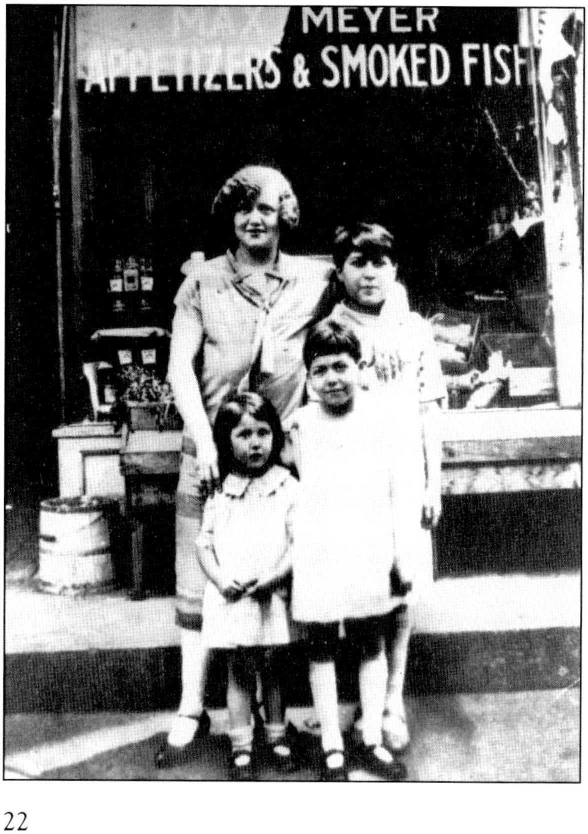

Max Meyer ran an appetizer and smoked fish store on Pacific Street *c.* 1927. Pictured, from left to right, are the following: (front row) Bella and Leona Meyer; (back row) Dora and Evelyn Meyer.

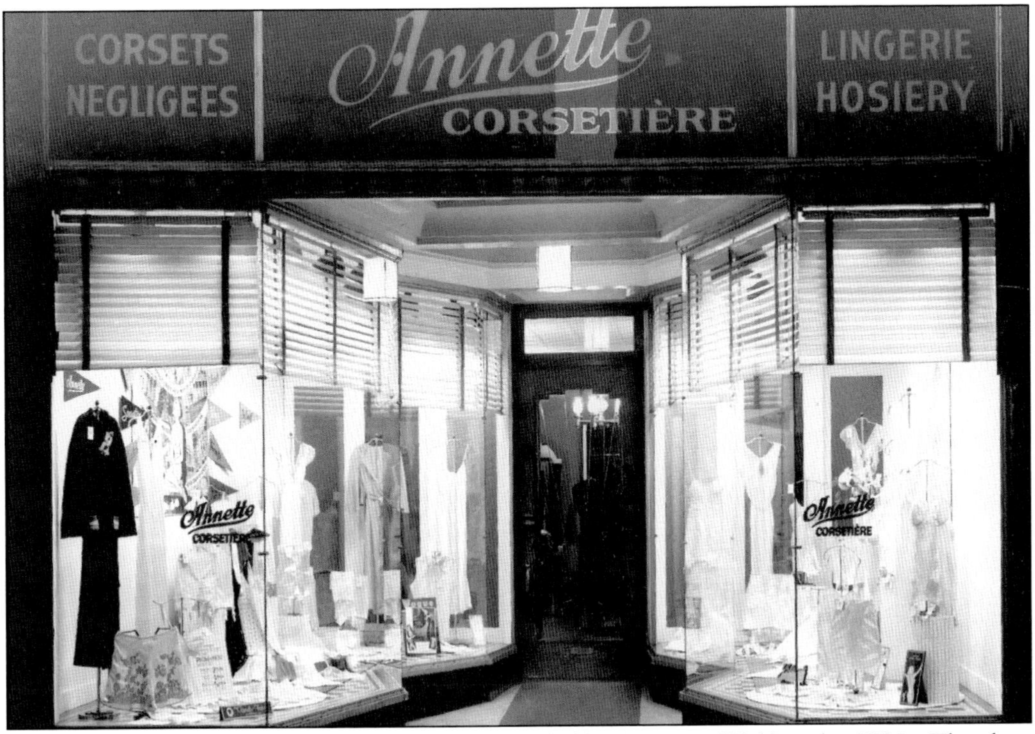

Annette's Corsetiere on Bedford Street was founded by Annette Wolf in the 1930s. The shop remained in business for 60 years.

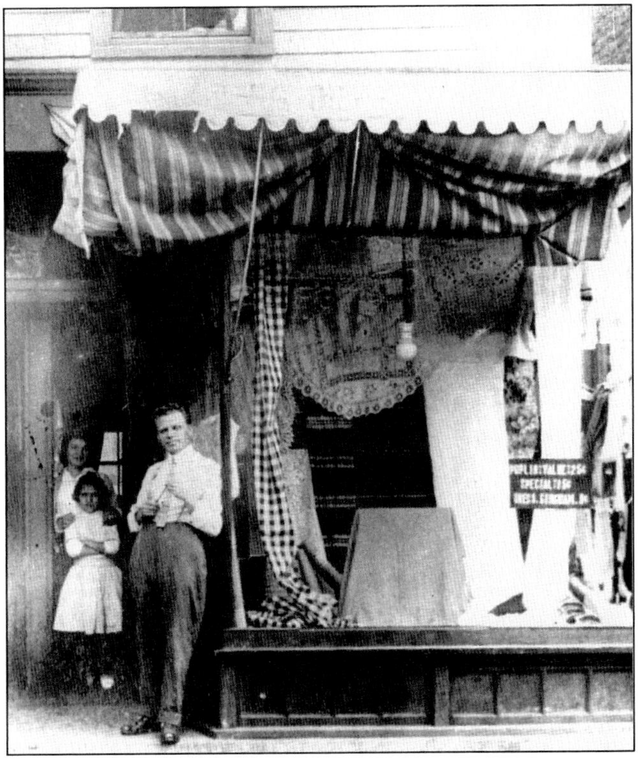

Nathan Gold is shown at his dry goods store on Canal Street *c.* 1920. The woman and child are unidentified.

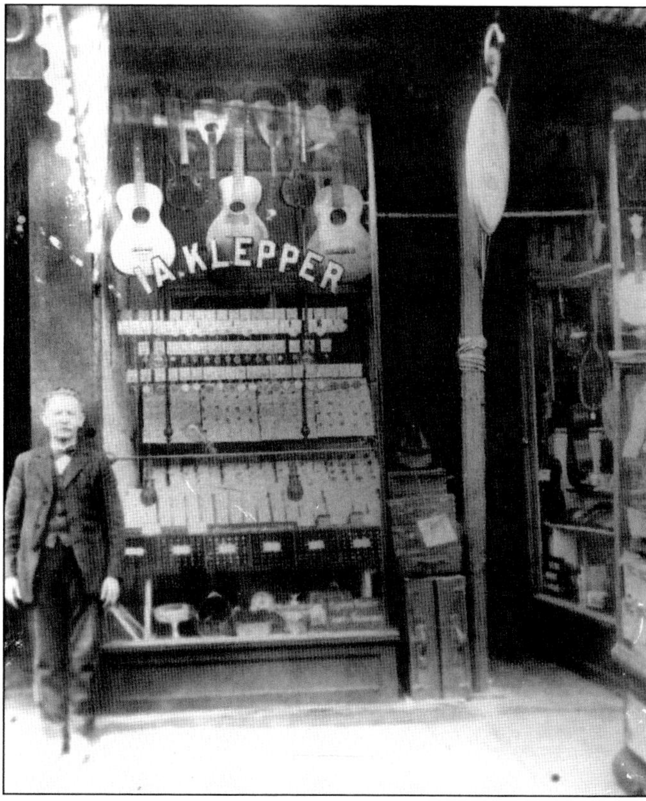

I.A. Klepper stands in front of his pawnshop.

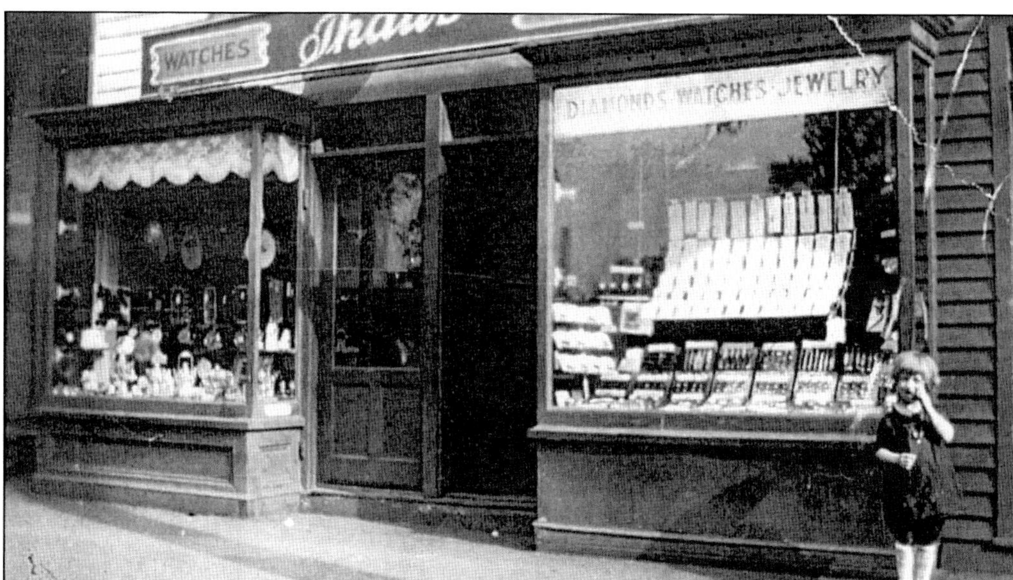

Jacob Koffler's jewelry store was located on Main Street opposite West Park. This photograph was taken *c.* 1920.

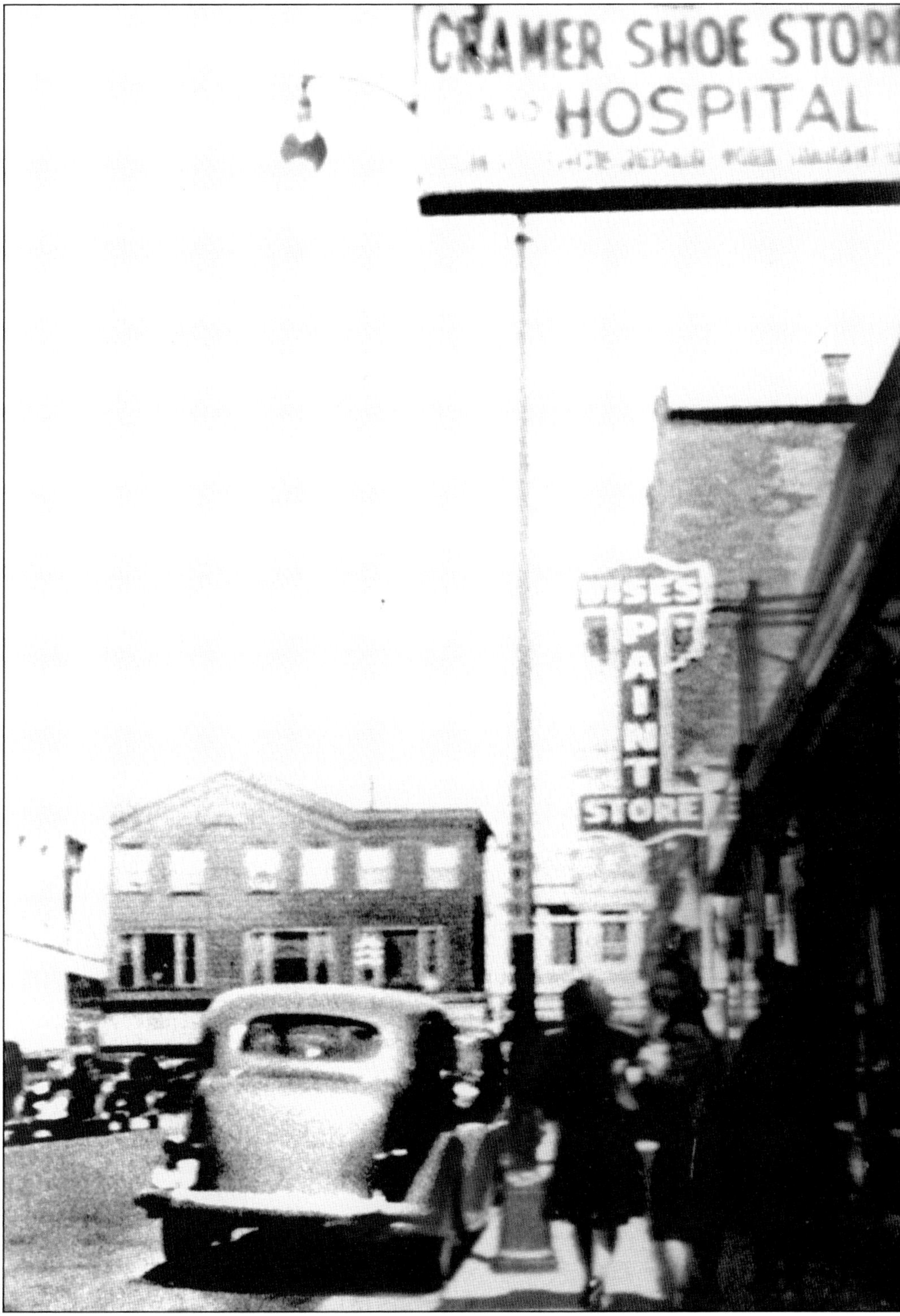

In this 1939 view of Pacific Street, the Cramer Shoe Store and Shoe Hospital is in the foreground next to Wise's Paint Store.

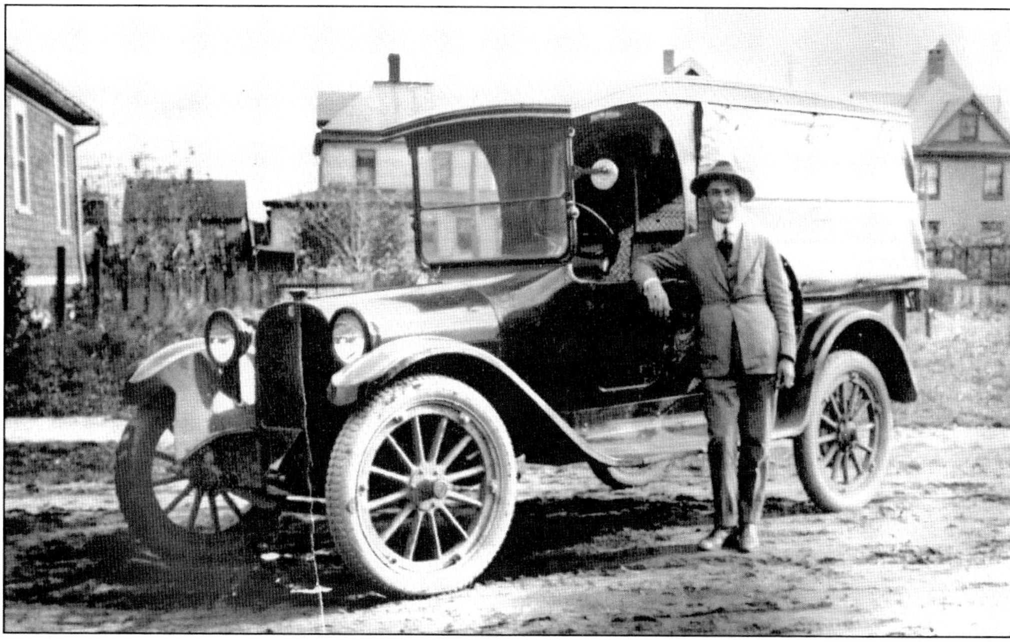

Philip Plotkin delivers lumber in 1920.

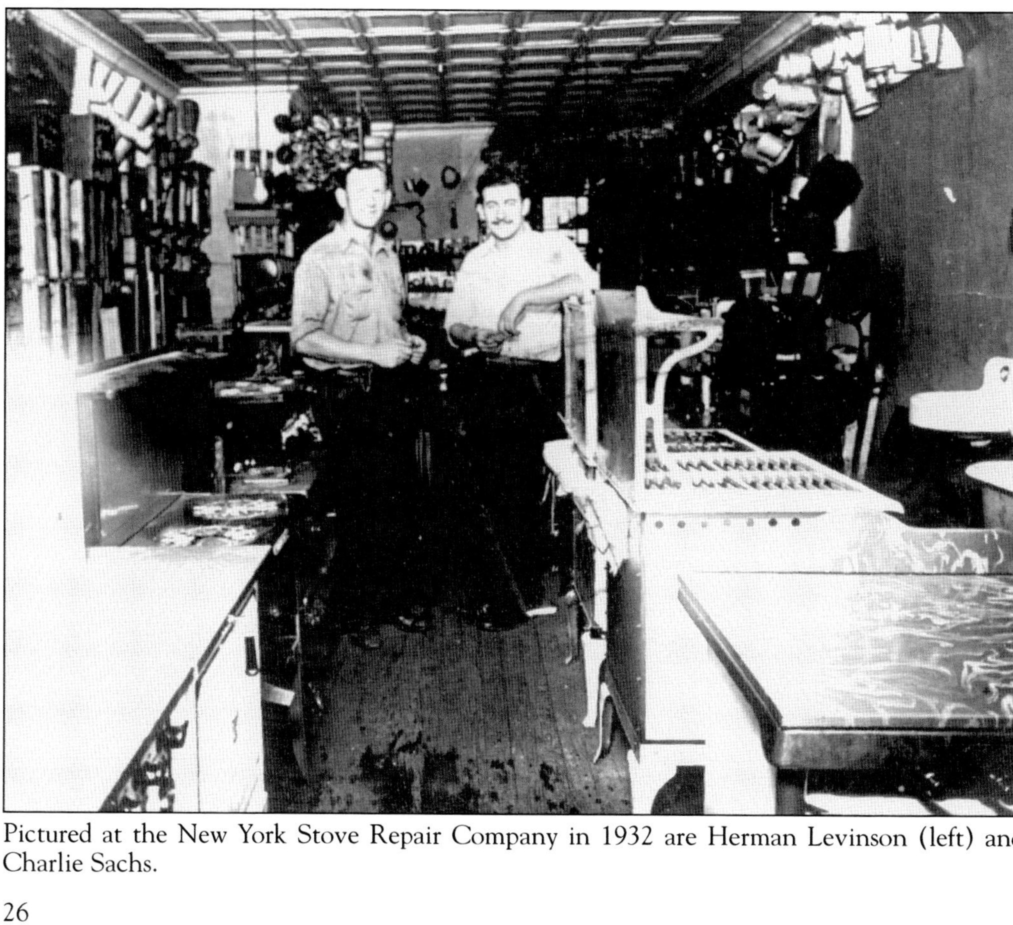

Pictured at the New York Stove Repair Company in 1932 are Herman Levinson (left) and Charlie Sachs.

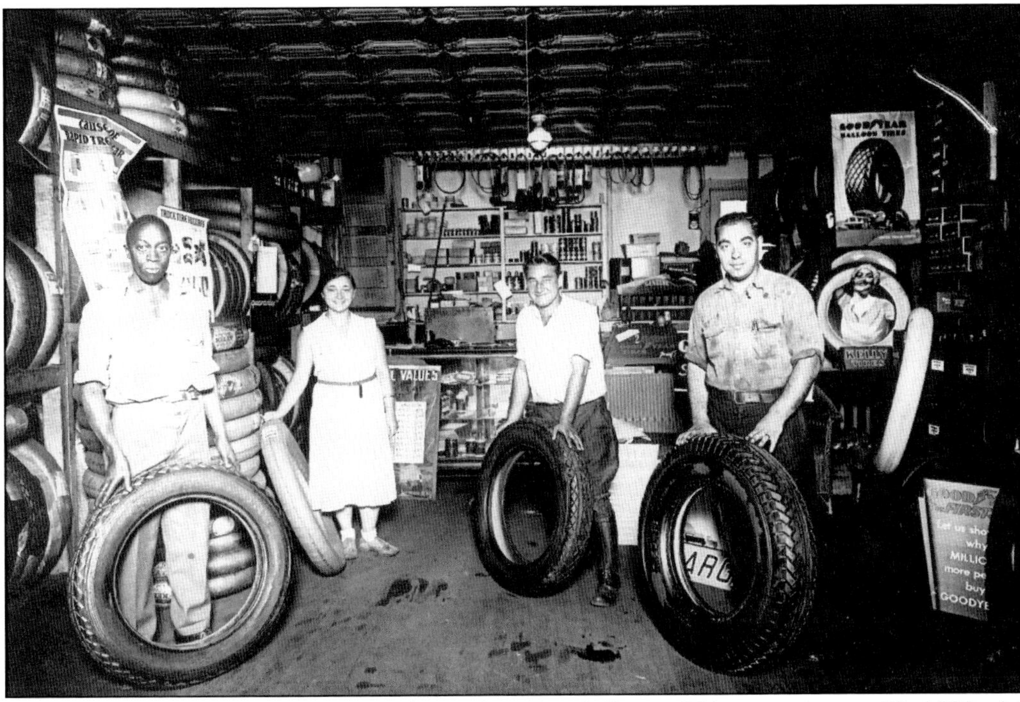

Epstein Brothers Tire Company was located on Brook Street. Taken on August 29, 1932, this photograph shows, from left to right, a Mr. Fitch and Sarah, Louis, and Max Epstein.

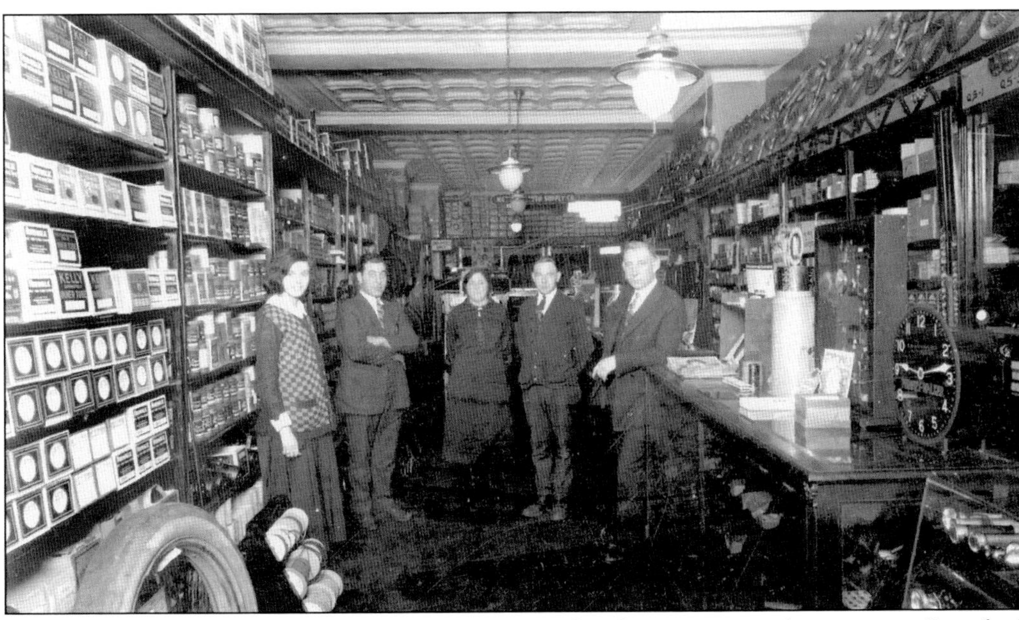

Kweskin Auto Supply on Atlantic Street was the first auto supply store in Stamford. It was located next to Karp's Hardware and was across the street from the post office. Pictured c. 1925, from left to right, are Esther Fine, Abe Epstein, Bessie L. Kweskin, Bob Bowes, and Morris Kweskin.

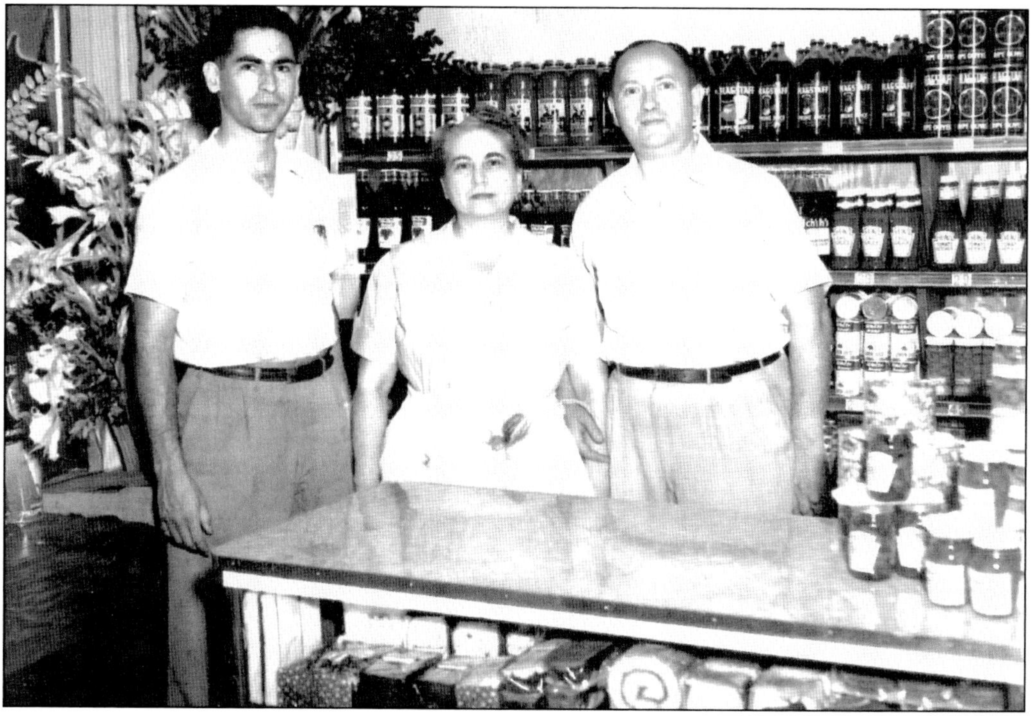

Bruce Gordon poses with his parents Rose and William Gordon at their grocery store in 1947. The store was located on Mason Street in Greenwich. Bruce Gordon, a certified public accountant, served as chairman of the Greenwich Housing Authority for many years.

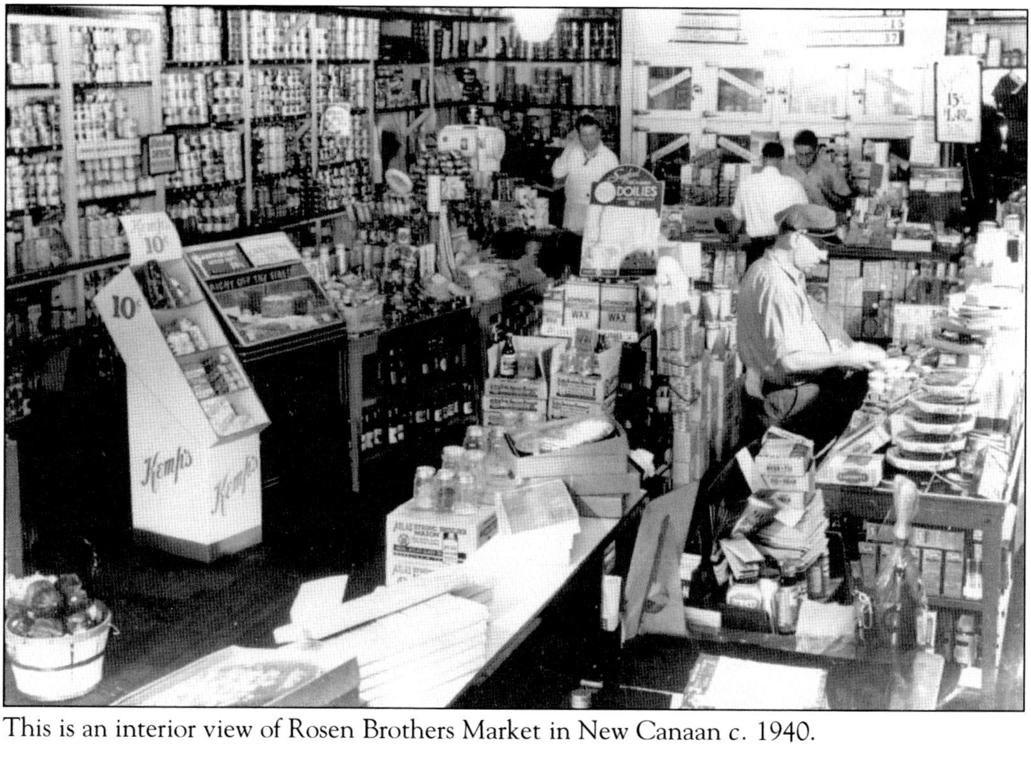

This is an interior view of Rosen Brothers Market in New Canaan *c.* 1940.

Two

The Way We Lived

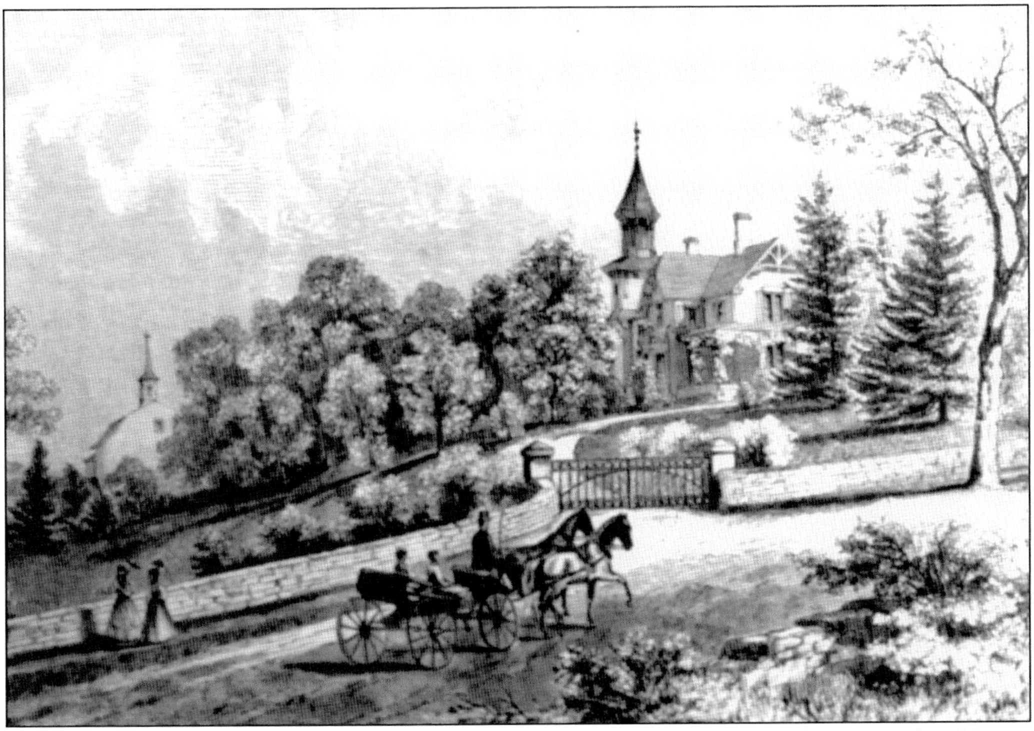

This is the former Wilcox Estate viewed from the foot of Noroton Hill just north of Lawn Avenue on the Post Road, currently East Main Street. The estate, pictured in 1867, was owned by the Frohman brothers Charles, Daniel, and Gustave. The brothers were renowned Broadway theatrical managers and producers. The house was the primary residence of their parents, Barbara and Henry Frohman, and was used by the sons as a country retreat from 1885 to 1897.

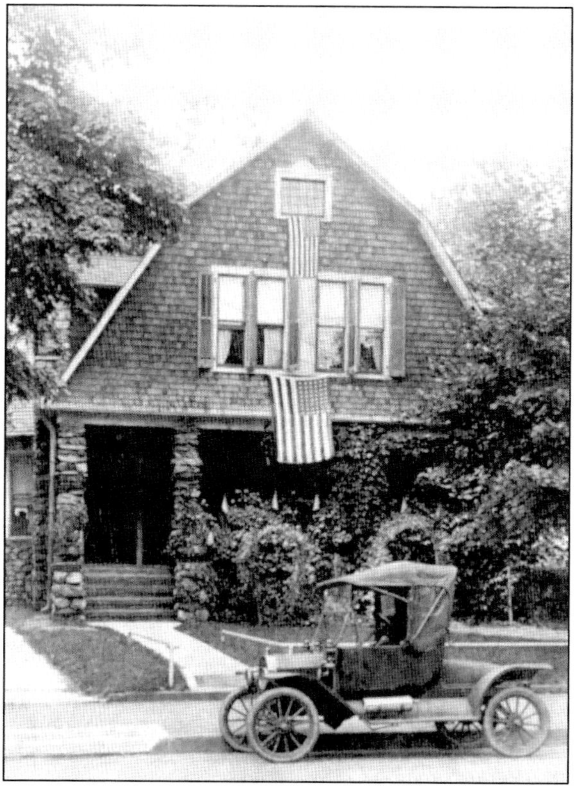

This 1912 photograph shows Dr. Jacob Nemoitin's home and office, at 96 Main Street.

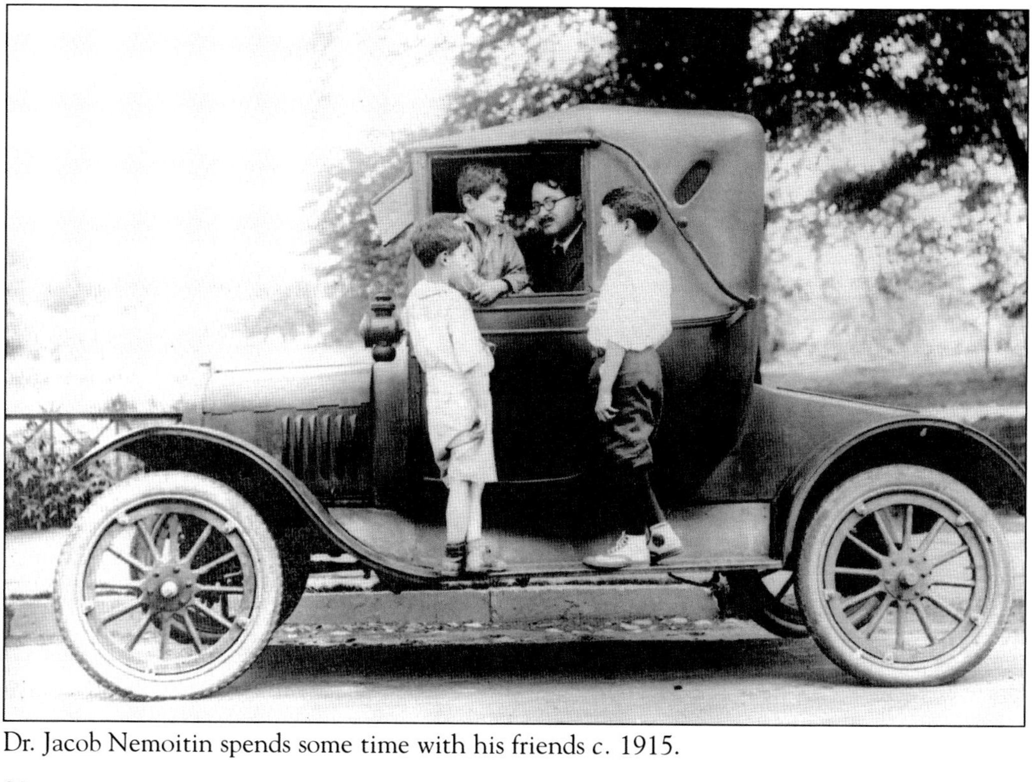

Dr. Jacob Nemoitin spends some time with his friends *c*. 1915.

Sam and Anna Goldberg lived in the second-floor apartment on the left side of this tenement on Hawthorne Street. Their son George was a founder of the Jewish Historical Society of Greater Stamford. Other tenants were Celia Karp, Murray and Herman Karas, and a Mrs. Fleisher.

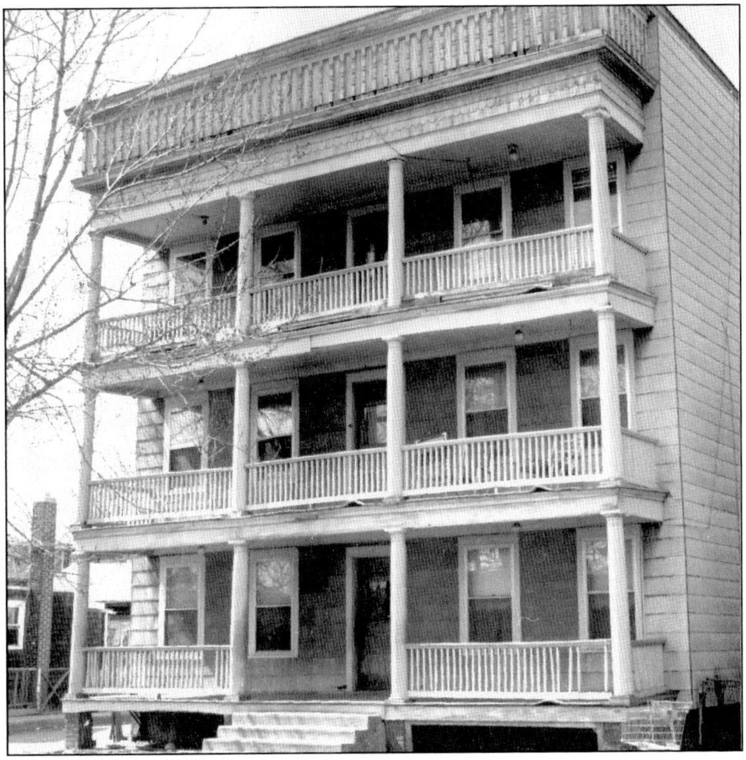

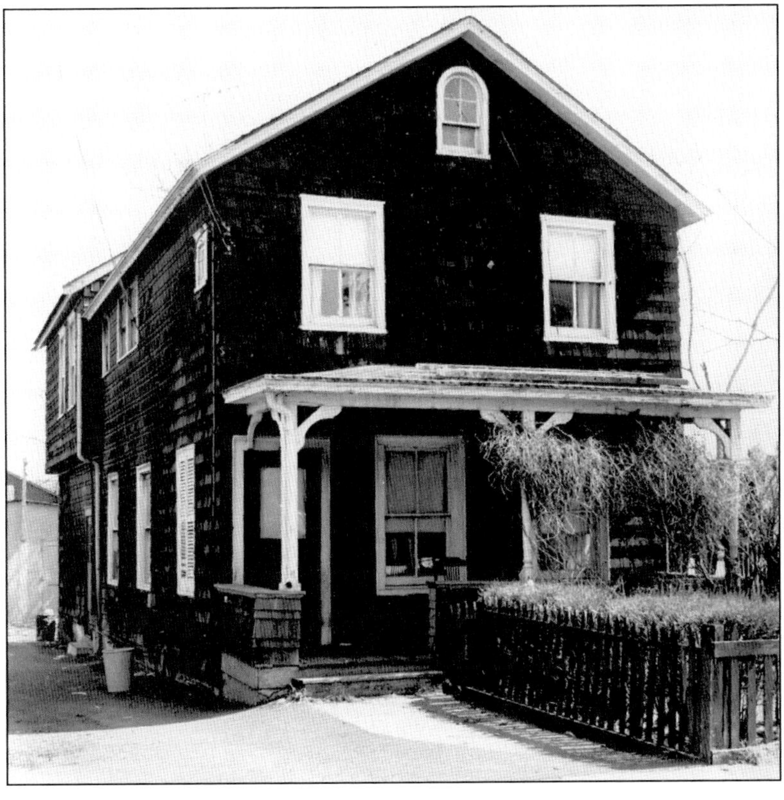

Pictured in 1968, this property at 42 Hawthorne Street was purchased by the Mangers, the parents of Marcia Lieberman, in 1918. Sen. Joseph Lieberman was born here in 1942 and lived in the house with his family until 1950.

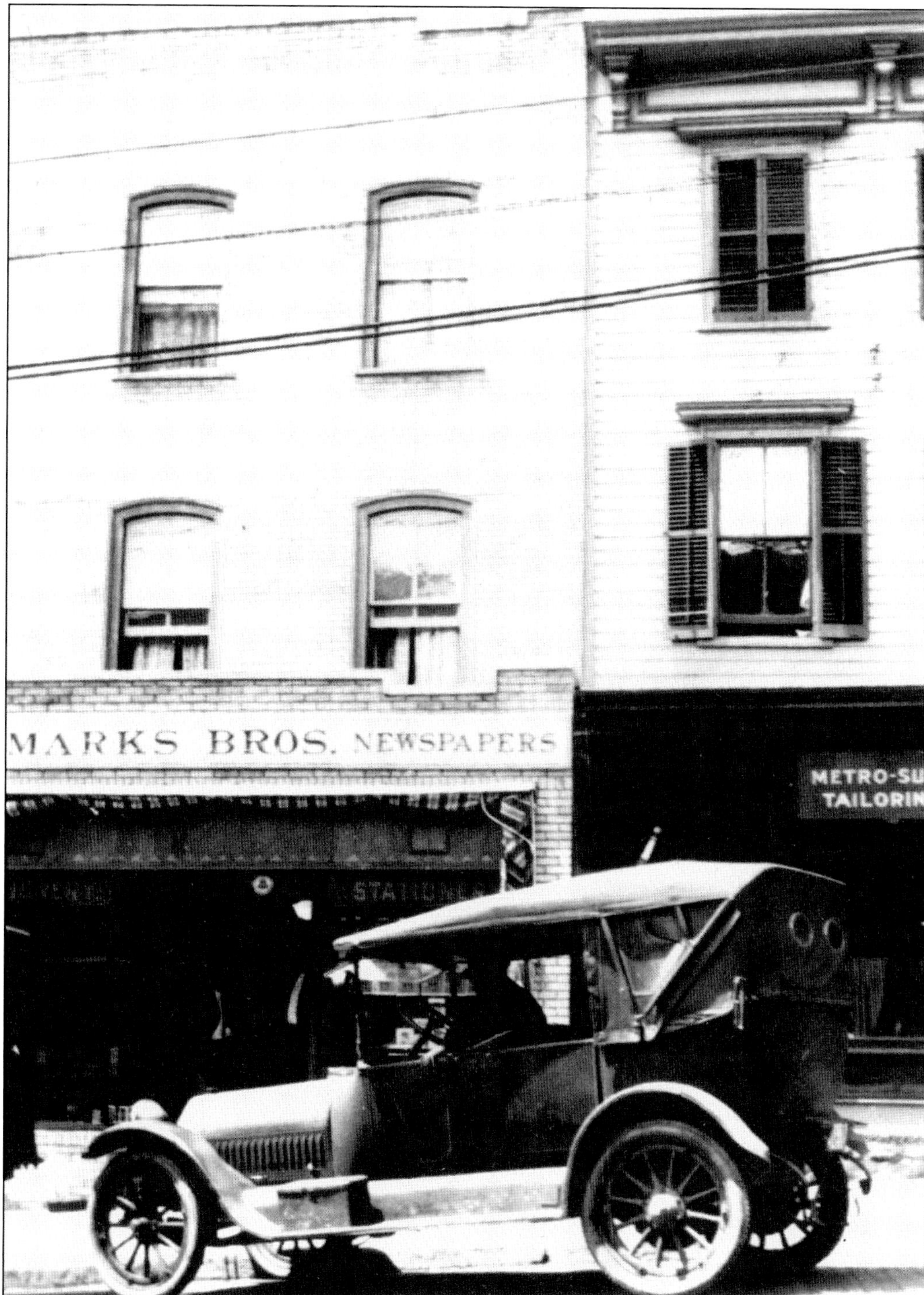

Above the stores on Greenwich Avenue, there were apartments where many Jewish merchants lived. Pictured is the Marks Brothers' newspaper and stationery store, founded in 1907. The Marks family was one of the earliest Jewish families to settle in Greenwich.

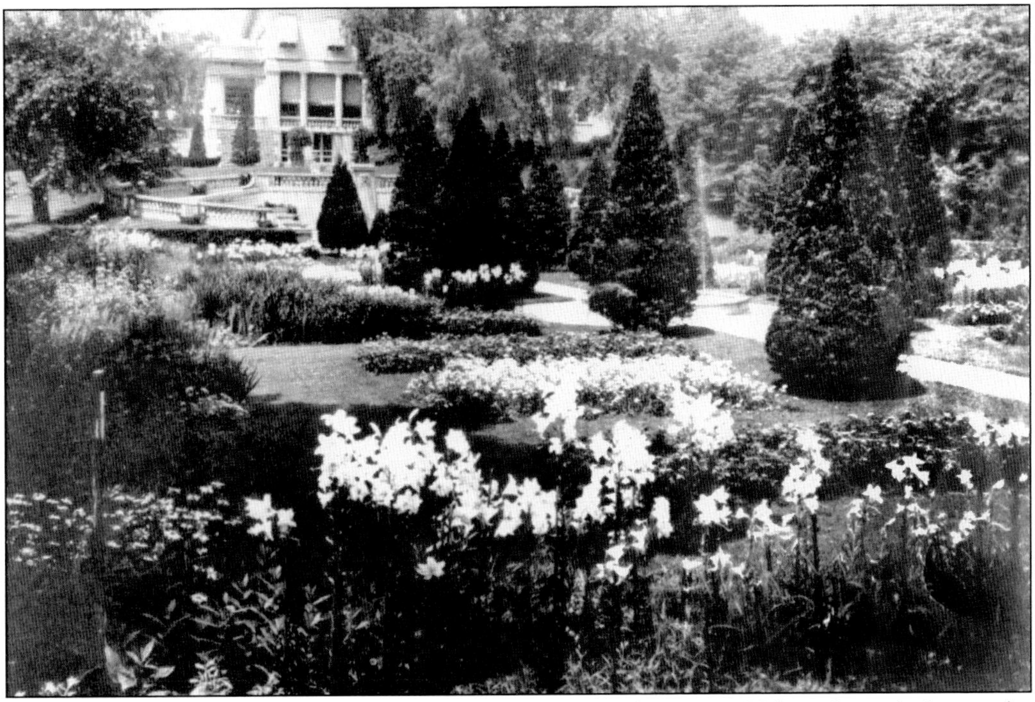

The estate of Valerie Langeloth of Greenwich is pictured *c.* 1929. Valerie Langeloth was the widow of Jacob Langeloth, the founder and president of American Metals Climax and a well-known Jewish philanthropist.

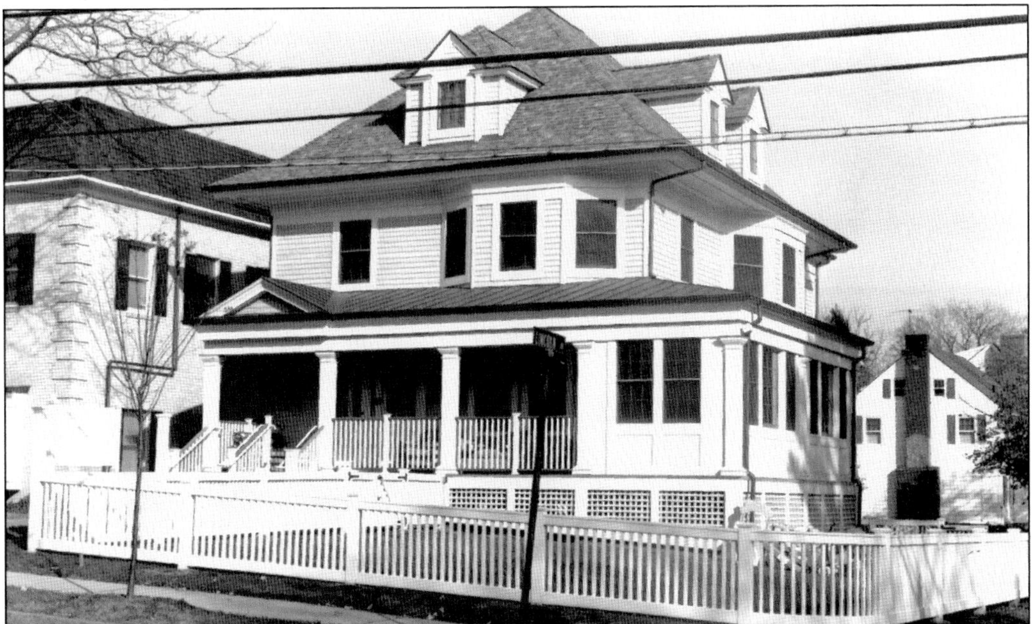

This is a current view of 75 Mason Street, Greenwich. The house was once owned by Morris and Sadye Steinberg. It was considered one of the "merchant mansions" on Mason Street. Chabad Lubavitch (a sect within the Hasidic movement, emphasizing Jewish learning) of Greenwich recently purchased and refurbished the building.

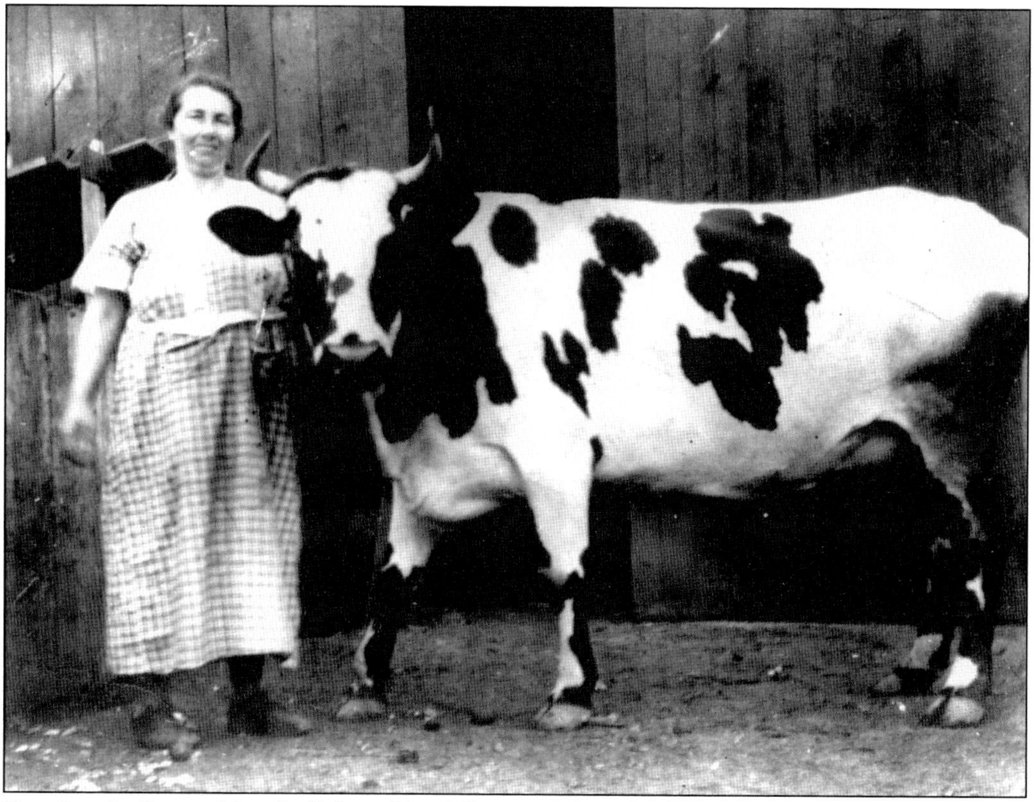

Standing in front of her "villa" on Virgil Street in Stamford, Mrs. Epstein proudly shows off her cow *c.* 1910.

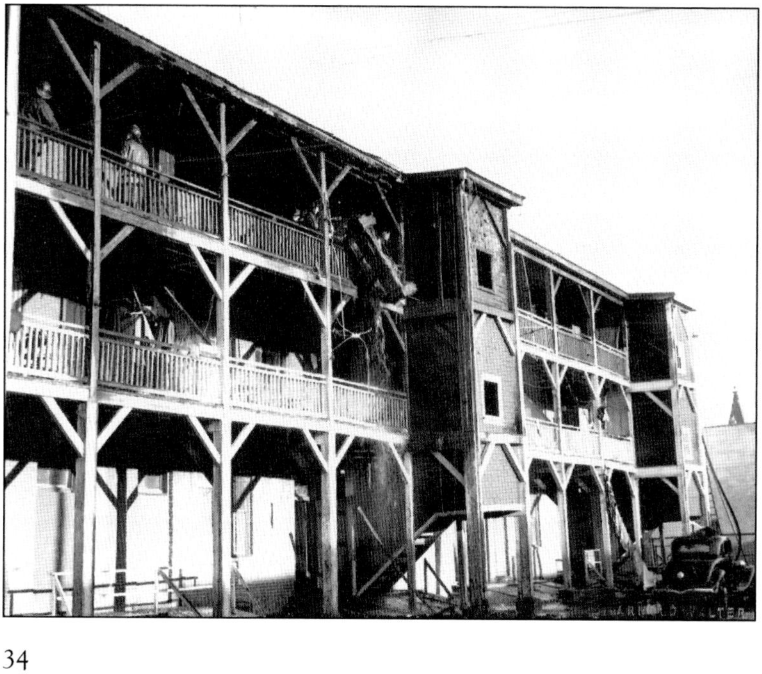

Shown is the rear of a Pacific Street tenement after a fire in 1940. The Jews were concentrated in and around Pacific Street in the early days of the eastern European migration.

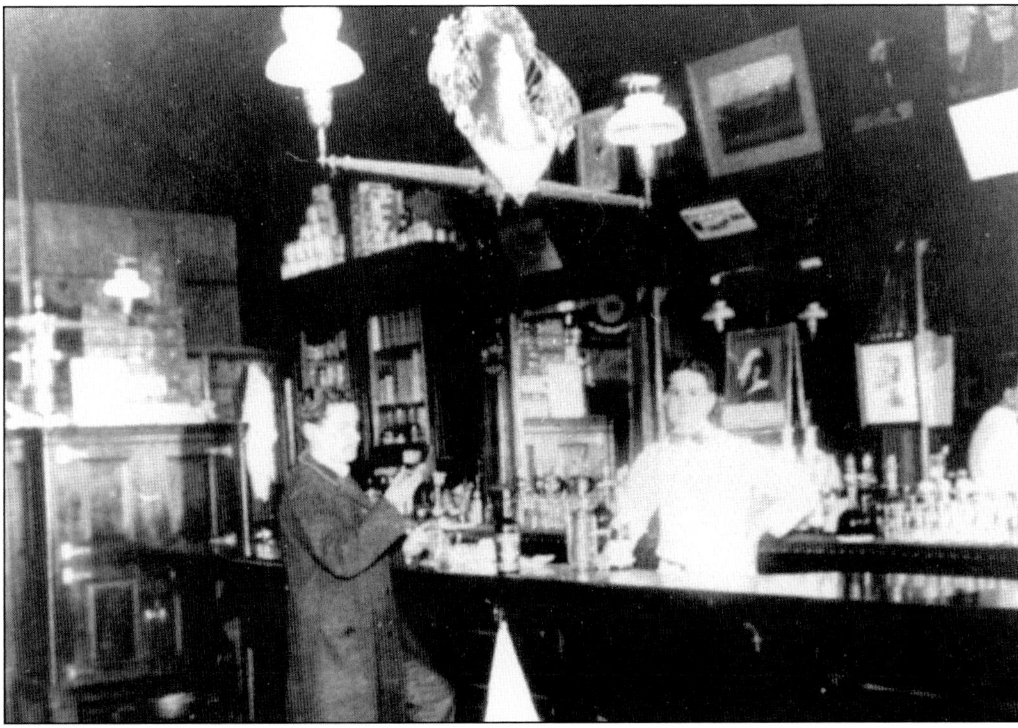

The Sandhaus Brothers' Saloon was located on Pacific Street in 1906.

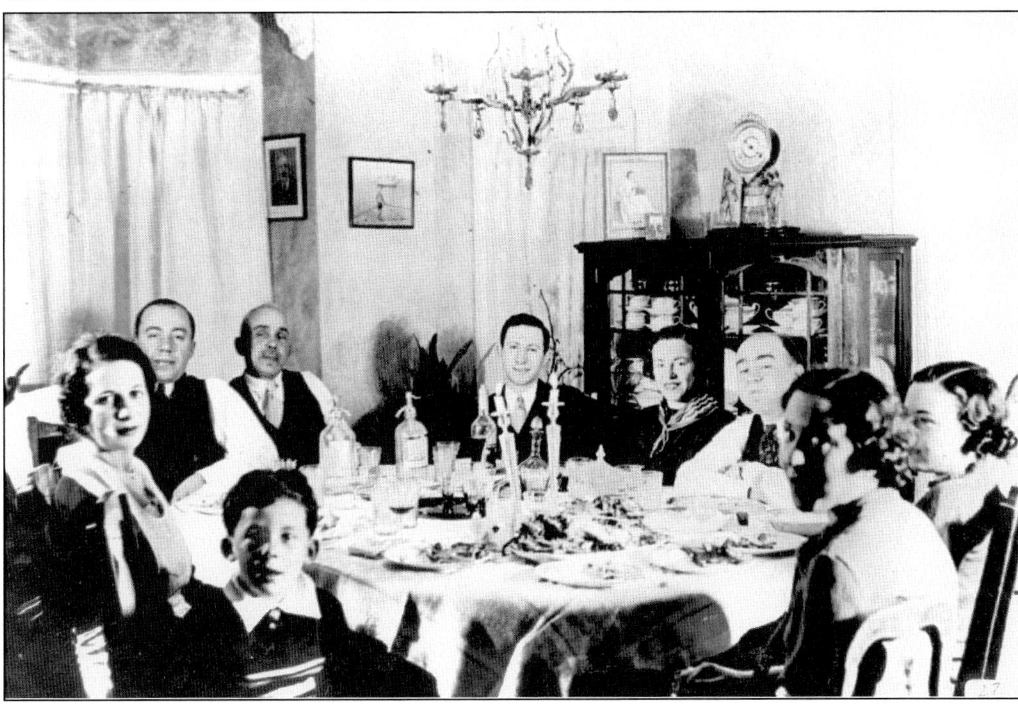

The Sherman family is gathered around the *yontif* (holiday) table in 1948. Counterclockwise from the front left are Billy, Gert, Joe, and Grandpa Sherman, Phil Infeld and his wife Syd, an unidentified person, and Rose and Mary (Sherman) Levine.

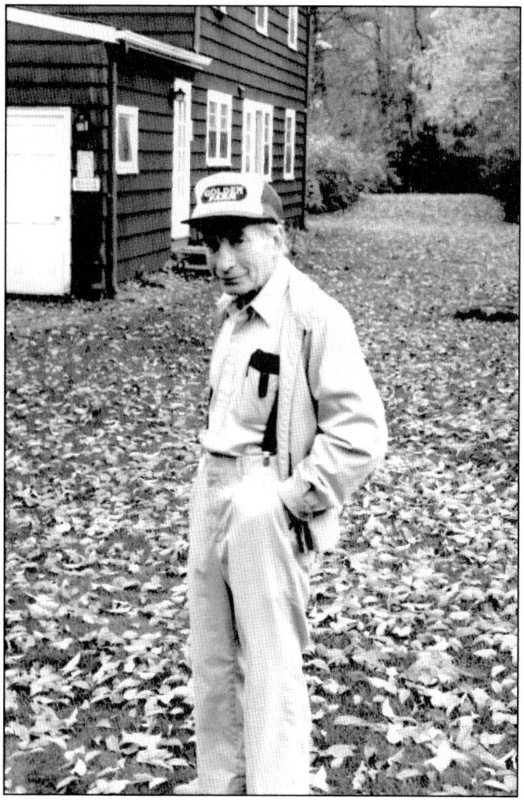

Dr. Walter R.C. Golden was a pathologist, a graduate of Yale in biochemistry, a director of Stamford Hospital Laboratory for 25 years, and a chicken farmer. He was born in New Milford in 1914. He started his chicken farm in 1946 on Turn of River Road and moved to 722 Rockrimmon Road in 1952. He was the last farmer in Stamford.

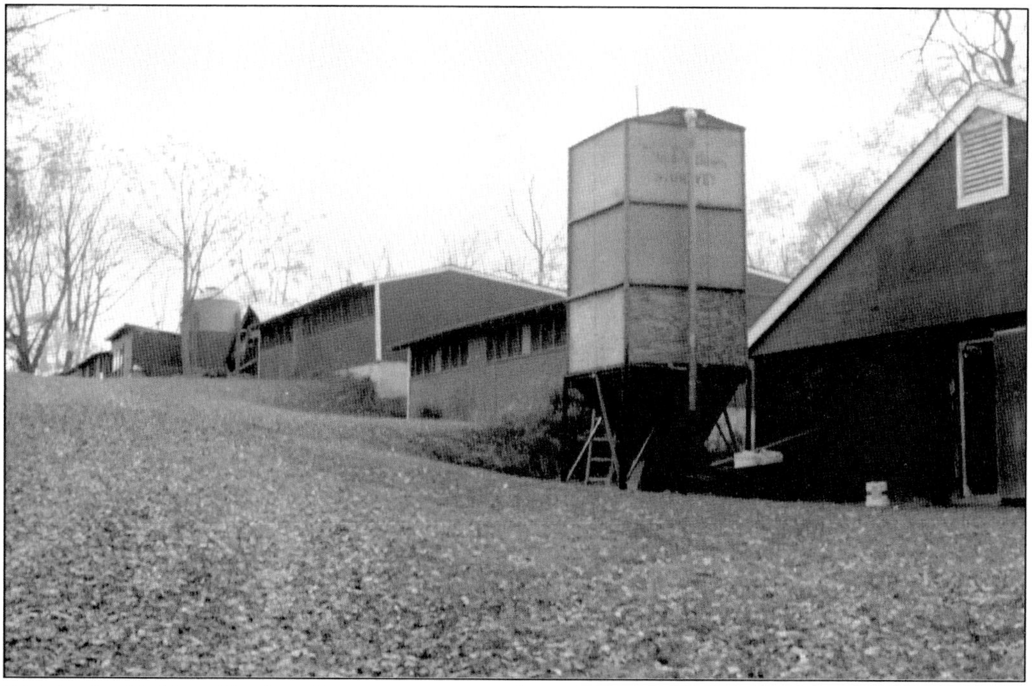

This is the Golden Chicken Farm as it appeared in 1991.

Sarah Epstein stops her motorcycle, complete with sidecar, on Brook Street. Her family owned Epstein Brothers' Tire Company.

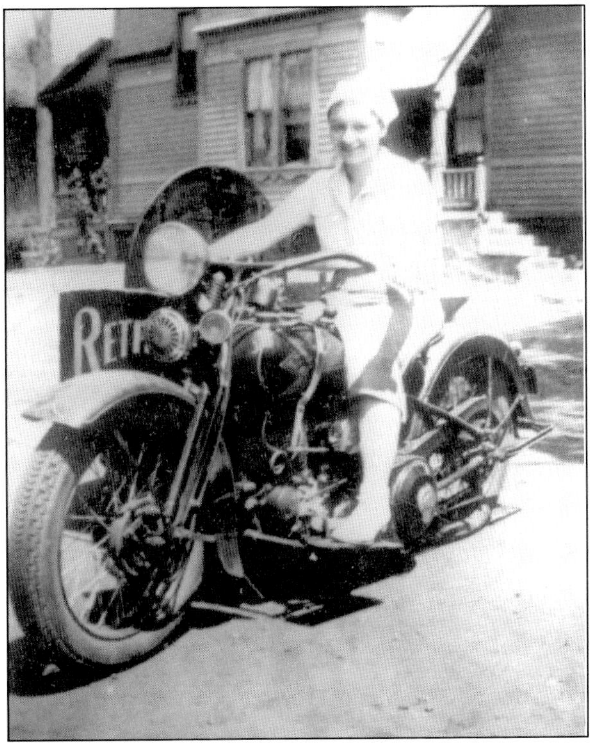

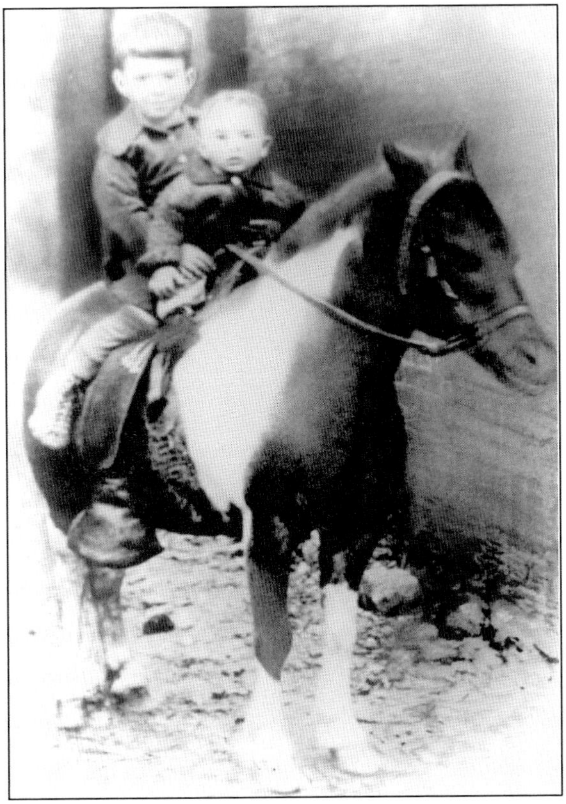

The parents of David and Irving Blum had their children's photograph taken with a pony by an itinerant photographer in a Pacific Street alley c. 1920. As an adult, David Blum served on the Stamford Board of Representatives.

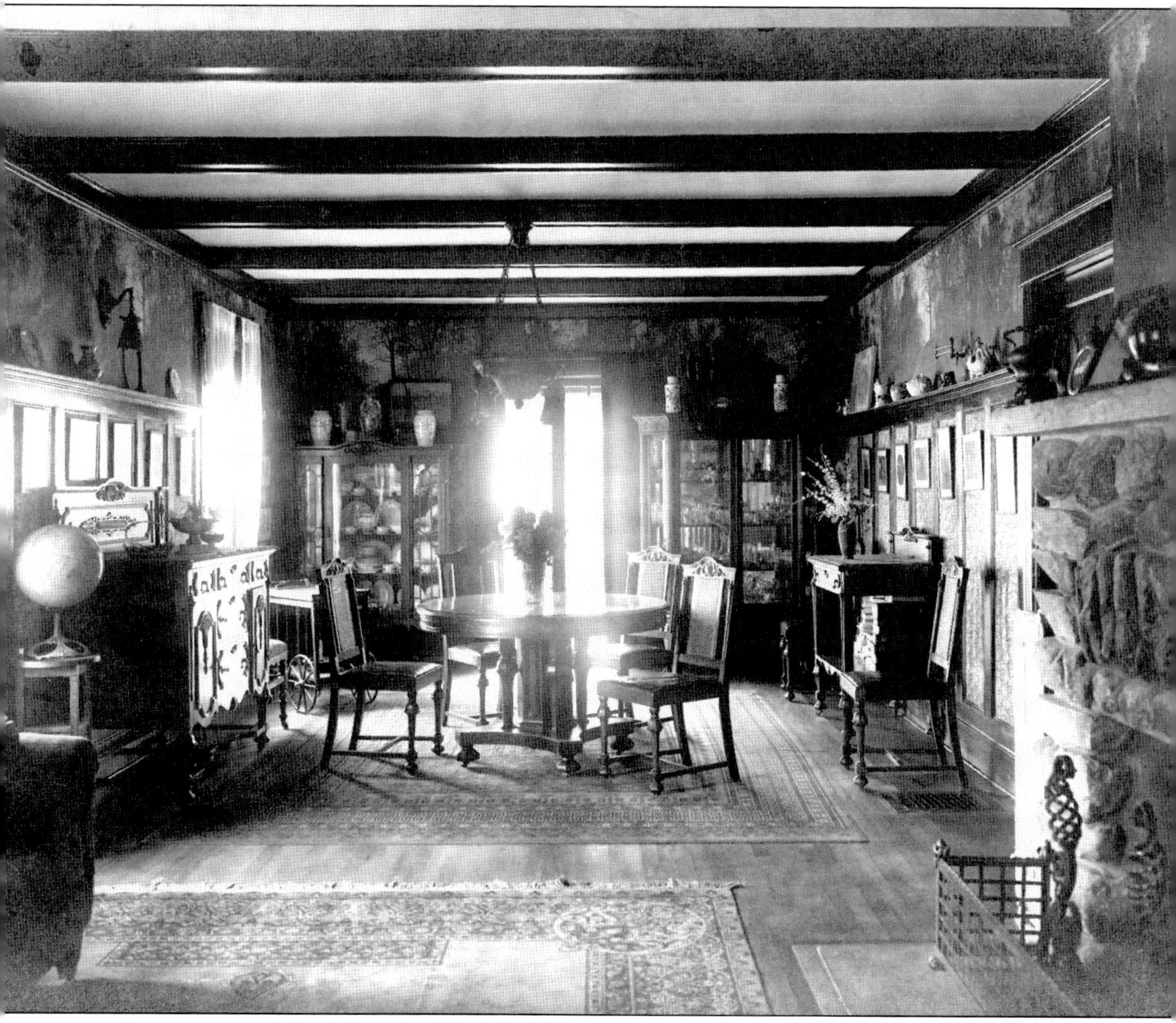

The interior of the Nemoitin home on Home Court in Stamford reflects the culture and aesthetics of the era *c.* 1918.

Three

Portraits from Our Past

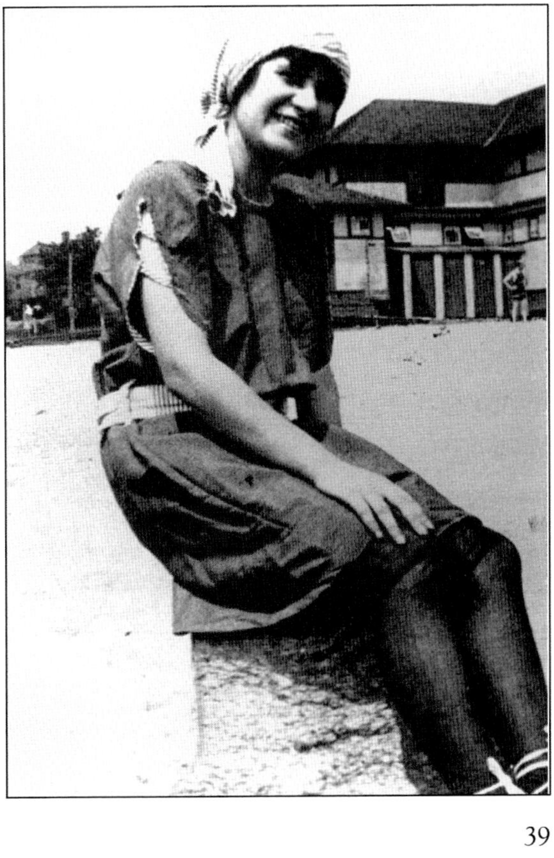

Dressed in the latest beach fashion, Betty Cohen sits in front of the pavilion at Spelke Beach c. 1920.

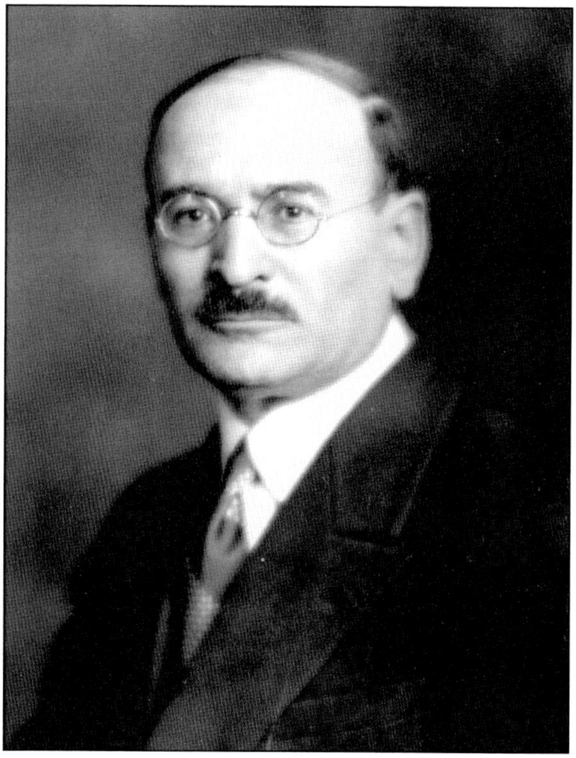

Jacob E. Berger owned an electrical supply store on Pacific Street. He also served as head of education at the Hebrew Institute for many years.

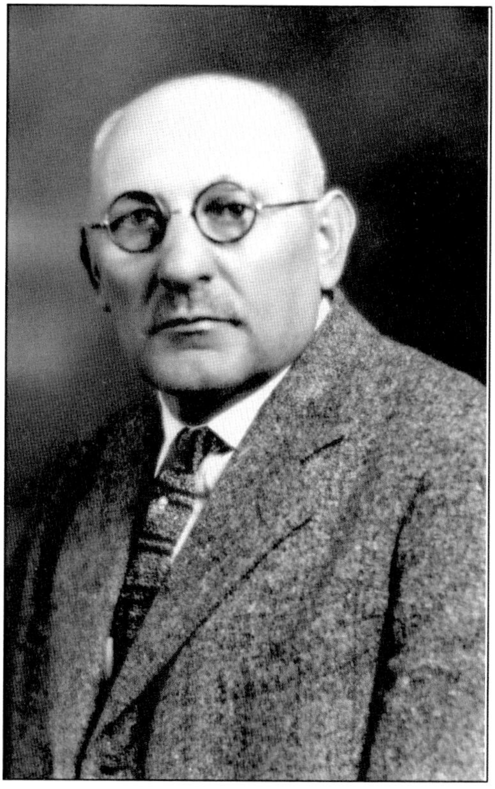

Morris Epstein was a partner in Epstein-Nevas Wholesale Grocery Distributing Company and first vice president of the Stamford Jewish Community Center *c.* 1930.

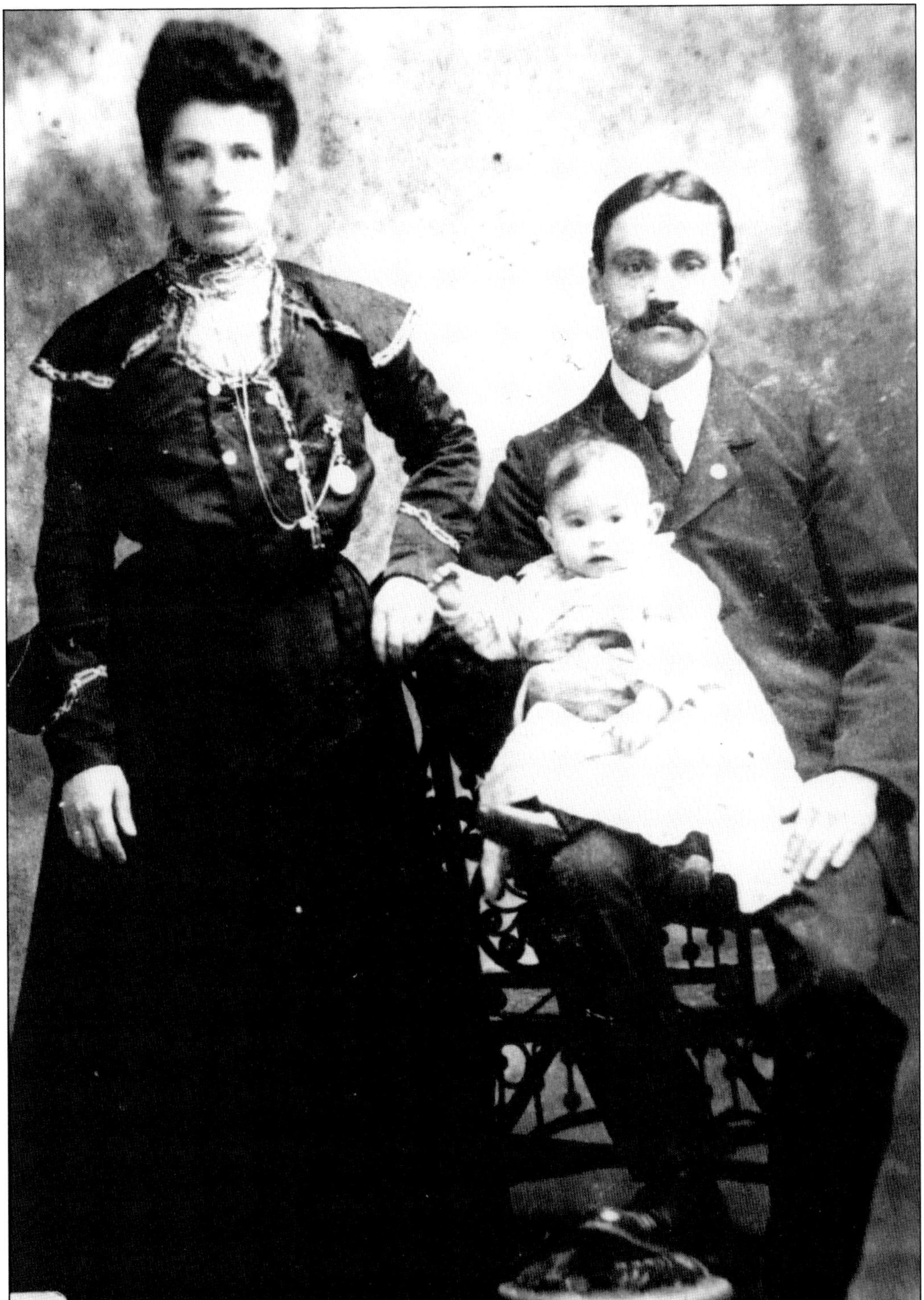

Yetta and Morris Sandhaus and their child pose for a portrait in a photographer's studio. Yetta Sandhaus's elegant "waist" was the height of fashion *c*. 1905.

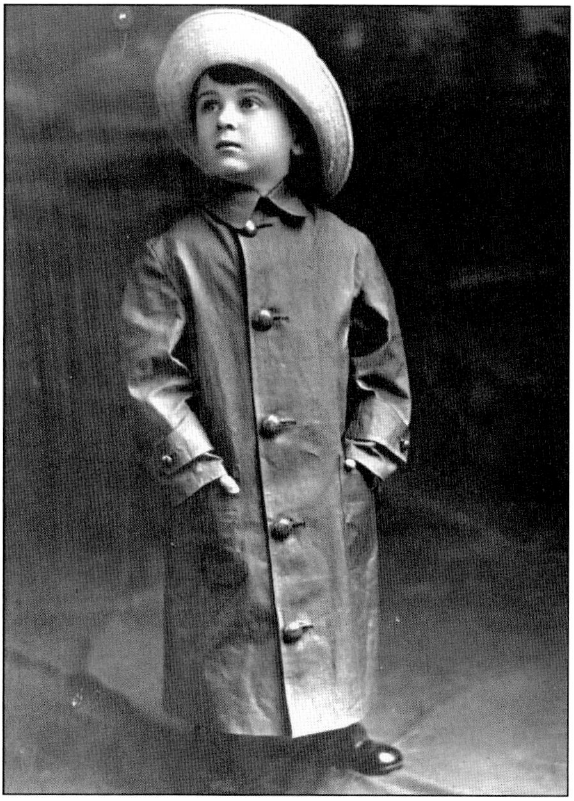

Bernard Nemoitin is pictured in 1912 at the age of four.

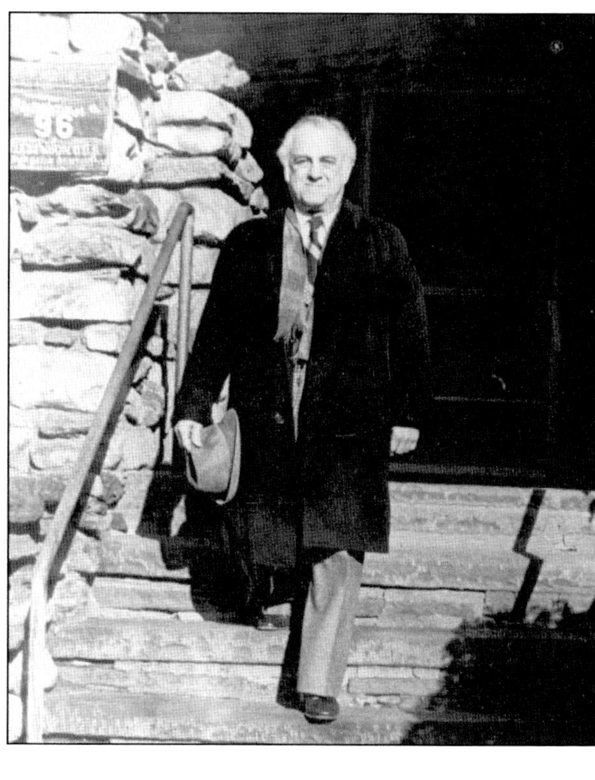

In 1983, at age 75, Dr. Bernard Nemoitin is shown leaving the office he shared with his late father, at 96 Main Street in Stamford.

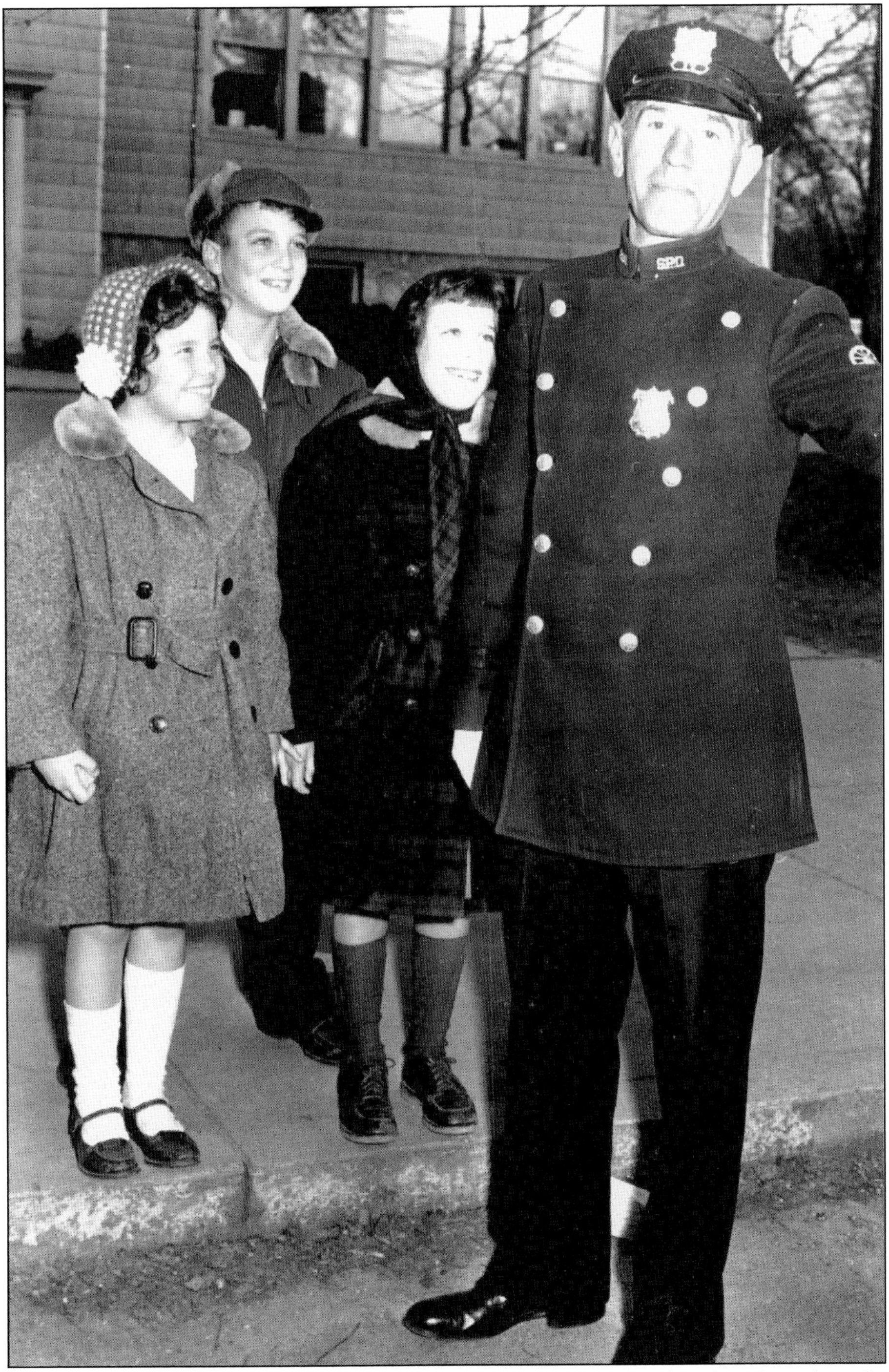

Harry Spelke (right), the son of Isaac and Rachel Spelke, was the first Jewish policeman in Stamford. He was appointed a supernumerary in 1928 but did not receive a permanent appointment until January 1937. He continued on the force until his retirement in September 1963. The children pictured with him in front of Springdale School are, from left to right, Jill Goldman, Alan Kruchkow, and Diane Kruchkow.

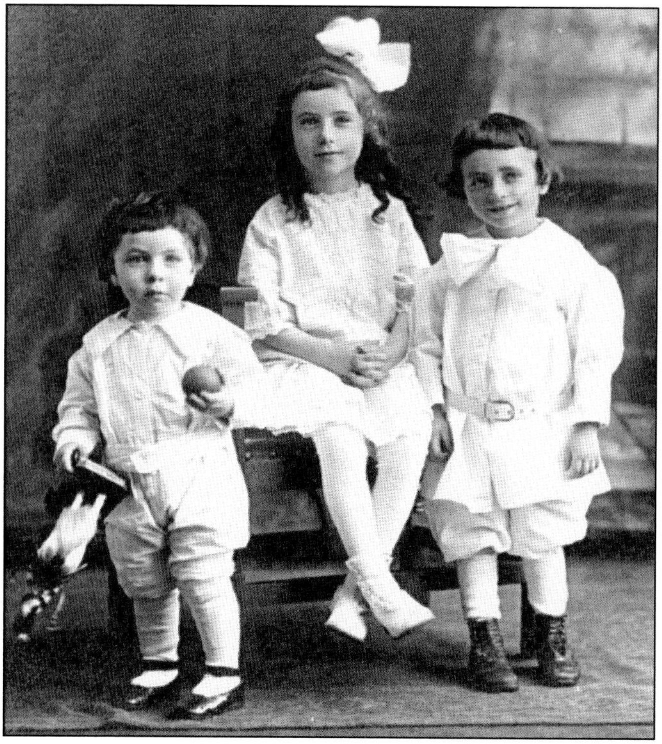

The Gilden children pose for a photograph in 1915. Little Joe Gilden (right) was a sickly child who was not expected to survive. He lived to be 85 years old.

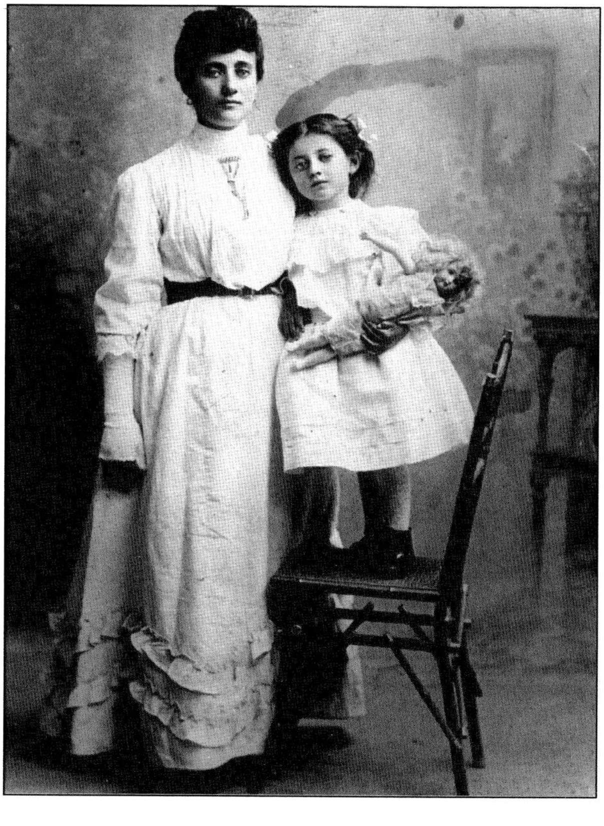

Sarah Beningson poses with her mother *c.* 1900.

Celia Cohen and her daughter Betty are pictured in 1910. Celia Cohen owned a dry goods and clothing store.

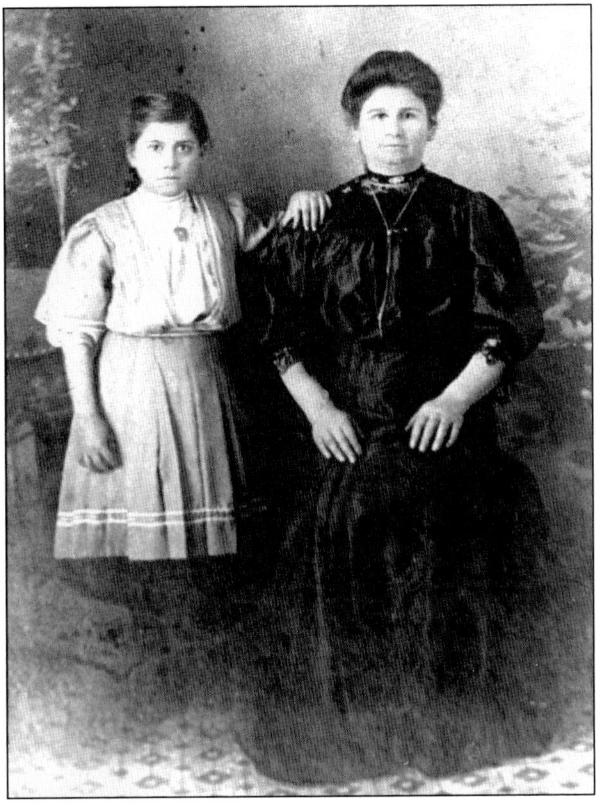

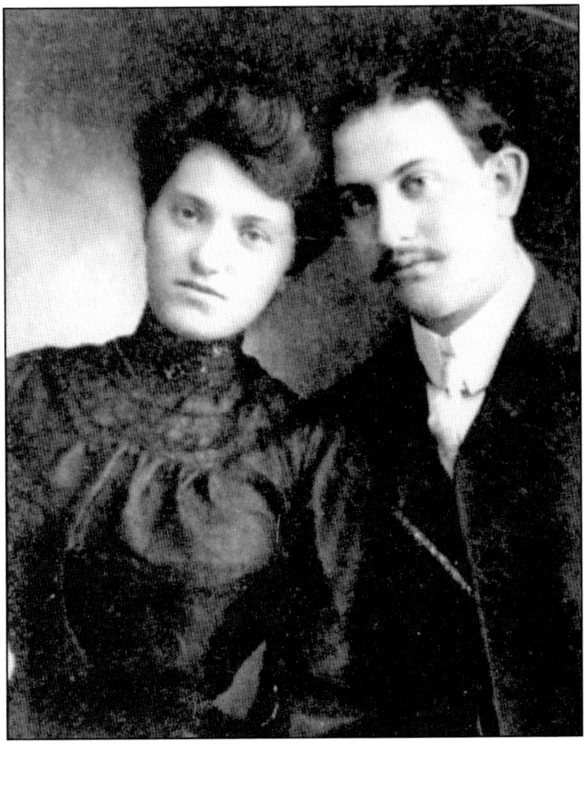

Dr. Charles Dichter and his wife, Celia, settled in Stamford in 1908.

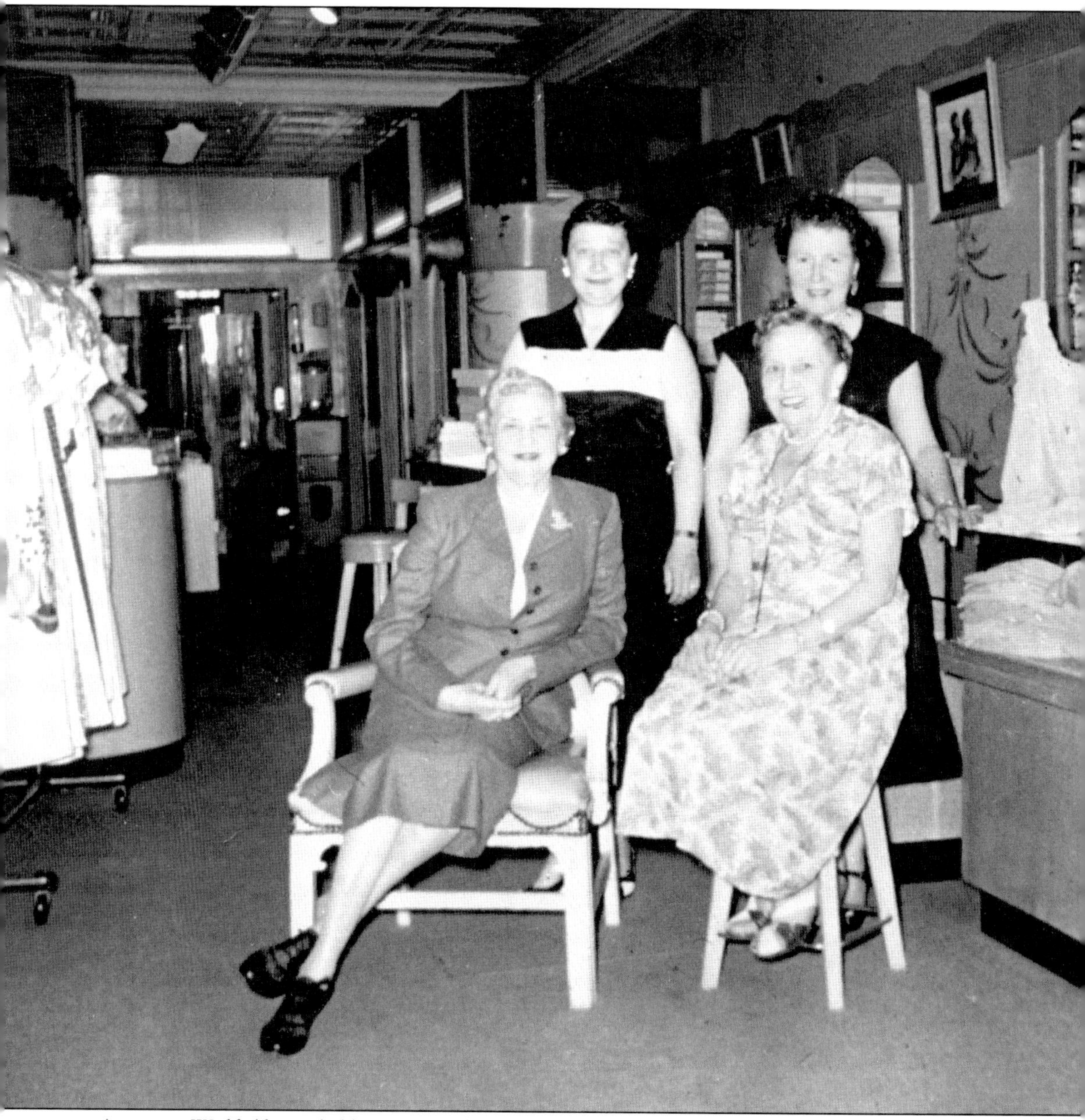

Annette Wolf (front left) poses with her staff in 1940. The Annette Shop in downtown Stamford sold women's corsets and undergarments. Annette Wolf opened the shop in 1933, and when she retired, Betty Mackey took over the business and ran it until March 1997, when it closed.

Shown are Betty Brownstein (left) and Betty Cohen c. 1920.

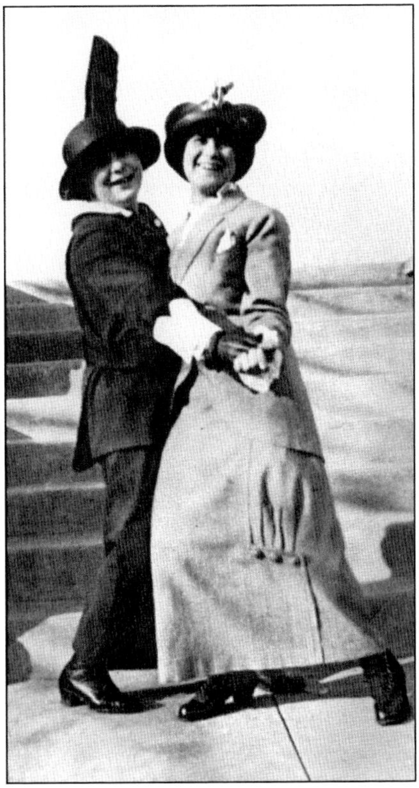

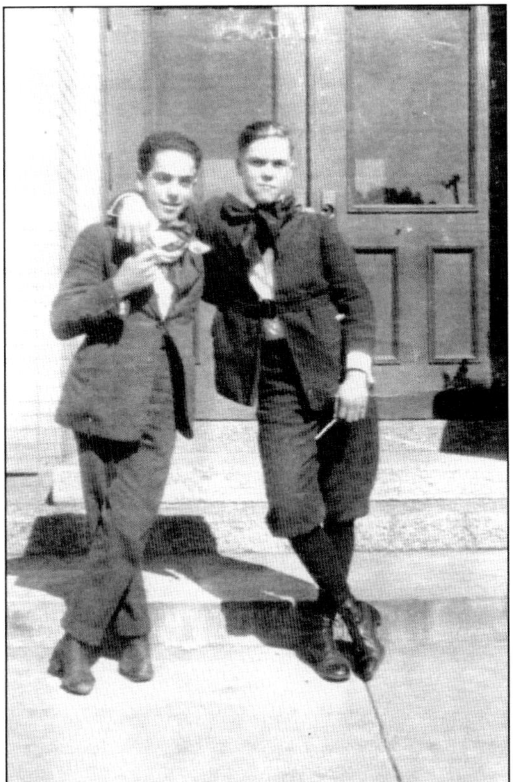

Max Taylor (left) and Joe Lockwood stand in front of the Havemeyer School in Greenwich. The Taylor family owned a Landmark store in Cos Cob and was one of the earliest Jewish families to settle in Greenwich.

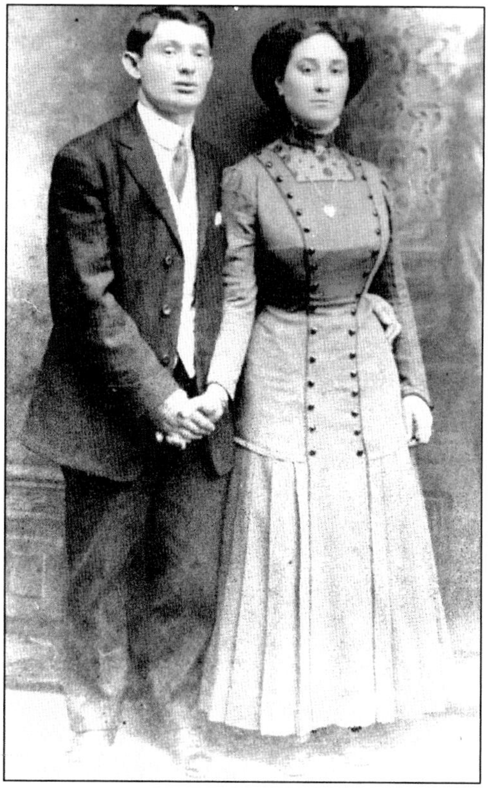

Isaac and Anna Goldberg were an uncle and aunt of George Goldberg, one of the founders of the Jewish Historical Society of Greater Stamford. Isaac Goldberg, a local cattle dealer and meat wholesaler, owned an abattoir on West Hill Road near the cemetery of Congregation Agudath Sholom.

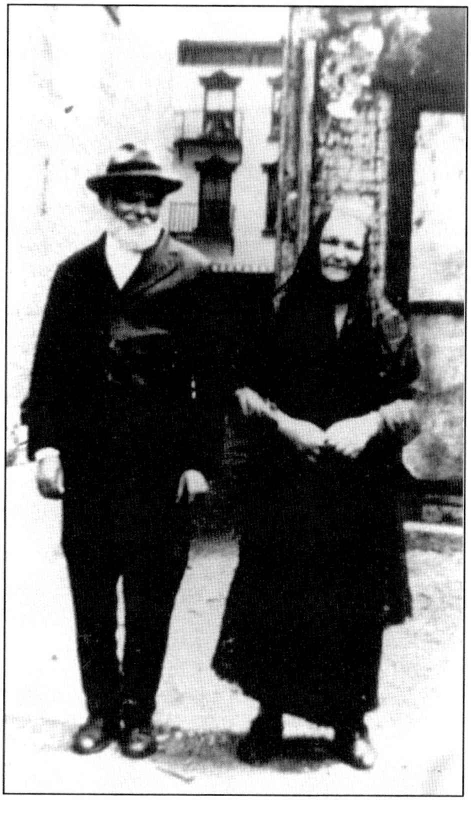

Pictured are the parents of Hyman Brazel of kosher meat market fame.

Betty Gordon of Greenwich, daughter of Rose and William Gordon, is shown in her Wave uniform *c.* 1943.

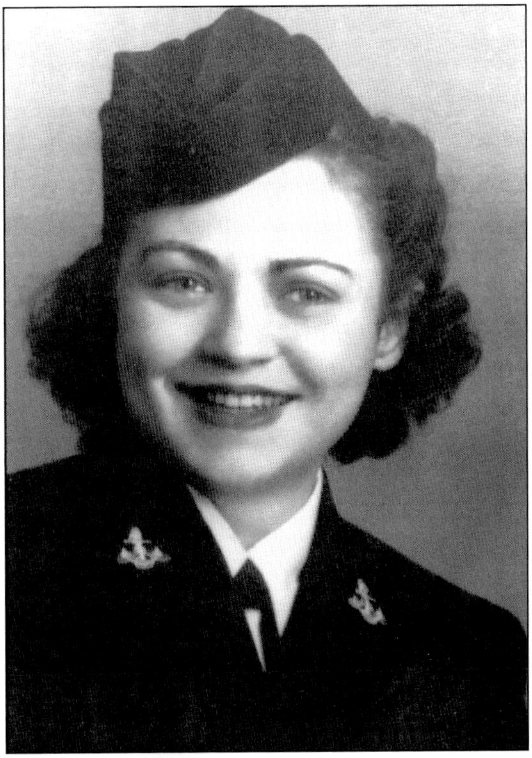

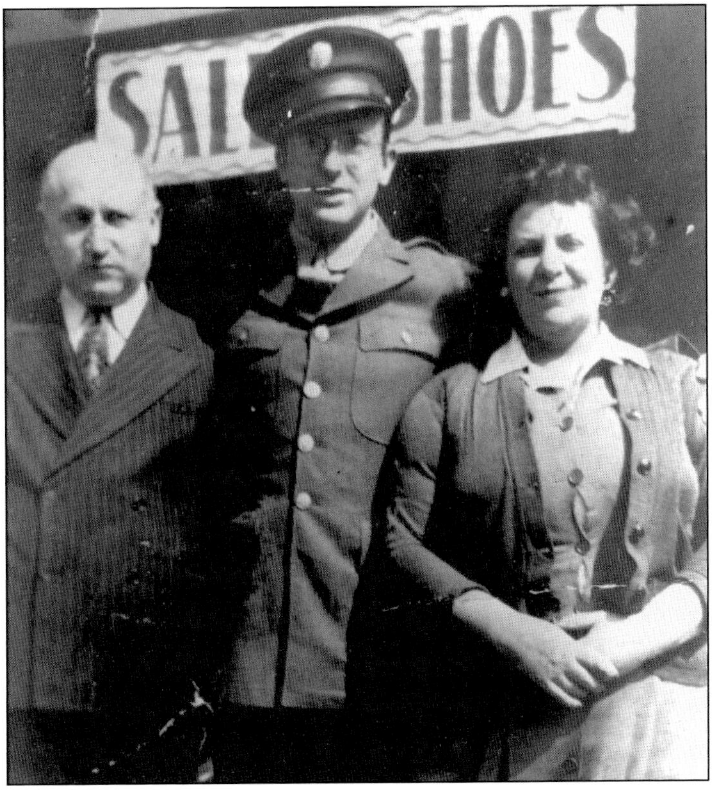

Isadore Shapiro, his son Michael, and his wife, Anna, pose in front of their clothing store at 114 Pacific Street in 1944. They later moved to Atlantic Street, where the store was known as Cousin Shapiro's.

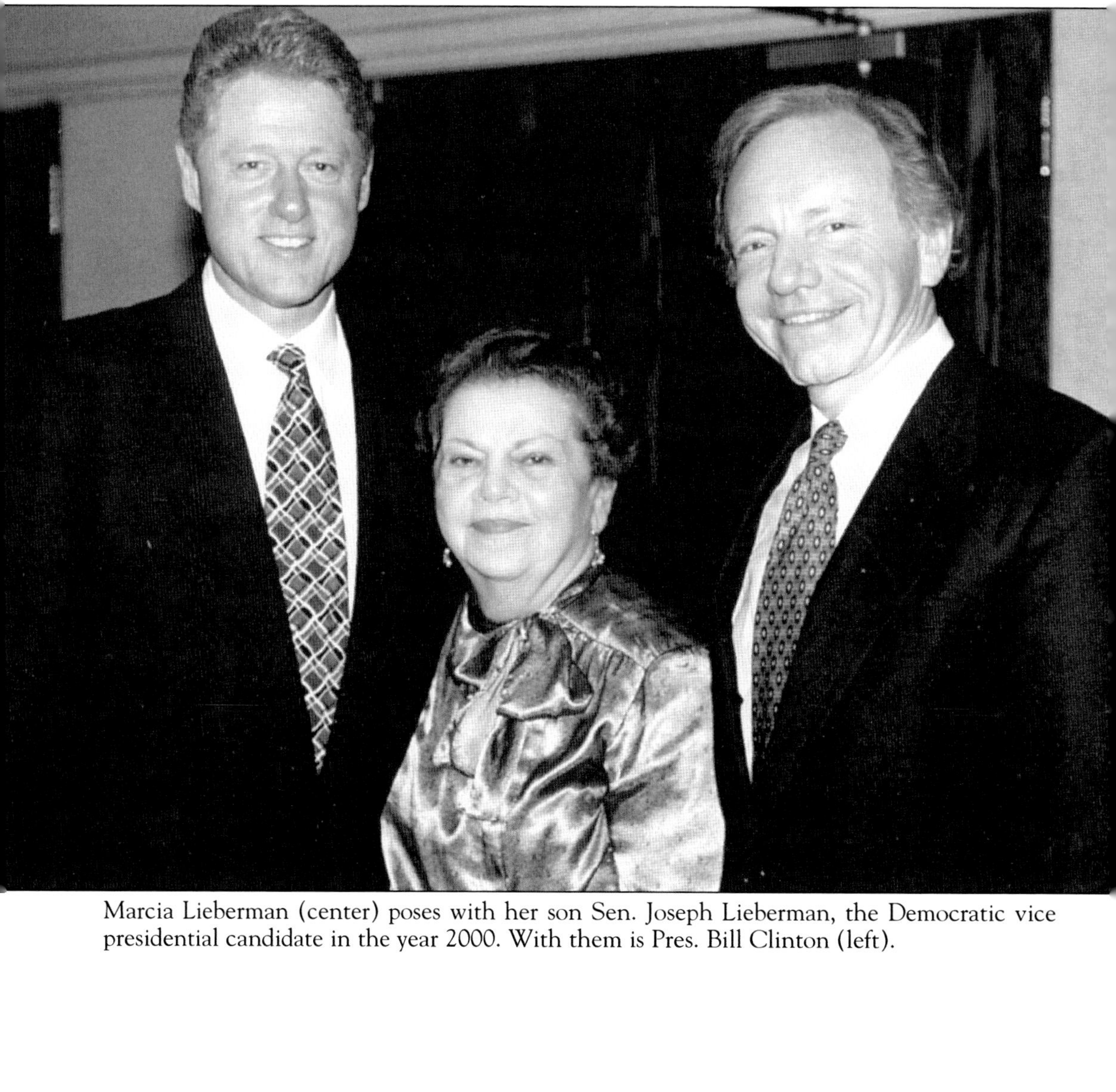

Marcia Lieberman (center) poses with her son Sen. Joseph Lieberman, the Democratic vice presidential candidate in the year 2000. With them is Pres. Bill Clinton (left).

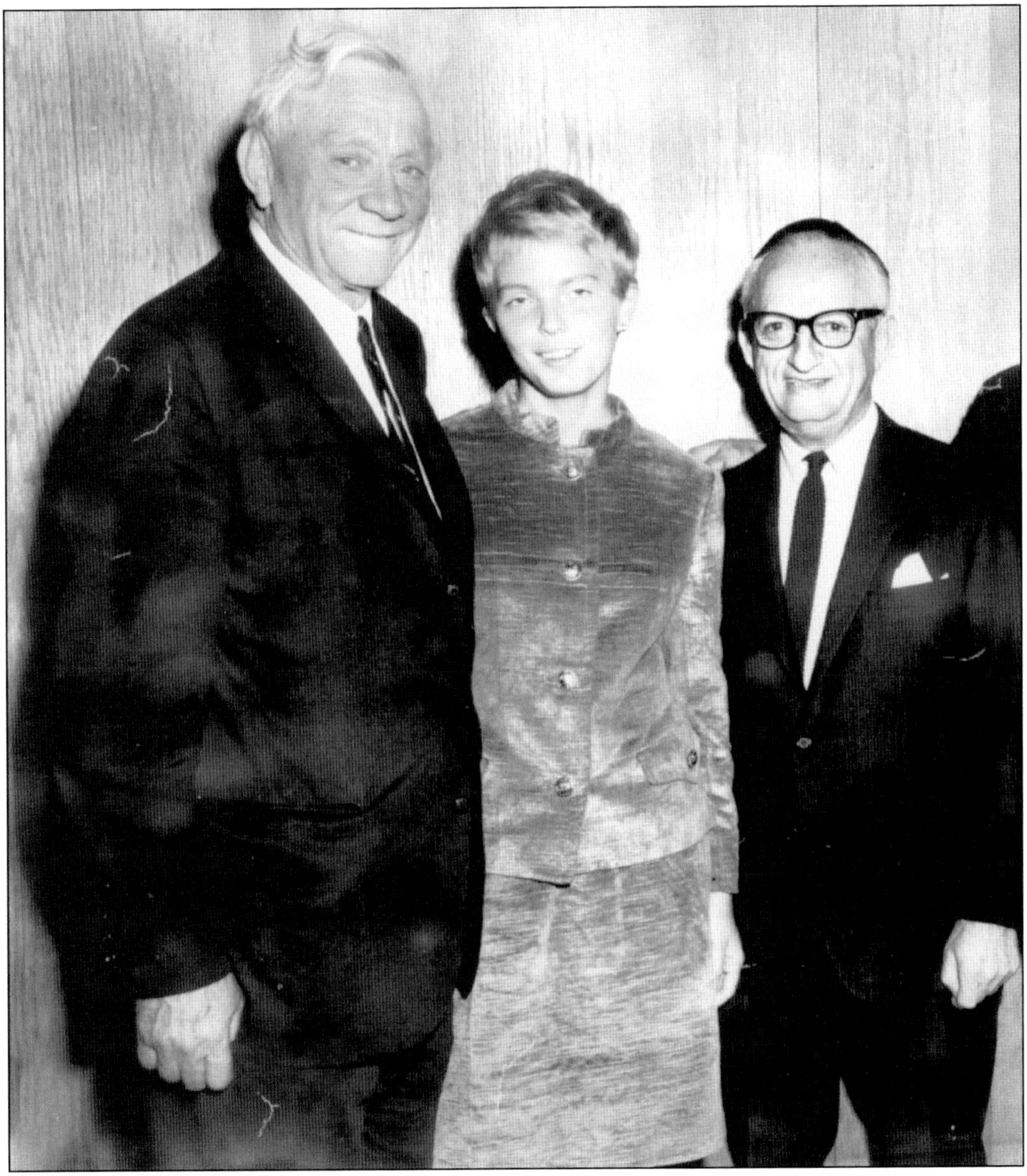

U.S. Supreme Court Justice William O. Douglas (left) is pictured with Mrs. Douglas and Harry Rosenbaum in 1964.

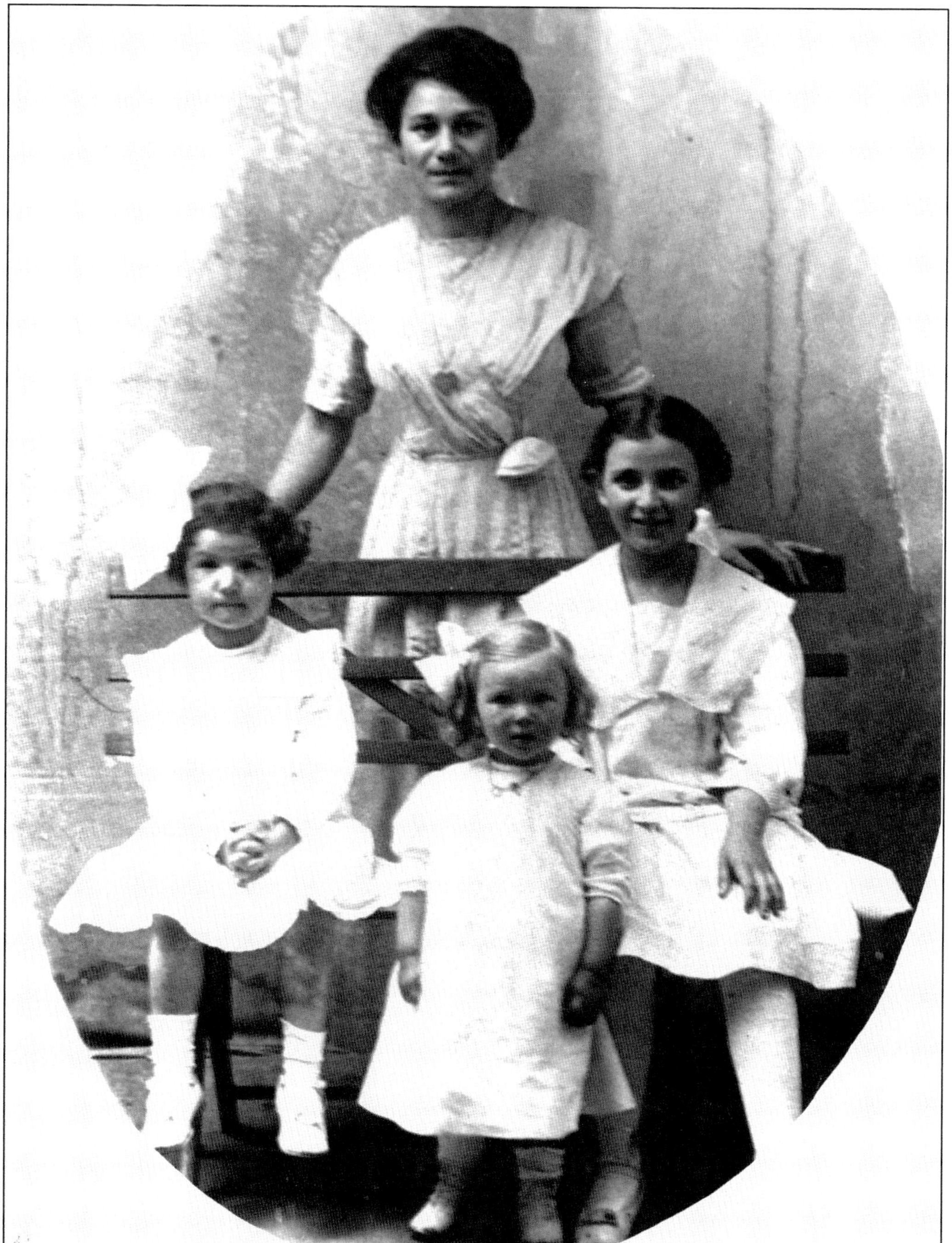

The Freeds were among the more prosperous members of the Jewish community. Posing with their governess, Julia Bauer, in 1913 are the daughters of Henry and Mary Freed, from left to right, Katherine Freed, Cora Freed (Duckman), and Stella Freed (Taylor).

Four

Our Communal Experiences

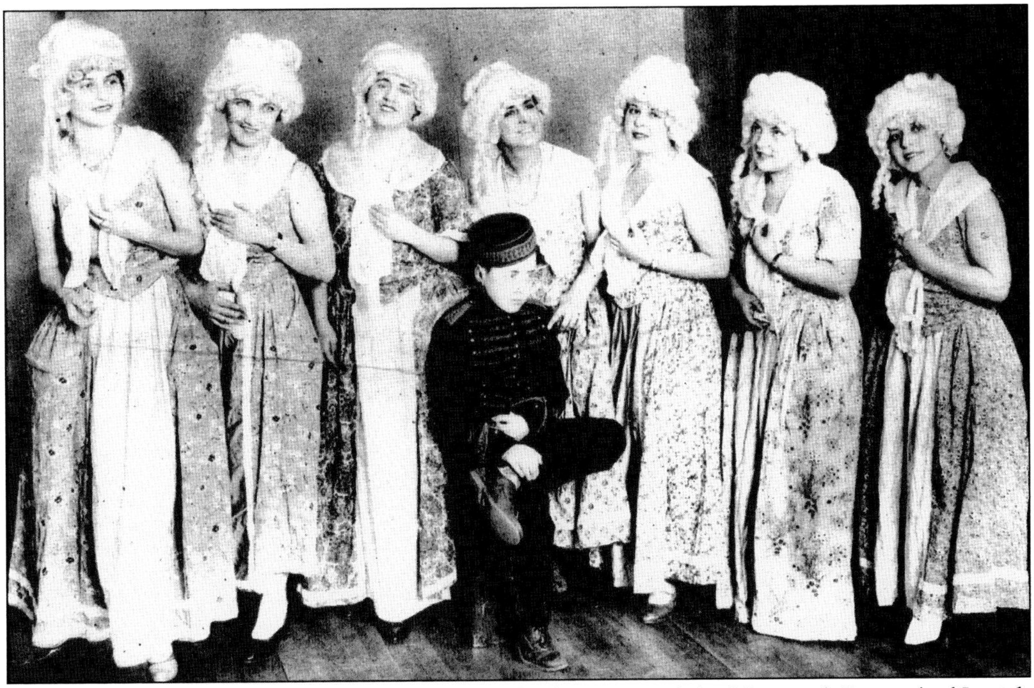

The Follies of 1929 was presented by the Stamford Section of the National Council of Jewish Women at the Jewish Community Center. Among those participating in the production is Mrs. Simeon Weissman (second from left).

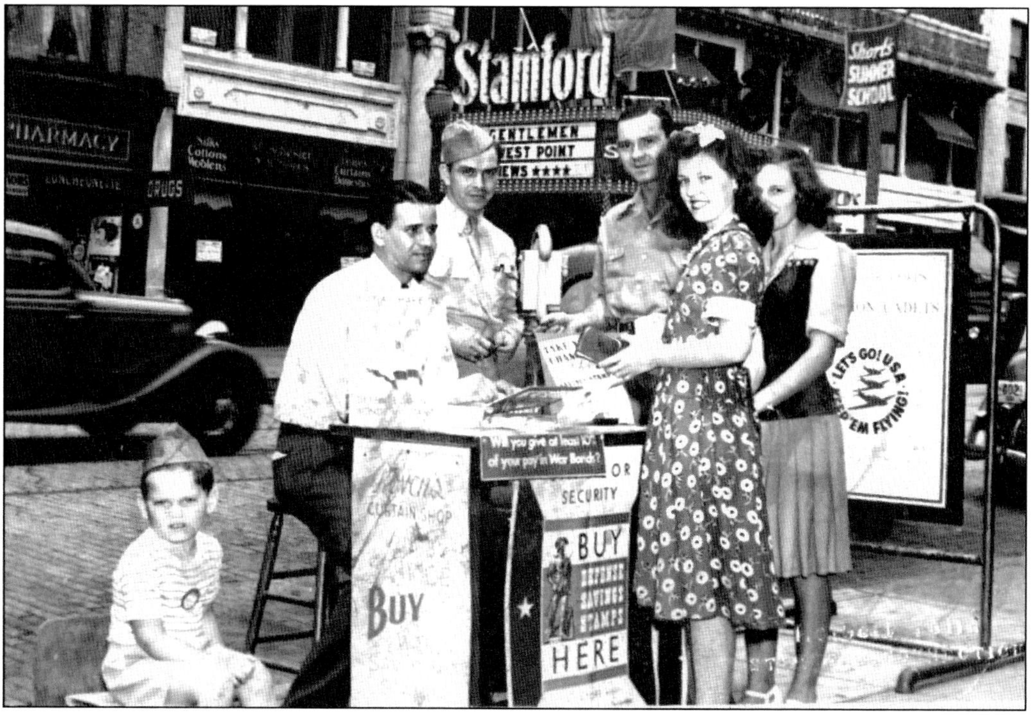

Al Roven and his son Larry Roven sell war bonds on Atlantic Street in 1943.

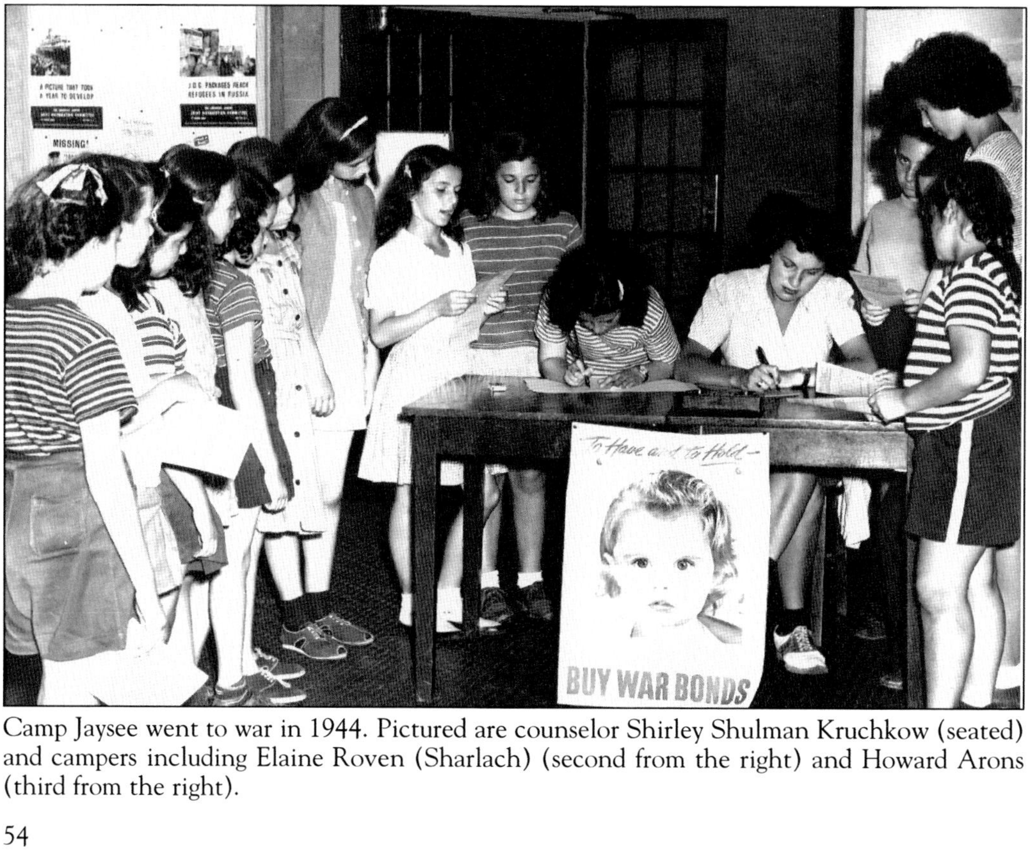

Camp Jaysee went to war in 1944. Pictured are counselor Shirley Shulman Kruchkow (seated) and campers including Elaine Roven (Sharlach) (second from the right) and Howard Arons (third from the right).

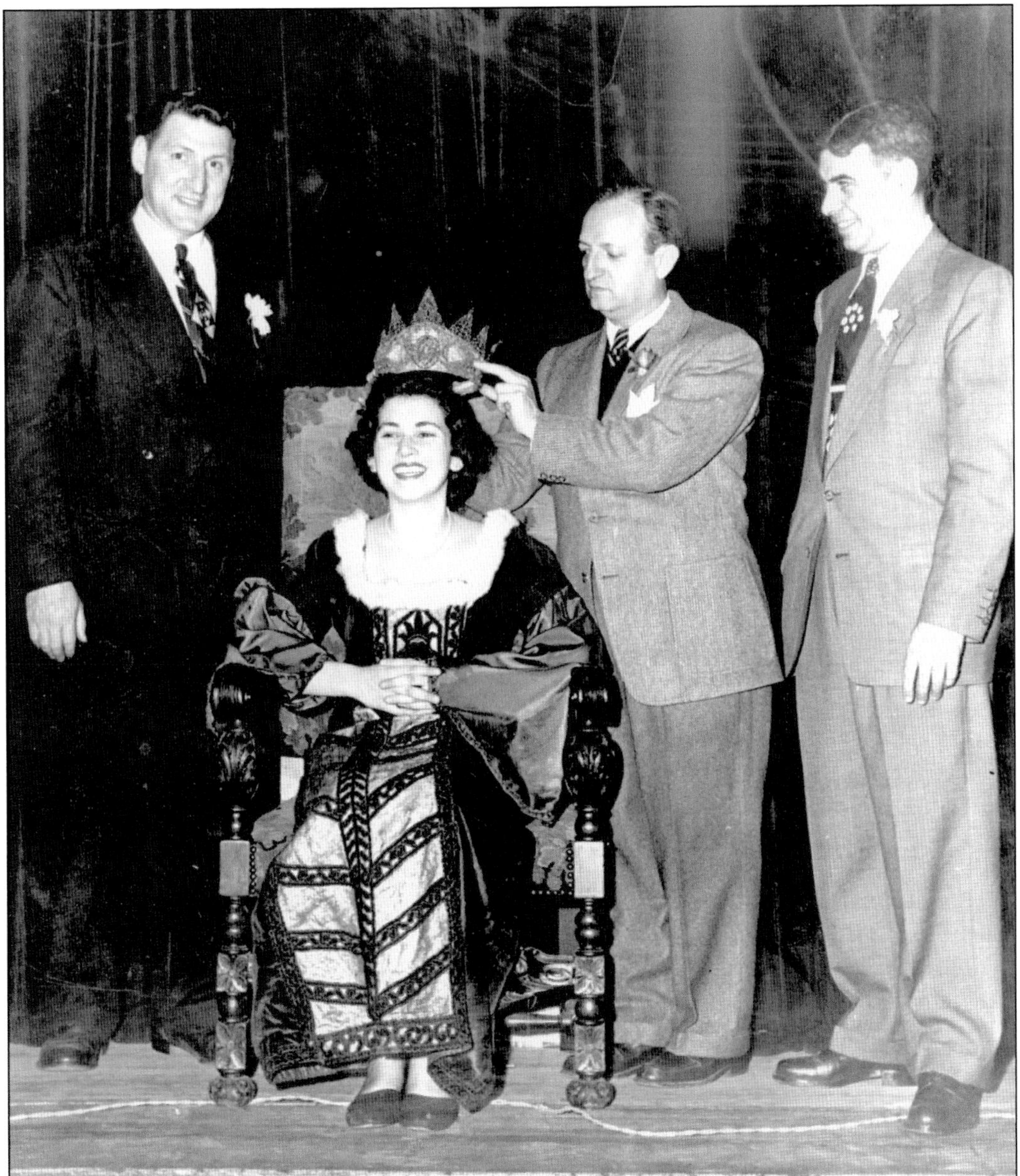

Purim queen Rosalind Bloomfield (Ziskin) is crowned in 1949. With her, from left to right, are Jewish Community Center director Morris Kronenfeld, Harry Rosenbaum, and Dr. Elmer Rosenblum.

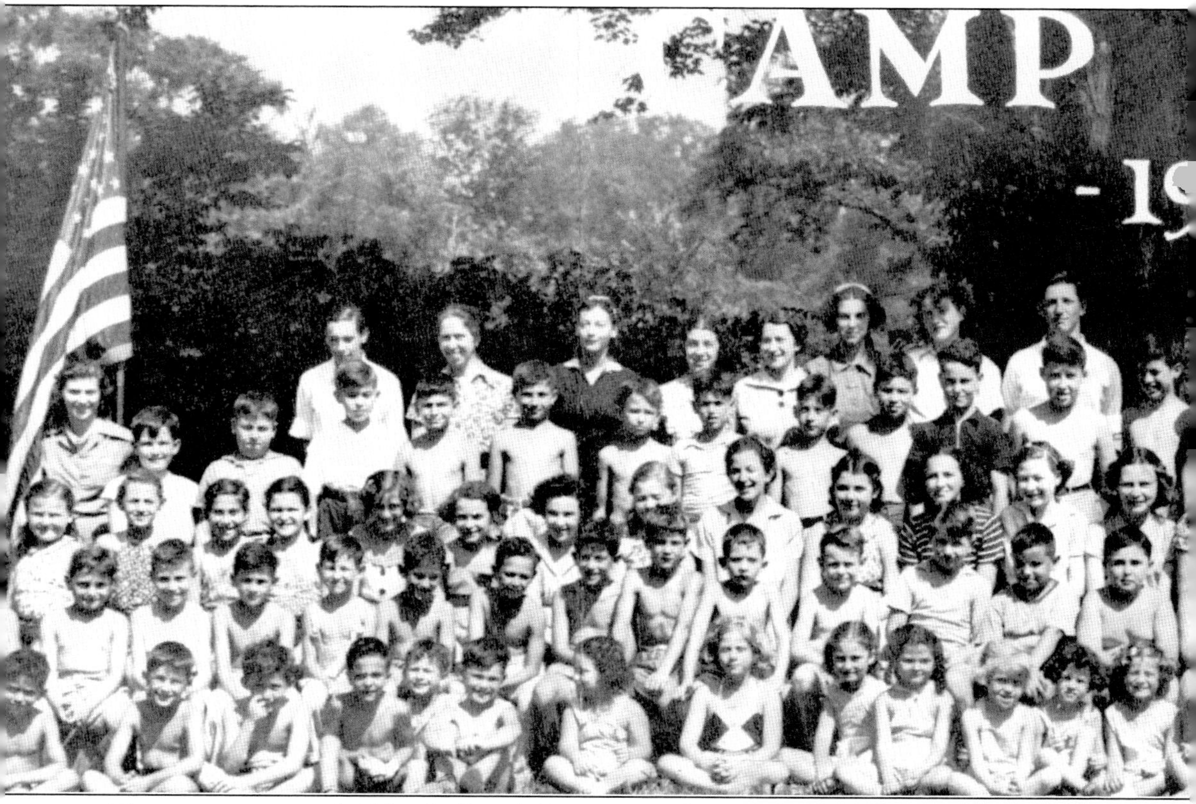

The cornerstone was laid for the Jewish Community Center of Stamford in 1928. The building, at 132 Prospect Street, opened in 1930 and soon became the focal point of social, cultural,

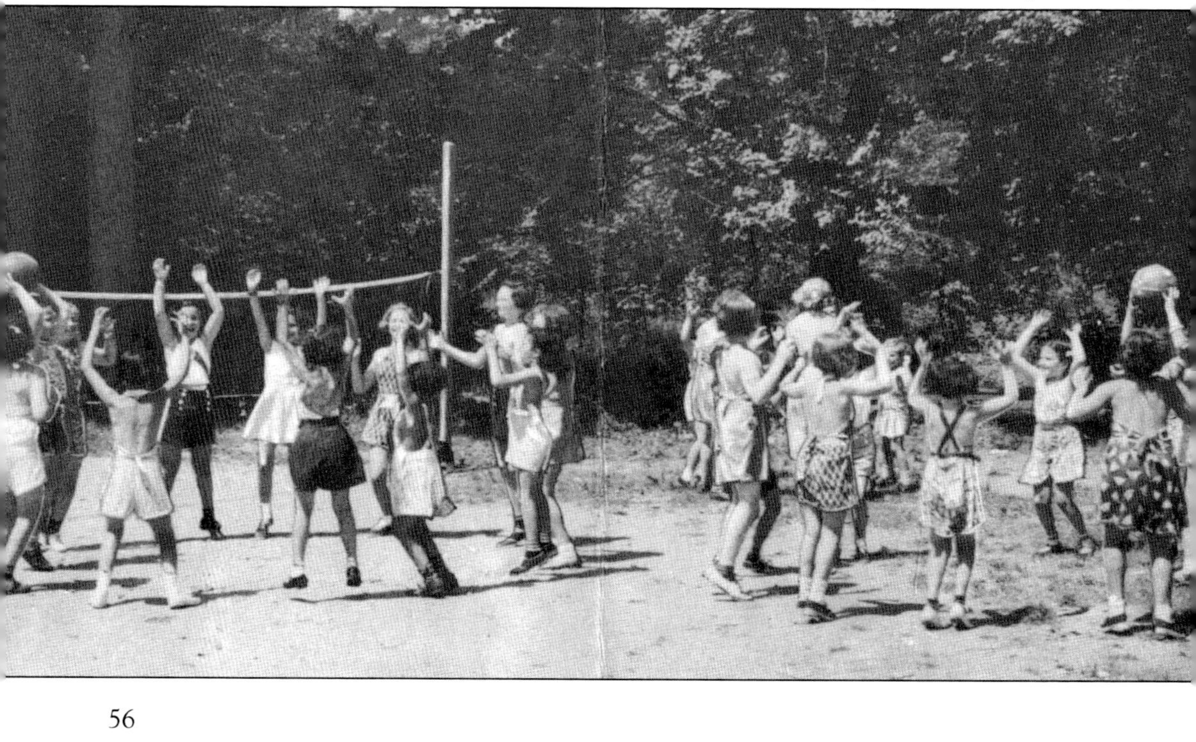

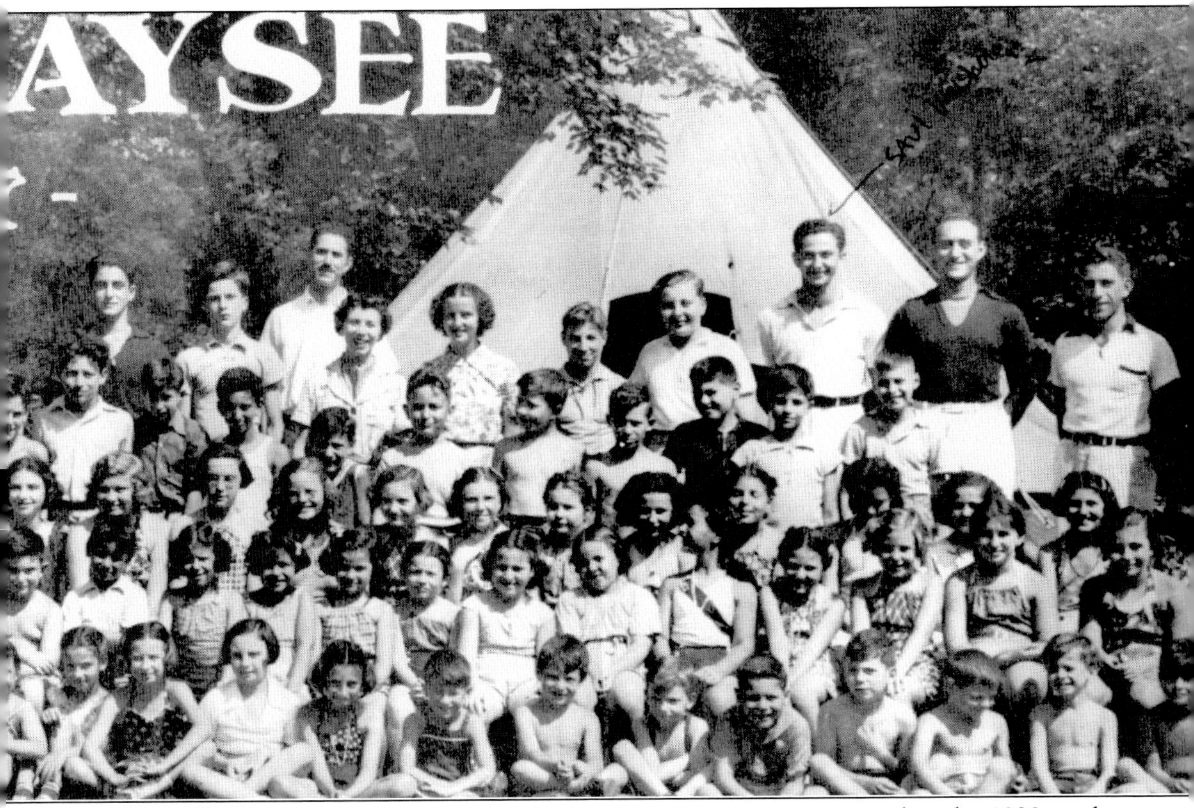

educational, and recreational activities. The summer camp programs started in the 1930s and continue to this very day. The 1937 camp brochure pictures happy campers and counselors.

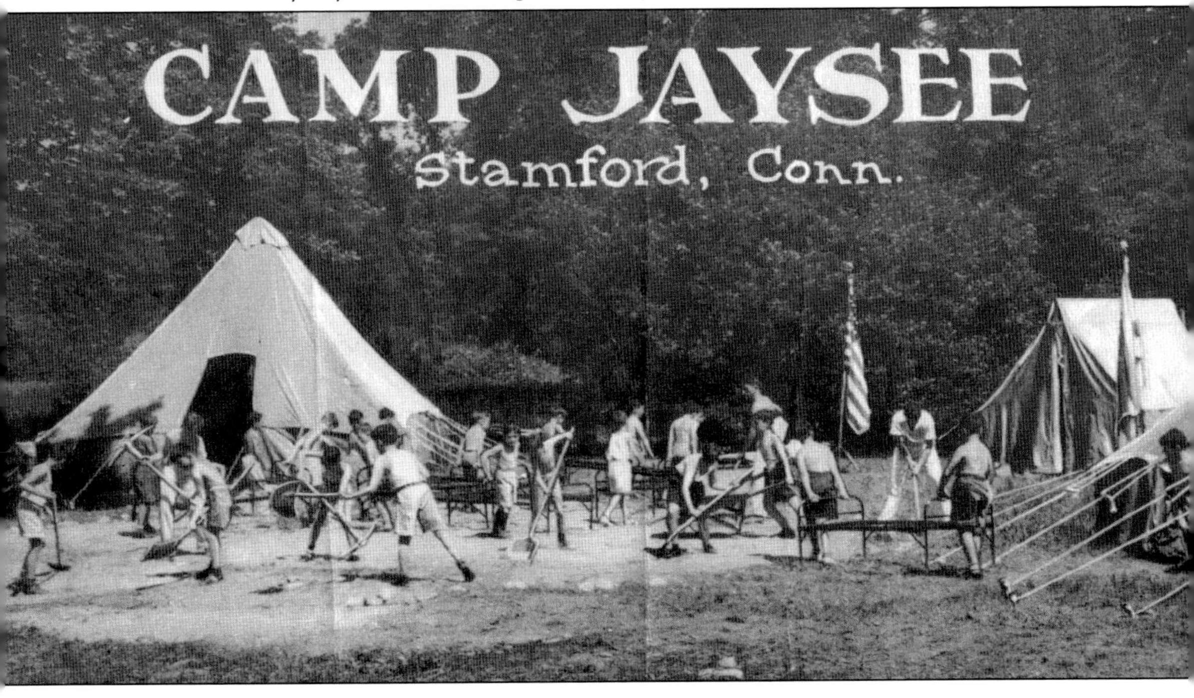

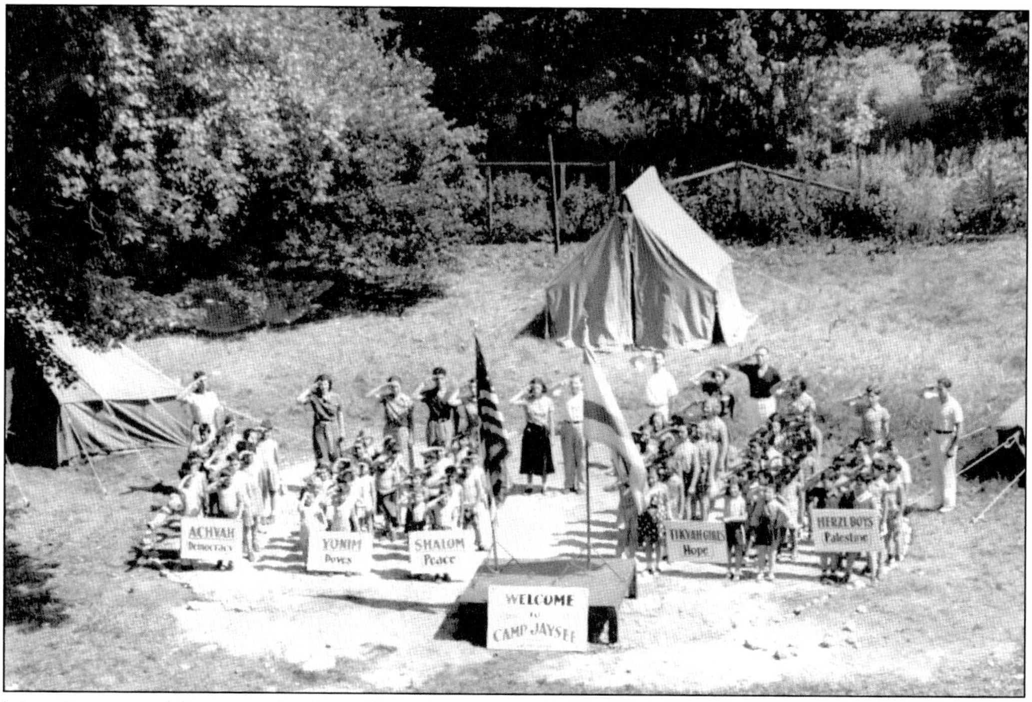

Morning assemblies were held at Camp Jaysee in 1940.

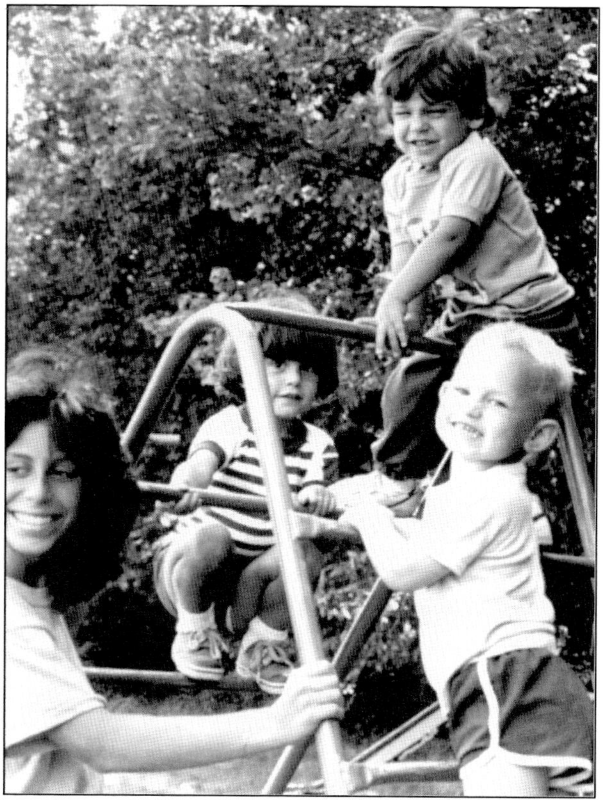

Jewish Community Center campers try out the climbing equipment in 1980.

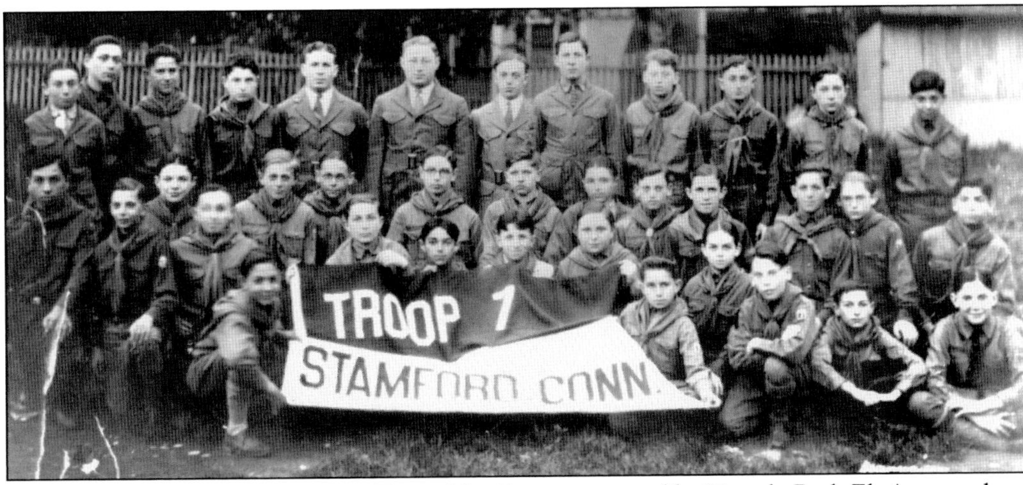

Photographed in 1924, Boy Scout Troop No. 7 was sponsored by Temple Beth El. Among those pictured are Elmer Rosenblum (middle row, far right), who became a dentist, scoutmasters Nathan and Sydney Martin (back row, fifth and sixth from the left), and Arthur Koffler (back row, ninth from left), who later became a noted physician in Stamford.

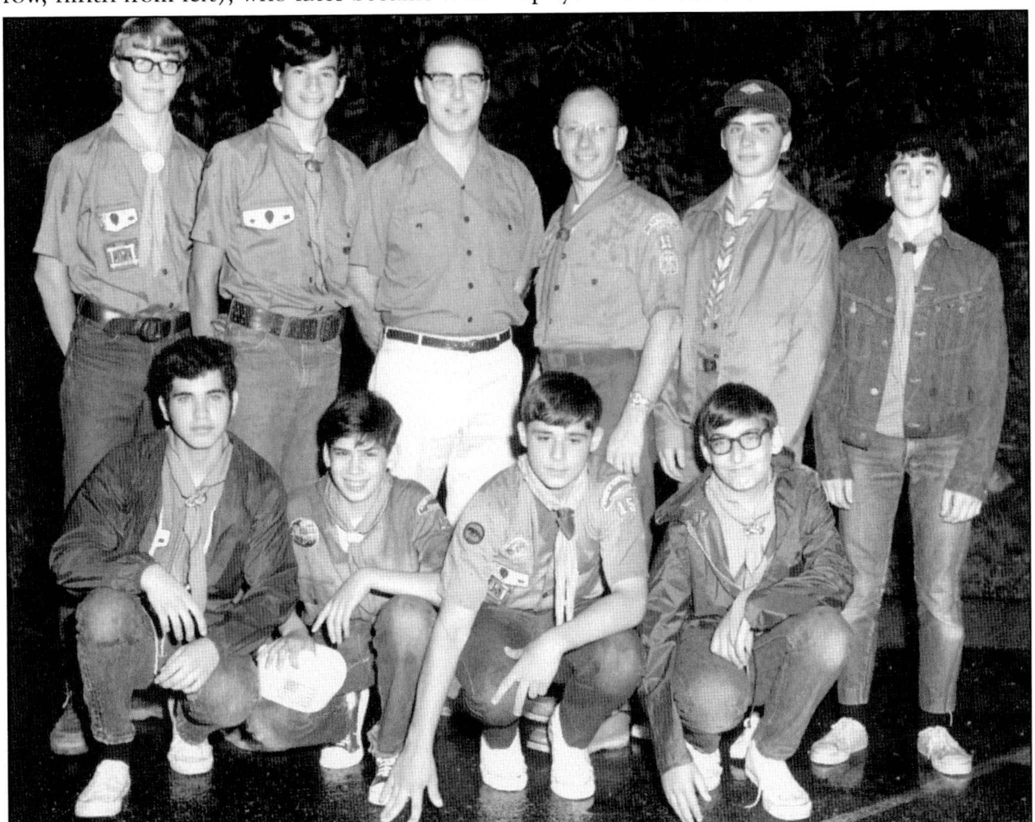

Boy Scout Troop No. 15 is pictured in 1971. From left to right are the following: (front row) Brian Sharlach, unidentified, Chester Goldberg, and Scout Rauh; (back row) Ray Herman, Barry Morris, assistant scoutmaster Dr. Ray Herman, scoutmaster Ross Gelb, Steven Gelb, and Mark Appel. The Jewish Community Center was the troop's sponsor.

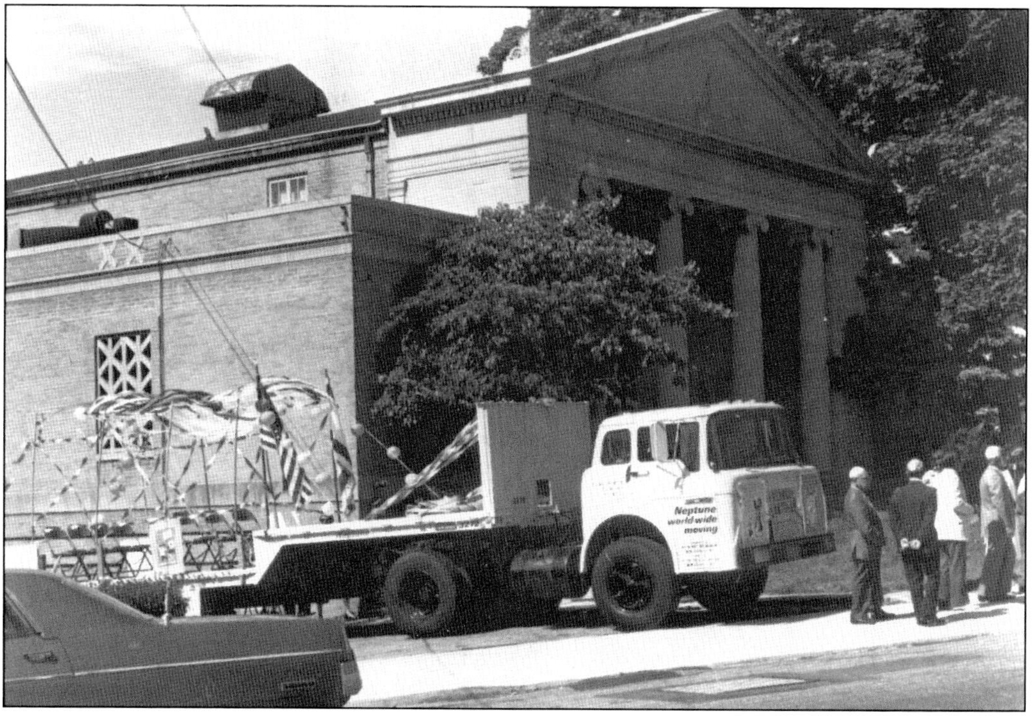

Moving day from Beth El Synagogue on Prospect Street to a new home on Roxbury Road occurred in September 1973. The seats on the flatbed trailer were for the dignitaries taking the four-mile ride to the newly completed synagogue.

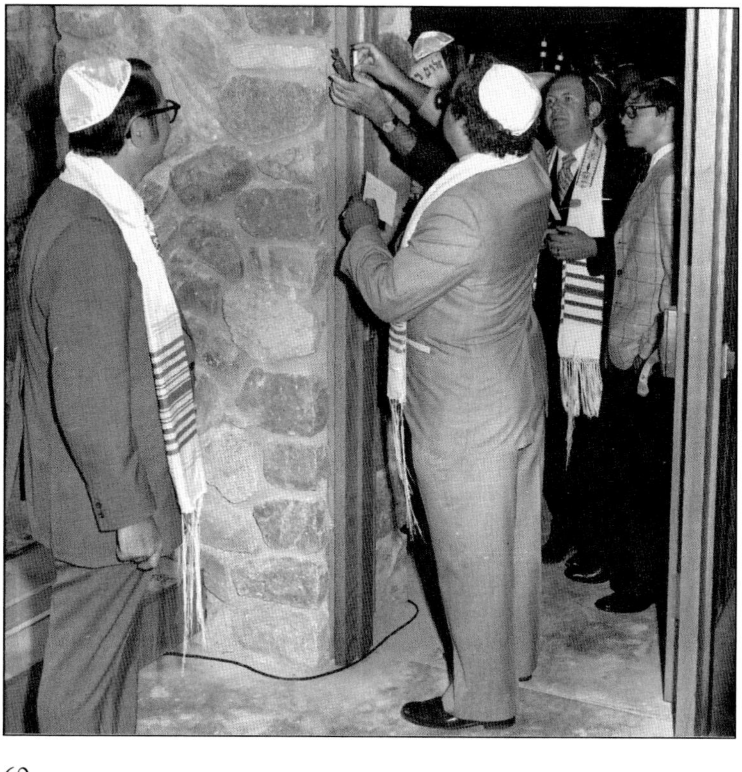

Gerald Sosnowitz affixes the mezzuzah to the doorpost of the main sanctuary at the new Temple Beth El on Roxbury Road in 1973. Al Golin looks on, and *Hazzan* Sidney Rabinowitz is in the background.

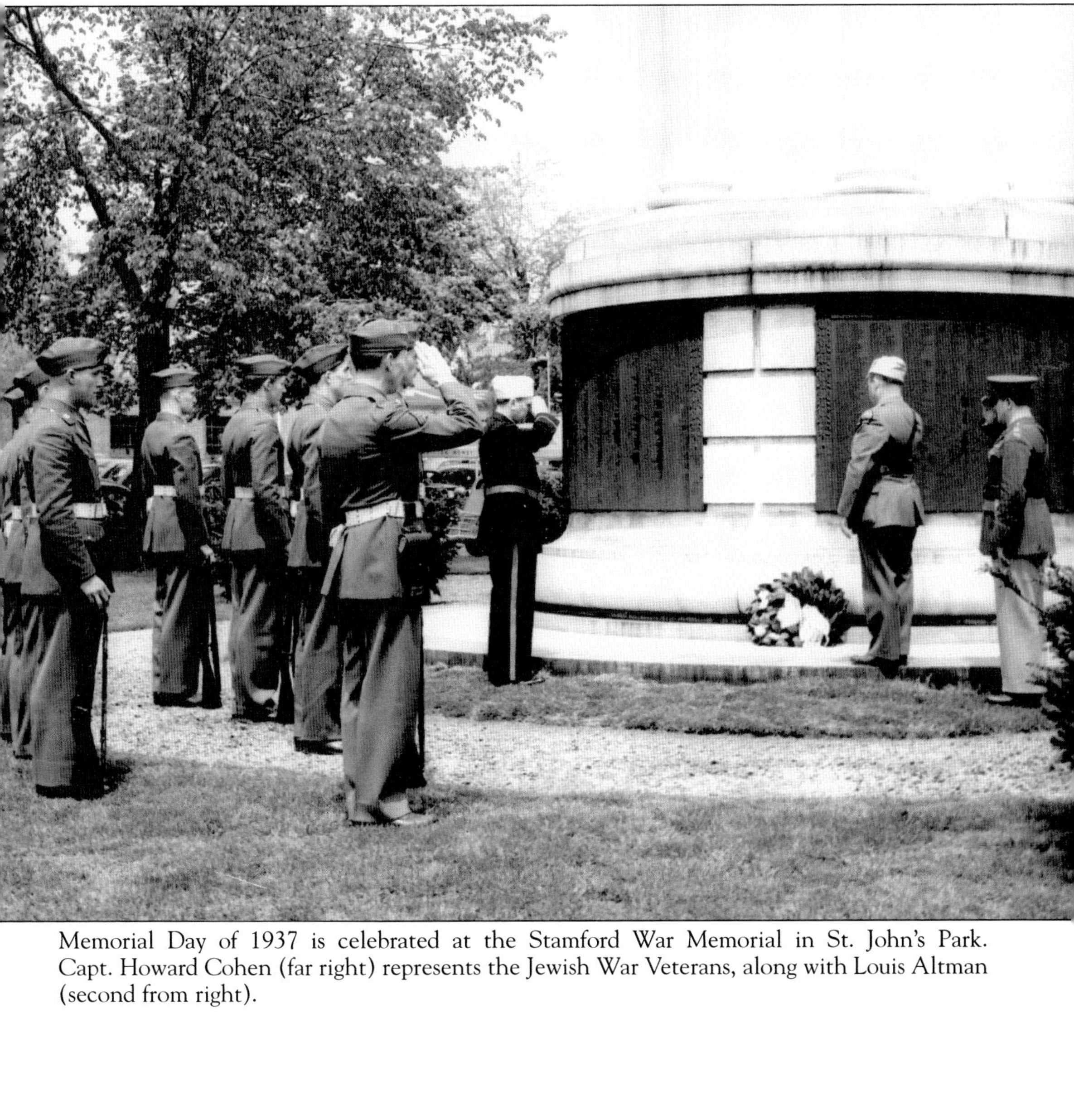

Memorial Day of 1937 is celebrated at the Stamford War Memorial in St. John's Park. Capt. Howard Cohen (far right) represents the Jewish War Veterans, along with Louis Altman (second from right).

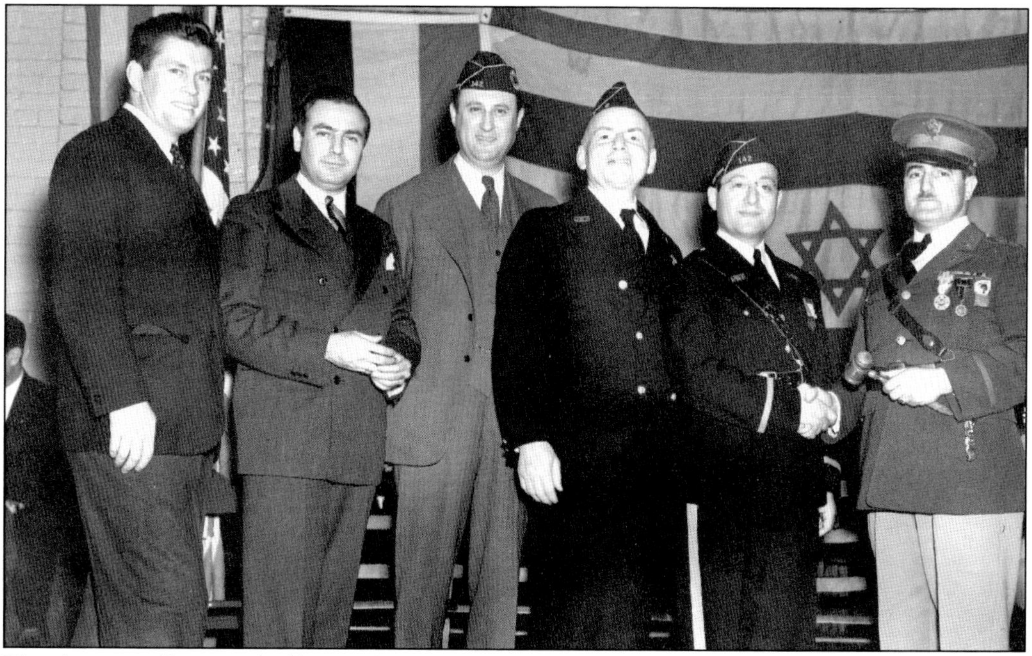

The first installation of officers of Stamford Post No. 142 Jewish War Veterans was held at the South Street State Armory on December 6, 1937. From left to right are Gene Tunney, ex-marine and former heavyweight champion of the world; Brian McMahon, assistant U.S. attorney general and later a U.S. senator from Connecticut; Max Spelke, master of ceremonies; Col. Morris J. Mendelsohn, special assistant to Homer Cumming, the U.S. attorney general; post commander Louis Altman; and Capt. Howard S. Cohen.

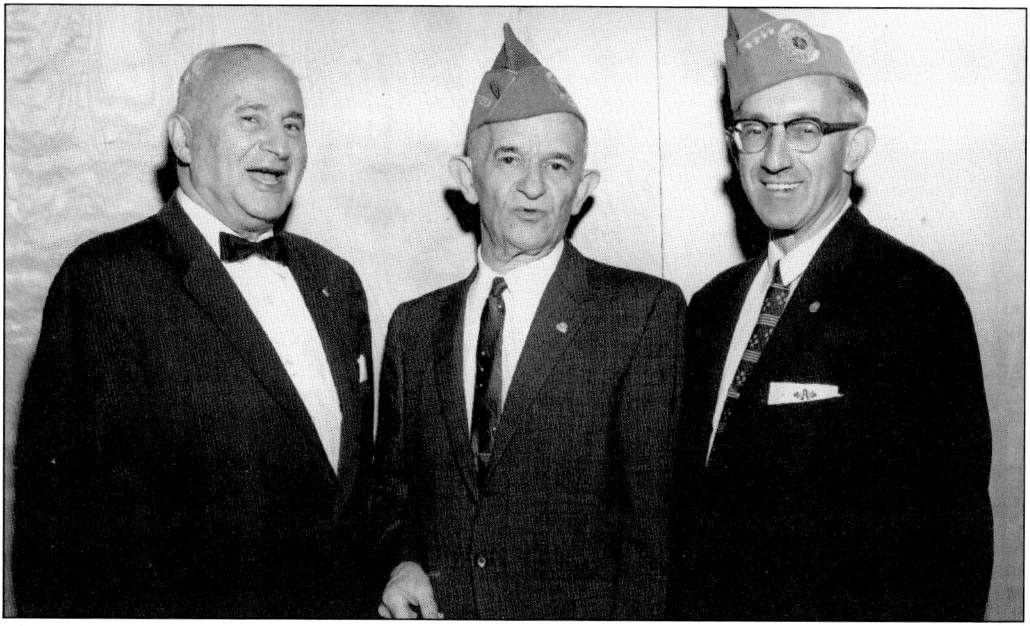

Shown *c.* 1956 are two members of the Jewish War Veterans: Benjamin Kaufman (left), Congressional Medal of Honor winner in World War I, and Fred Robbins (center), commander of Stamford Post No. 142 and national commander of the Jewish War Veterans.

The Confirmation service program of the Sabbath school was sponsored by the National Council of Jewish Women. Giving the keynote address and blessing was Rabbi David Levy, the leader of the reform Congregation B'nai Israel in Bridgeport. The school was founded in 1910 in accordance with the policy adopted by the National Council of Jewish Women in Chicago that year. The school was established for the children of immigrants. In Stamford the educational format was American Reform Judaism. Classes were held at the Odd Fellows Building, on Main Street and Relay Place. The Sabbath school merged with Temple Beth El when that congregation was founded in 1920.

CONFIRMATION SERVICES

SABBATH SCHOOL

Stamford, Connecticut, Section
COUNCIL OF JEWISH WOMEN

MAY 23RD, 1915-5675

SERVICE WITH RESPONSES
READING OF THE LAW
BENEDICTION BY CLASS
CONFIRMATION HYMN
PRAYER

Opening Prayer - - -	Daniel Rosenbloom
Address of Welcome - - -	Anna L. Phillips
Address to Parents - - - - -	Stella Freed
Meaning of Confirmation - -	Daniel Rosenbloom
Confession of Faith - - - - - - -	Class
The American Jewess - - -	Anna L. Phillips
Address and Blessing - -	Rabbi David Levy
Closing Prayer - - - - - -	Stella Freed

ENKELOHENU

CLASS

STELLA FREED DANIEL ROSENBLOOM ANNA L. PHILLIPS

MISS FRANCIS SIGLER, Teacher

PIANO SOLO—"Caprice Hongrois" DORA LANNIS
VIOLIN AND PIANO DUET "La Zingana"
FRANCIS GRUBER, EVA LEVINE
SONG "Just a Little Love, a Little Kiss" RALPH SOSNOWITZ
PIANO AND MANDOLIN DUET—"Carnival de Venice"
LOUIS SCHACHAT, HARRY DAVIDOFF
SONG "Il Trovatore" SARAH FREEDMAN

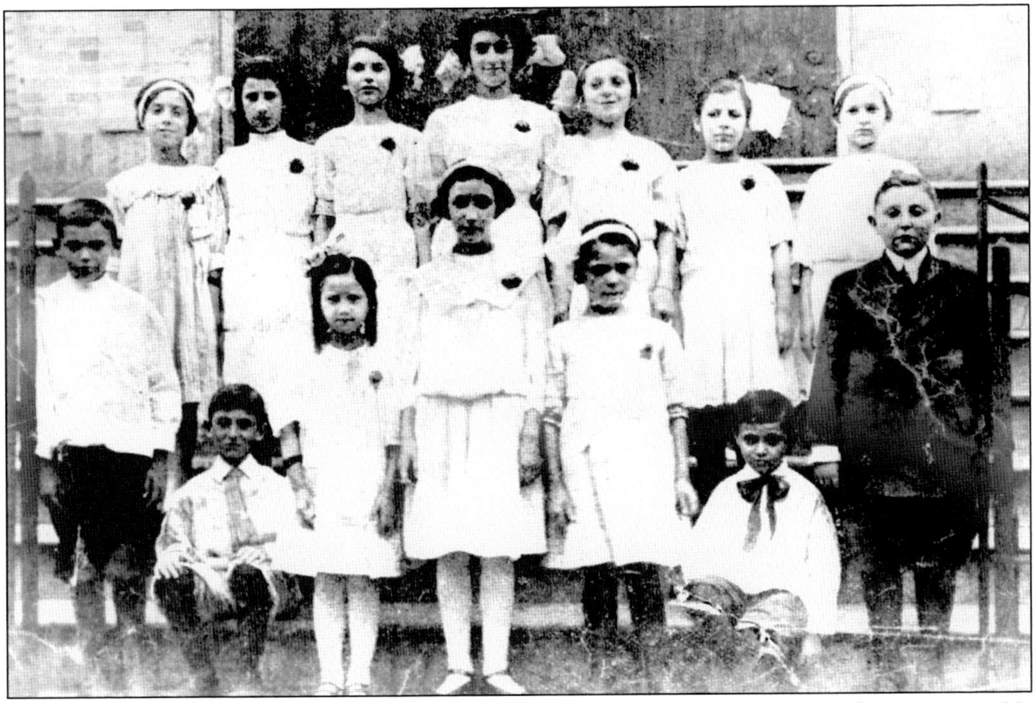

Students of the Hebrew school of Agudath Sholom Synagogue are pictured on August 22, 1911. From left to right are the following: (front row) Nathan Olshansky, Joseph Isenberg, Rose Sobeloff, Sadie Friedman, Rebecca Levine, Phillip Gold, and Myron Frankel; (back row) Elizabeth Silverman, Rebecca Alswanger, Rose Moore-Wise, Mary Sigler, Anna Gold, Essie Rosenblum, and Mildred Cohen.

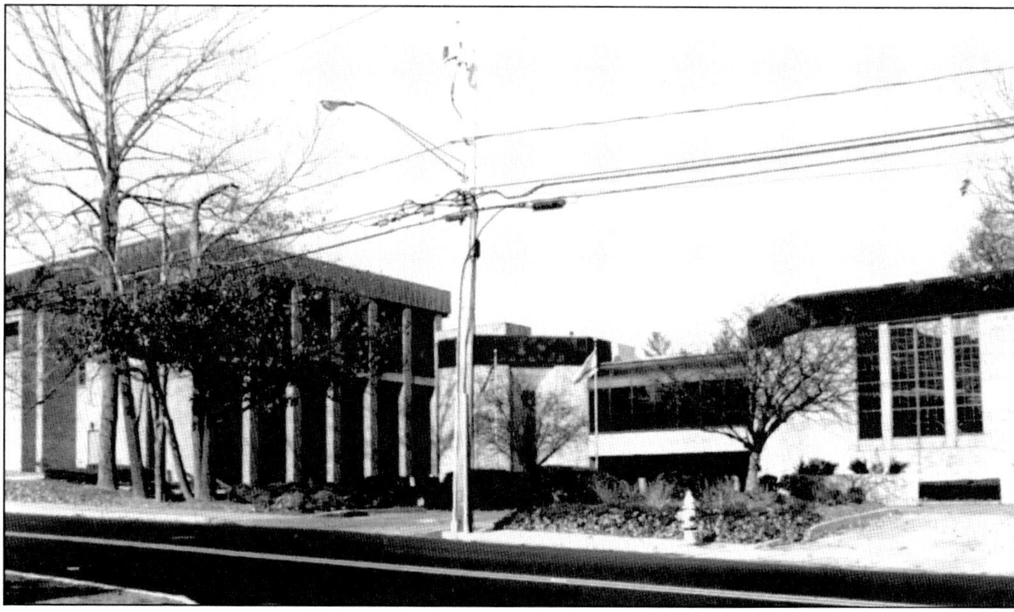

Agudath Sholom Synagogue, in 2001, is located on Strawberry Hill Avenue and Colonial Road. This is the congregation's third home in Stamford.

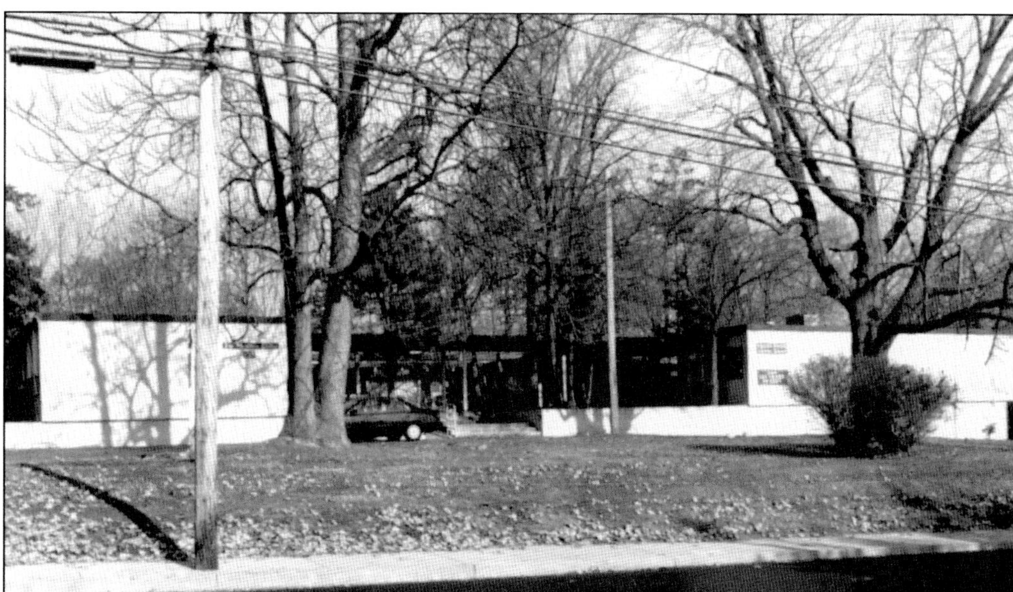

The Hebrew school of Agudath Sholom shares the building at 159 Colonial Road with the Gan Yeladim preschool.

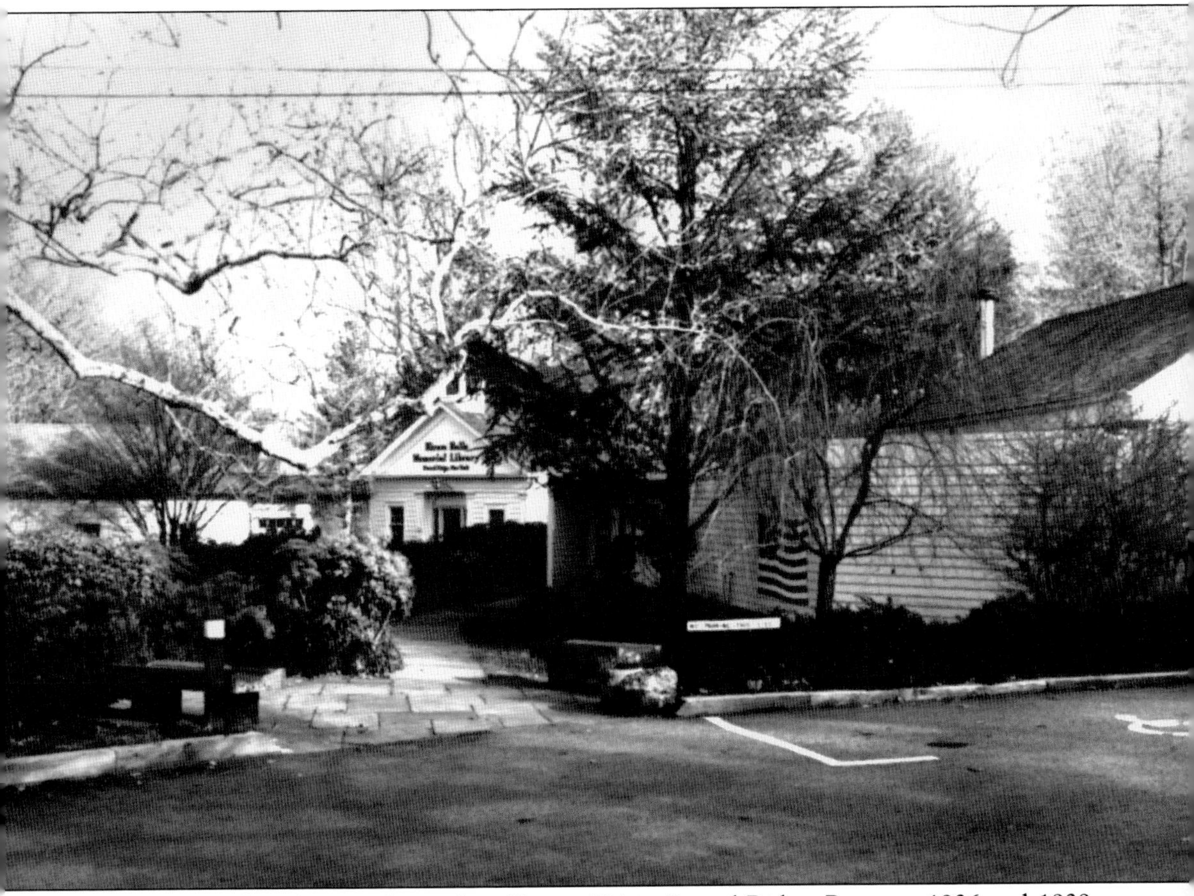

The Hiram Halle Library is located on Route 124 in Pound Ridge. Between 1936 and 1939, Hiram Halle organized his own personal Works Progress Administration. He purchased and remodeled many houses, employing German Jewish refugees as craftsmen. His sponsorship was critical in obtaining visas from the State Department for many people who otherwise would certainly have been caught up in the horrors of the Holocaust. Halle was one of the founders of the University in Exile at the New School. Conceived by Alvin Johnson and support by the Rockefeller Foundation and Hiram Halle's personal wealth, the university initiated a historic effort to rescue endangered scholars who had been dismissed from teaching and government positions by the Nazis. Among the 167 scholars and their families were Max Wertheimer, a founder of the Gestalt school of psychology, and economists Karl Brandt and Gerhard Colm, both to be named members of the President's Council of Economic Advisers. One of the University in Exile's first students was Franco Modigliani, who later received his doctorate at the New School and won a Nobel Prize in Economics. (Information courtesy of New School University – History.)

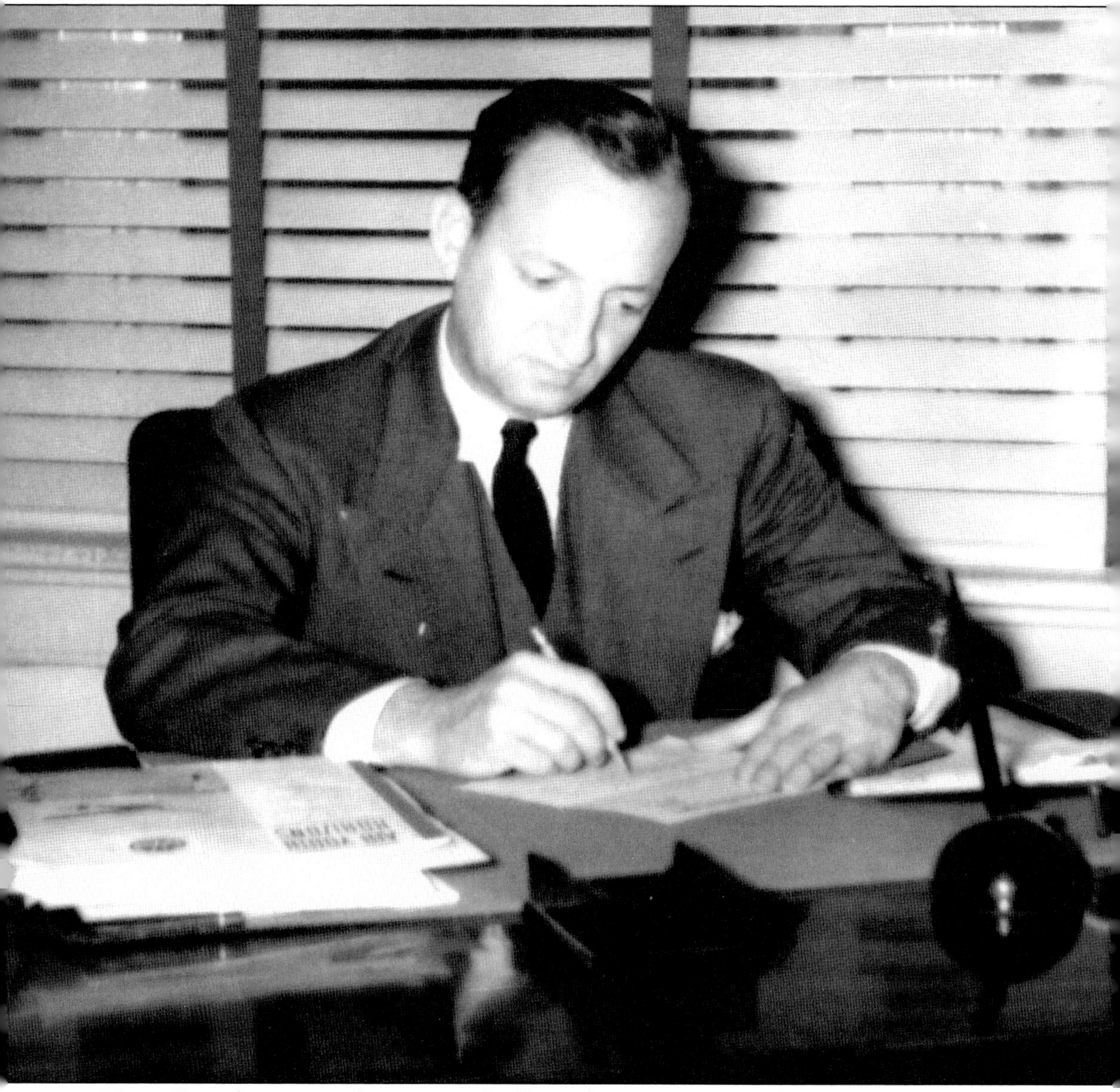

Harry Rosenbaum was born to umbrella maker Morris Rosenbaum and his wife, Bella Rosenbaum, on New York's lower east side. He was a clothing salesman and his first contact with Stamford occurred when he came to town to sell overcoats. Soon after that he opened a store and became deeply involved in the life of the community. When the depression cut sharply into his business, he organized a group of merchants for the purpose of sharing the cost of advertising handbills. With the aid of another Jewish businessman, Sid Karp, the clothing business took a backseat and the partners began building a publishing empire. Rosenbaum published the *Stamford Shopper and Weekly Mail* from 1935 until his retirement in the 1980s. In 1976, an anonymous donor gave a contribution for the establishment of a library to be named in honor of Harry Rosenbaum, publisher and community leader for 50 years. The library is a project of the Jewish Historical Society of Greater Stamford and is housed at the Jewish Community Center. From a dream that began with a donation and an *Encyclopedia Judaica* has grown a library of Jewish interest of significant size, variety, and content.

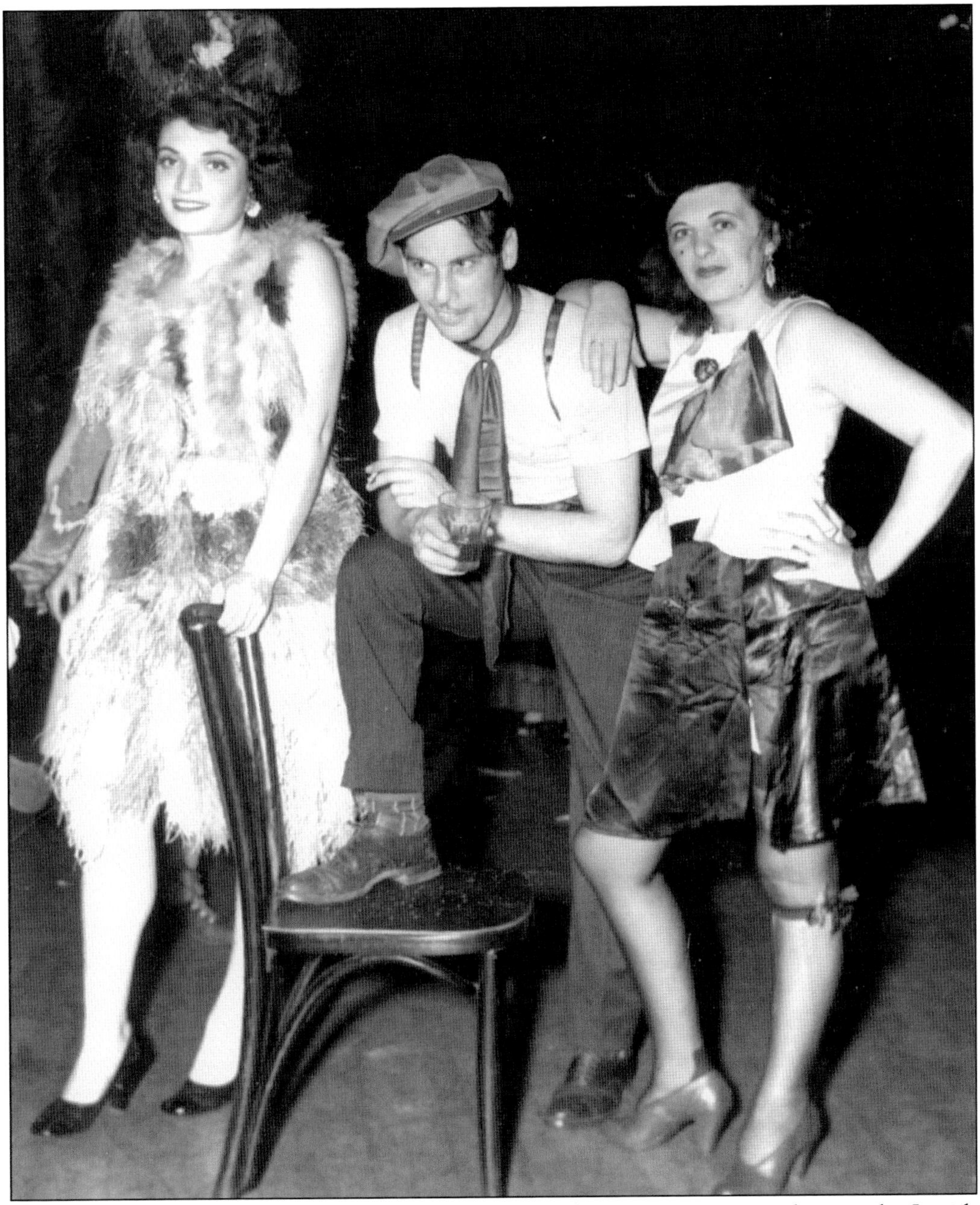

Sid Karp was a man of many talents. He is shown performing in a variety show at the Jewish Community Center on Prospect Street in 1940. With him is his wife, Gertrude Karp (right), and an unidentified woman.

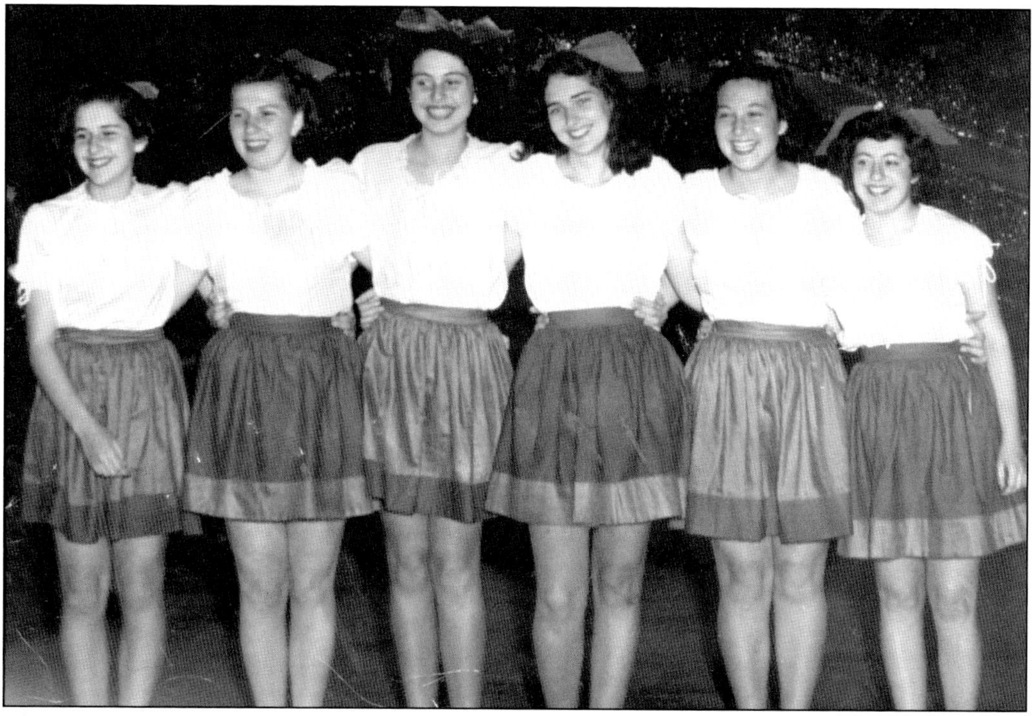

These are the girls in the chorus at the Jewish Community Center in 1949. From left to right are Ruthie Germaine, Rosalind Bloomfield (Ziskin), Elaine Roven (Sharlach), Jackie Glazer, Thelma Fogel, and Lois Levine.

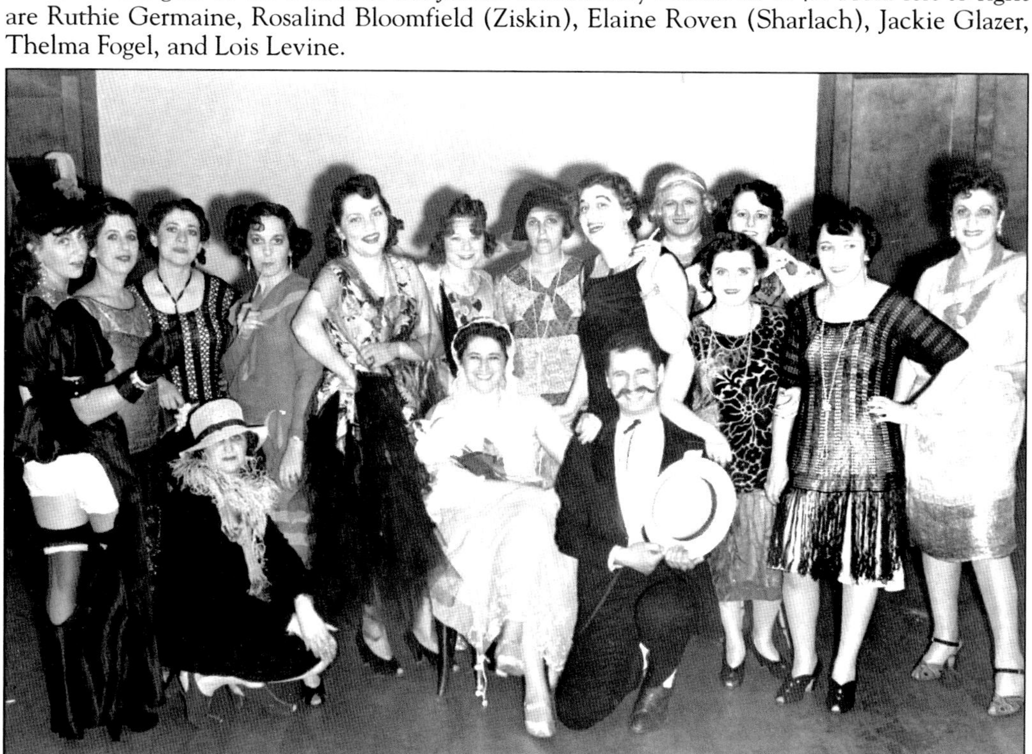

Members of the Jewish Community Center acting company are pictured in 1942.

Five

FROM THIS YOU CAN MAKE A LIVING

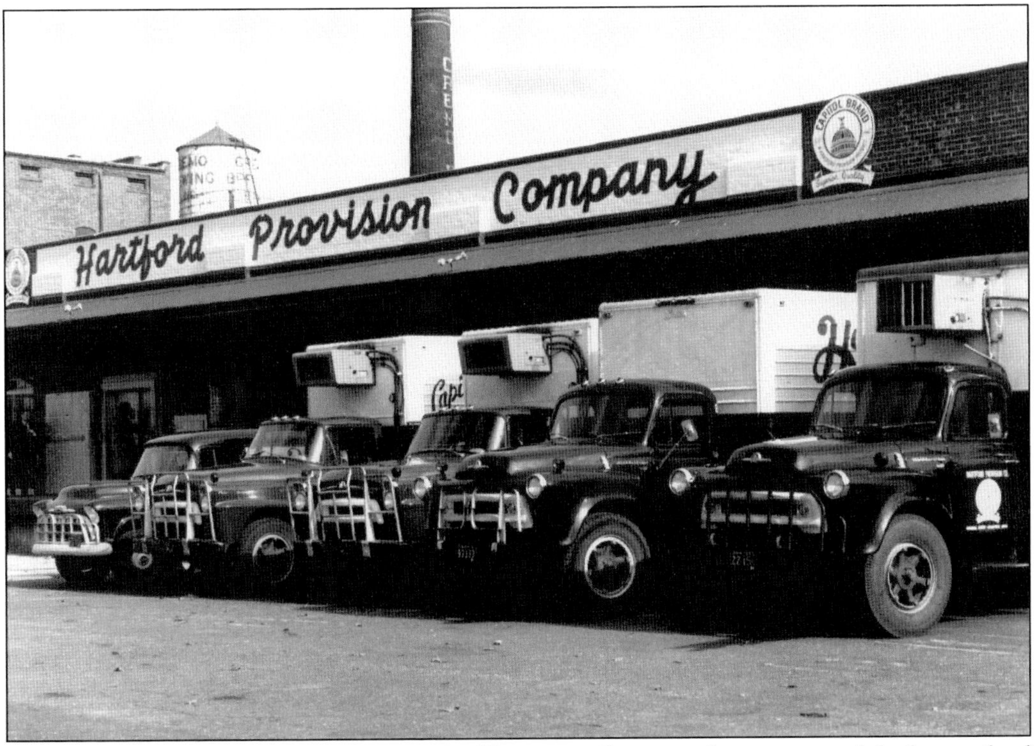

Starting as Sosnowitz and Lotstein, Hartford Provision Company became one of the largest food wholesalers in Connecticut. The Lotstein family also owned several Grand Central Markets in Old Greenwich, Stamford, and New Canaan.

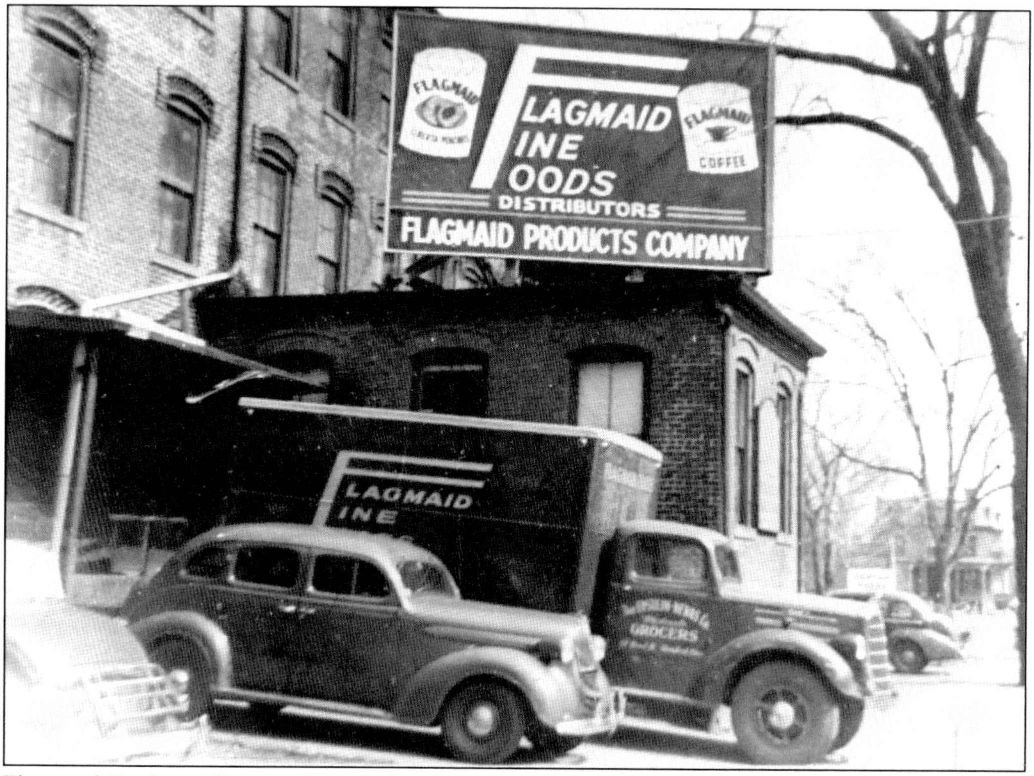

Flagmaid Products Company, a wholesale grocer on Broad Street between Bedford Street and Grey Rock Place, was owned by Harry Nevas and Morris Epstein in 1939. Later, the building housed the first store of the Dress Barn chain founded by the Jaffe family of Stamford.

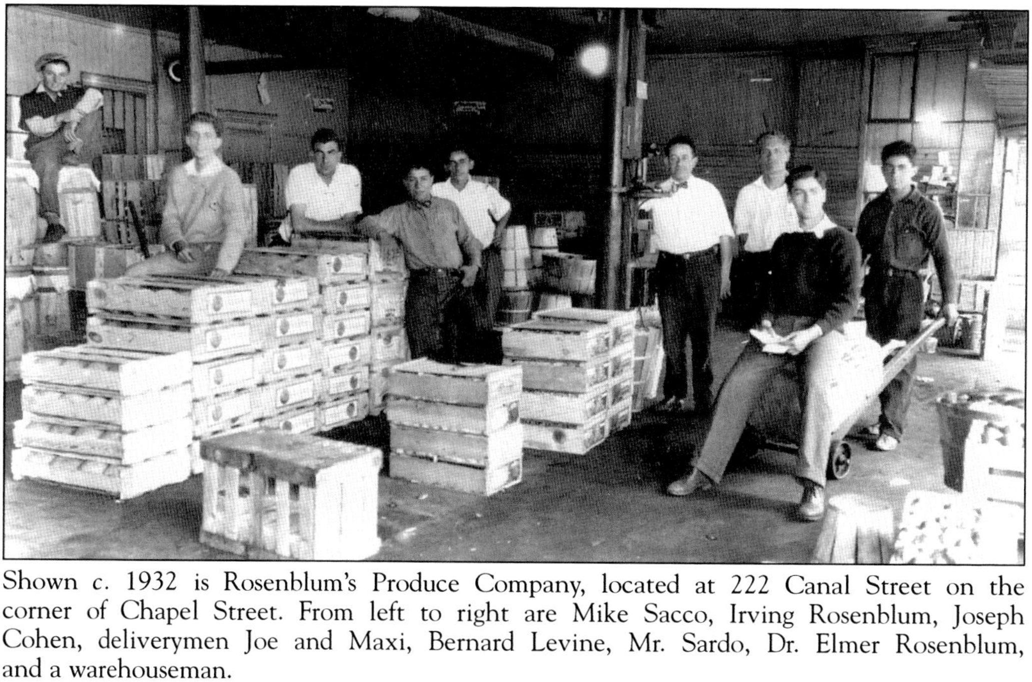

Shown *c.* 1932 is Rosenblum's Produce Company, located at 222 Canal Street on the corner of Chapel Street. From left to right are Mike Sacco, Irving Rosenblum, Joseph Cohen, deliverymen Joe and Maxi, Bernard Levine, Mr. Sardo, Dr. Elmer Rosenblum, and a warehouseman.

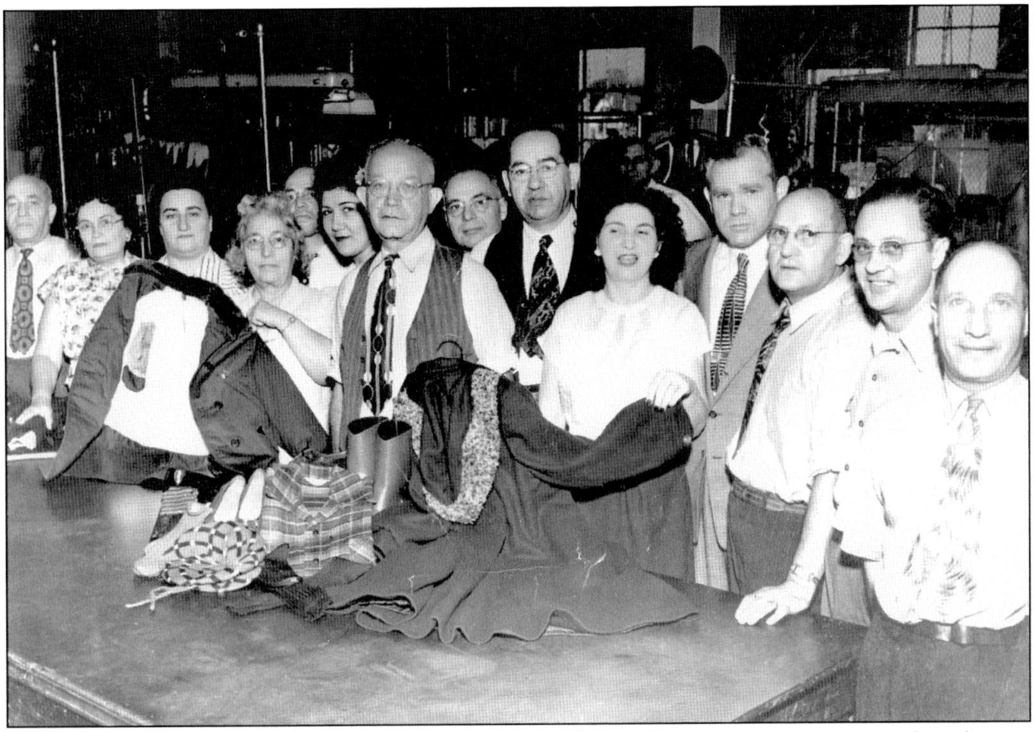

This picture was taken *c.* 1940 at United Coat and Suit Company, sometimes referred to as Gruber's. Among those pictured are owner Joseph Gruber (sixth from the right) and Isadore Schulman (far right).

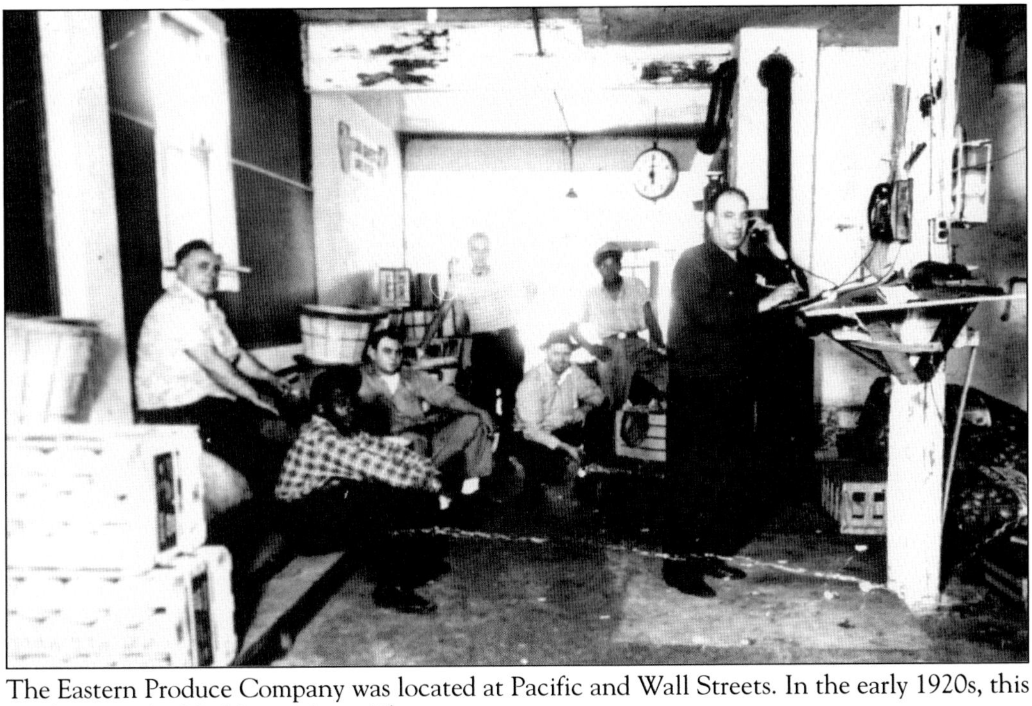

The Eastern Produce Company was located at Pacific and Wall Streets. In the early 1920s, this site became the Nicklette Movie Theater.

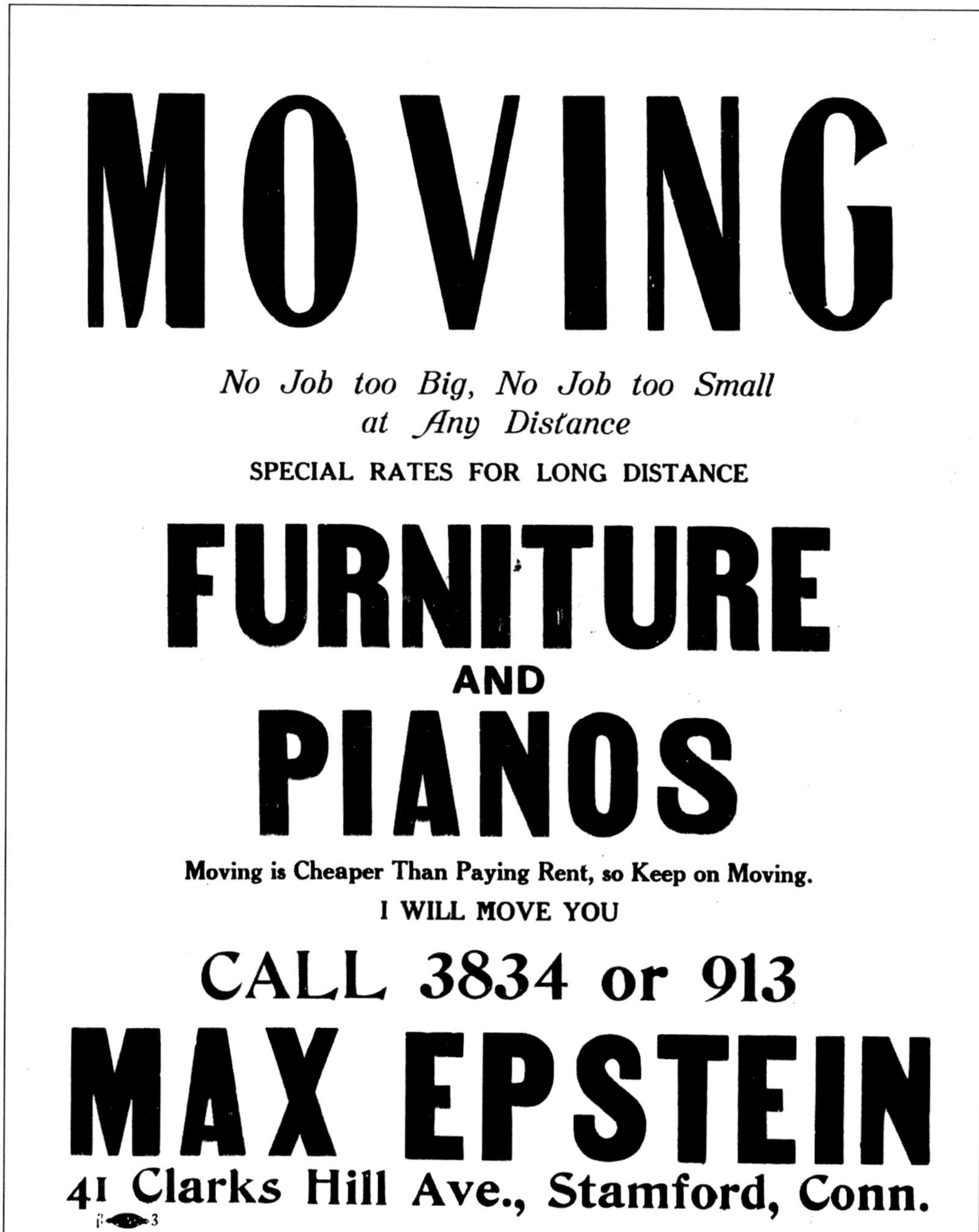

This poster advertises Max Epstein's moving company, 41 Clarks Hill Avenue, Stamford.

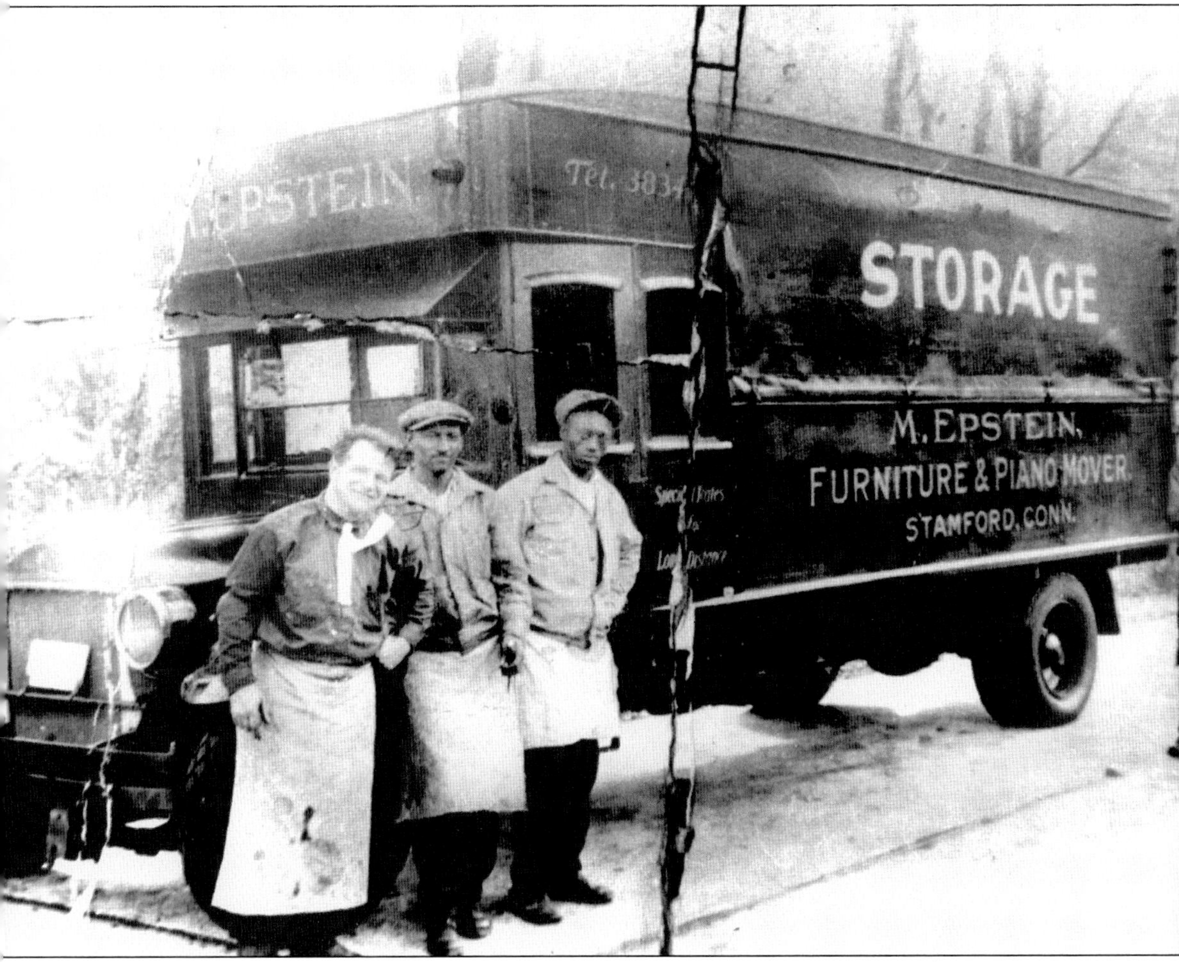

Max Epstein (left) is pictured with his staff and the truck for his furniture and piano moving business *c*. 1930. During the Depression it was frequently cheaper for a family to move to a new apartment if they were having trouble paying the rent. A new landlord would give one, two, or even three months' concession to get a new tenant. It was not uncommon for people facing economic hardship to move a number of times in a year.

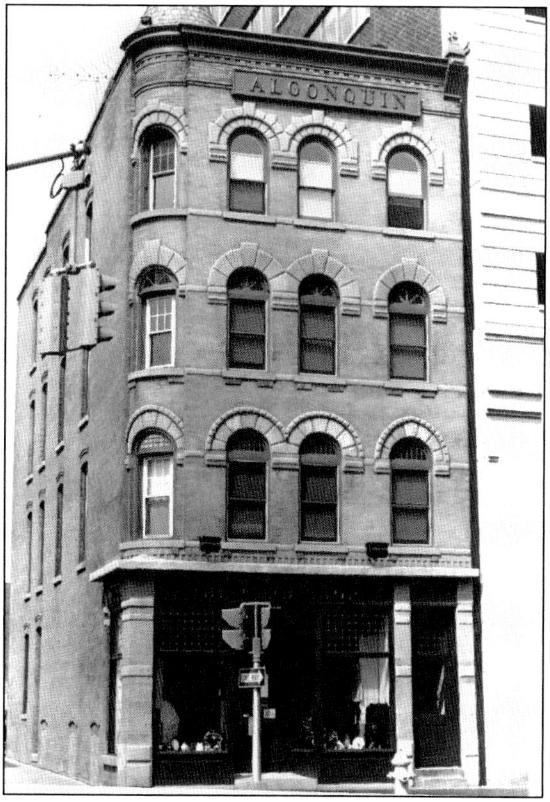

The Algonquin Building was constructed in 1894 by Saul Adams, the first Jewish real estate broker in Stamford. It is located at the corner of Main and Summer Streets and is the oldest existing structure built by a Jewish developer in Stamford. The photograph was taken in 1992, after the building underwent extensive restoration.

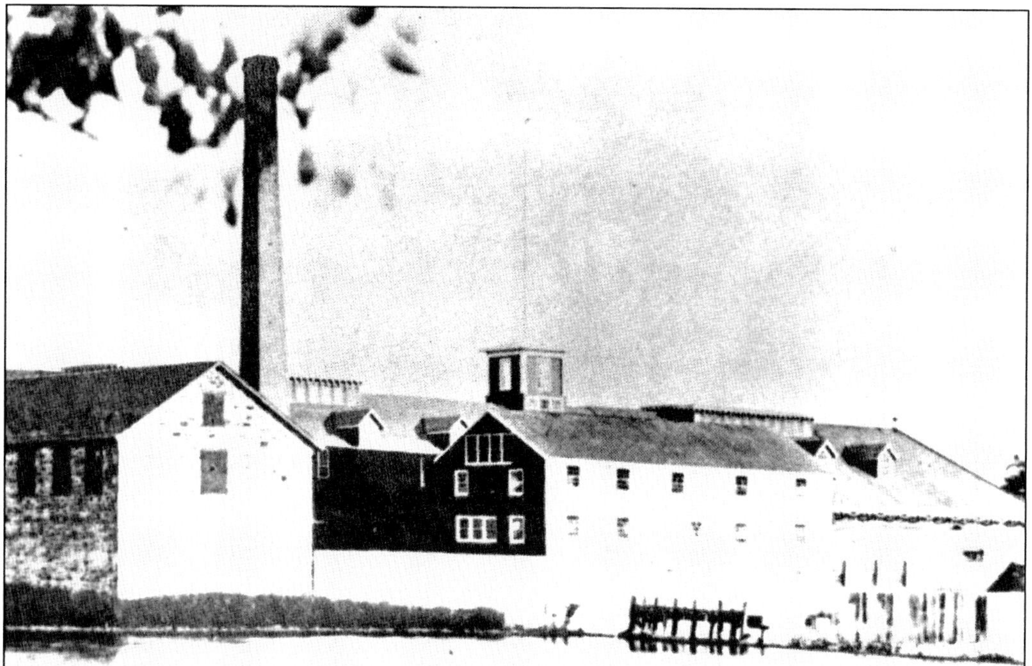

The woolen mill, pictured in 1881, was the site of the gristmill and home of Jacob and Esther (Levy) Hart from 1739 to 1763.

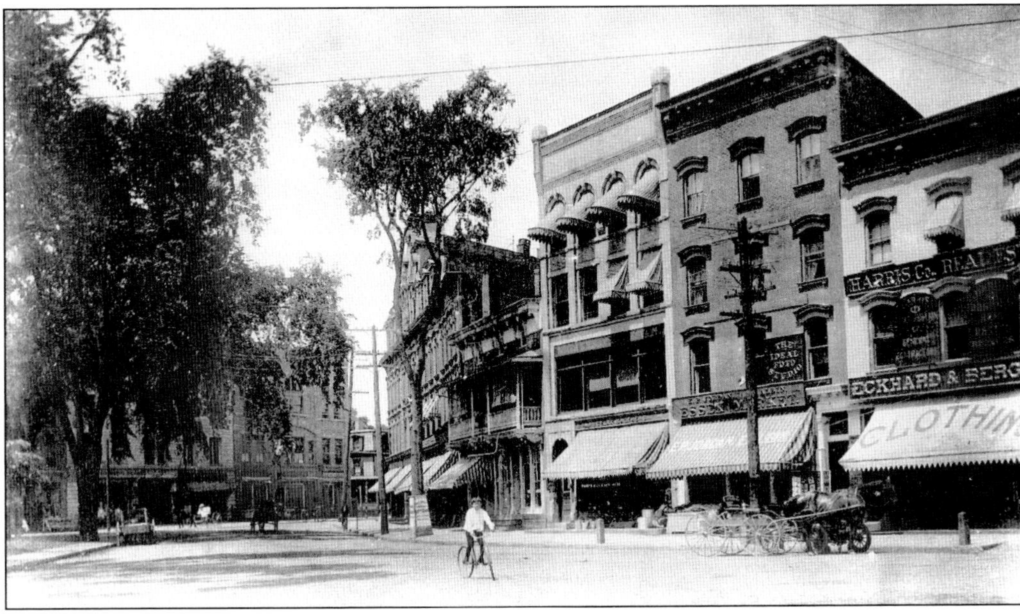

A number of Jewish business and professional offices were located on Park Row as early as 1874. Benjamin Harris, a real estate developer, had his office at 48 Park Row. He built Stamford High School on Strawberry Hill, Stamford Hospital, the Cos Cob School in Greenwich, and many of the commercial buildings on Atlantic Street. In this 1907 photograph, note the Harris Company Real Estate offices on the second floor over Eckard & Berges Fine Clothing store.

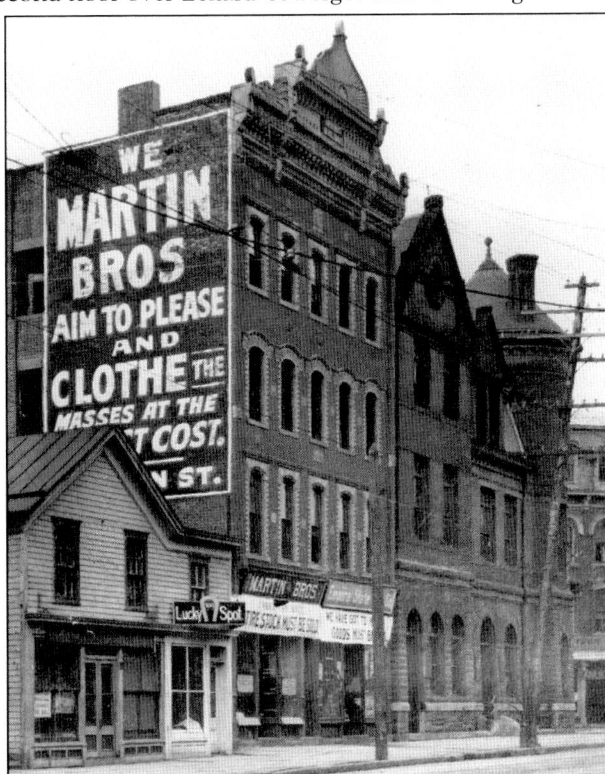

Frank and Israel Martin's store, in 1904, was located on Main Street just west of what is now referred to as the old town hall. The Martin brothers bought the store in 1892 from Saul Adams.

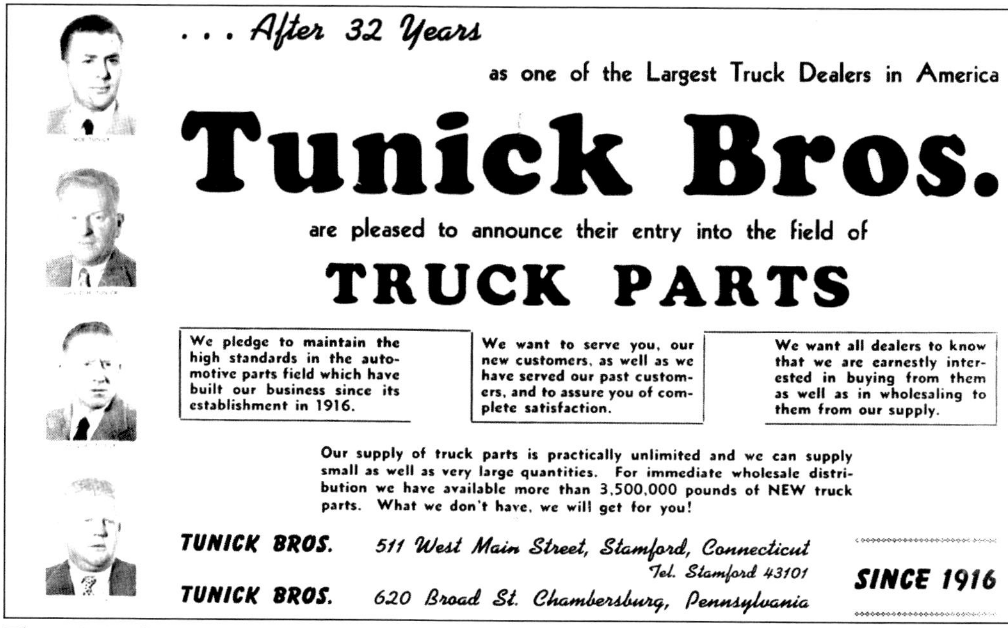

This 1948 advertisement is for Tunick Brothers Truck Parts. Pictured from the top are Moe, David, Jacques, and Abe Tunick.

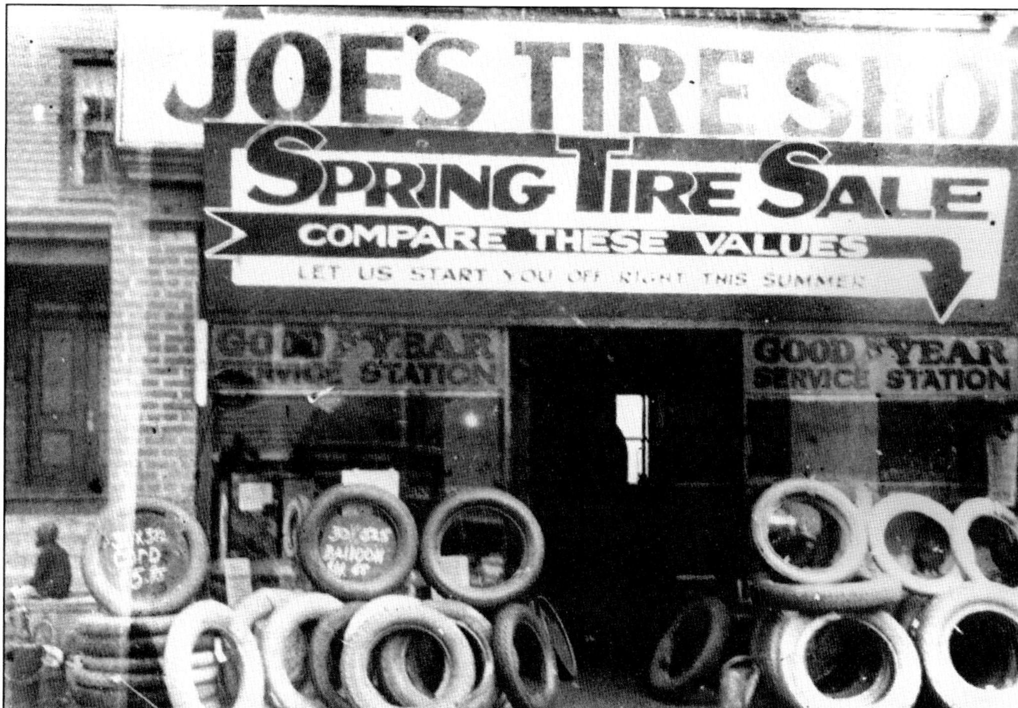

Tunick Brothers was not the only supplier of automotive parts. For the frugal shopper there was Joe's Tire Shop on Brook Street.

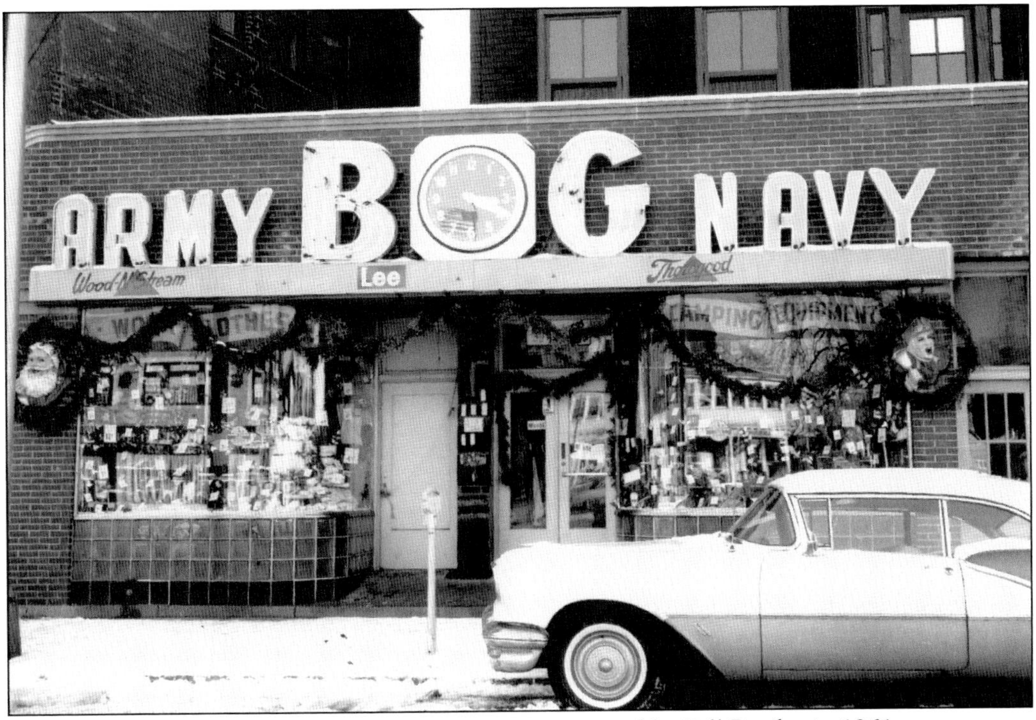

B. and G. Army & Navy Store on Main Street was owned by Bill Broder in 1961.

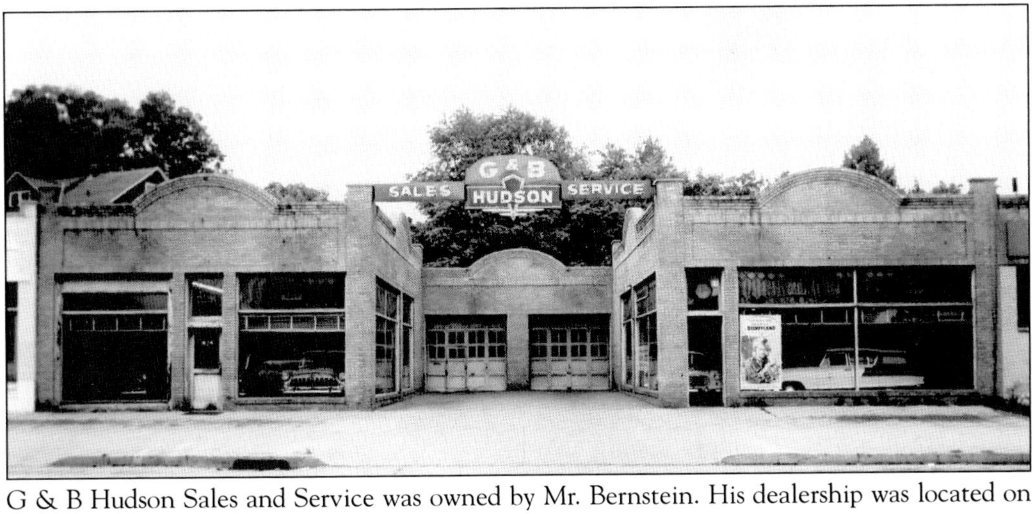

G & B Hudson Sales and Service was owned by Mr. Bernstein. His dealership was located on East Main Street in 1955.

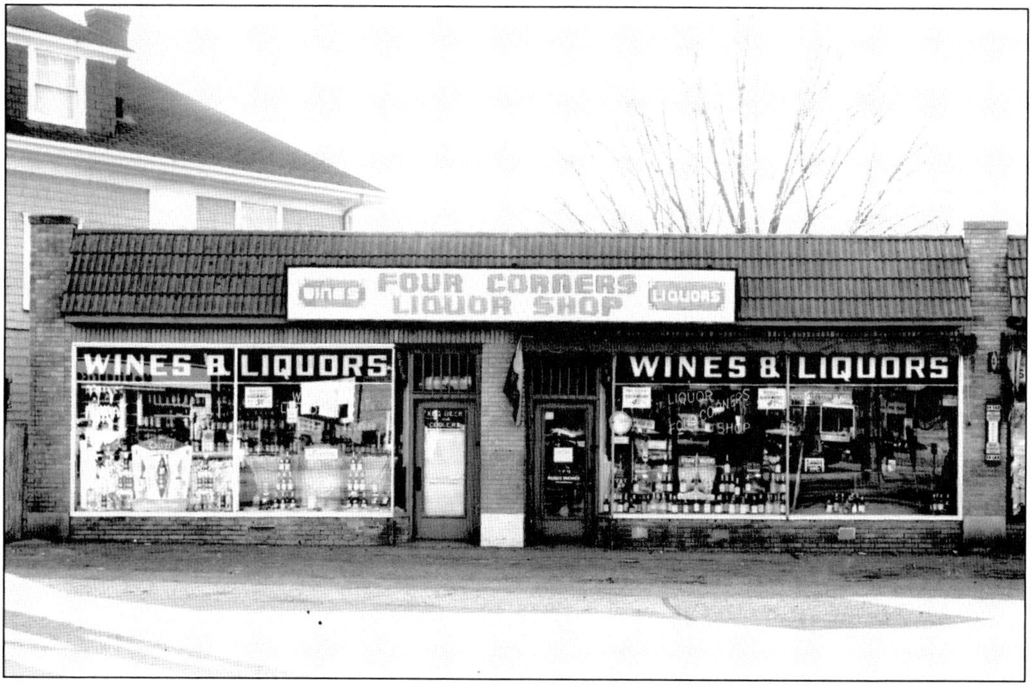

Four Corners Liquor Shop, located at Bulls Head, was owned in 1958 by Morris Brenner.

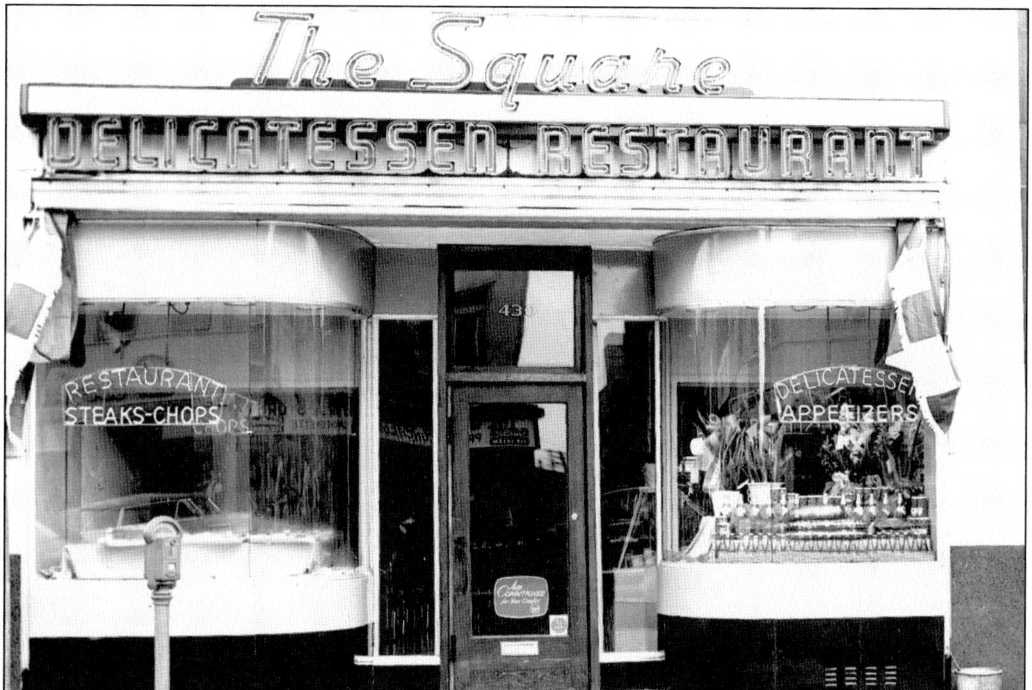

This is a 1958 view of the kosher-style Square Delicatessen. Located on Main Street, it was owned by Meyer Bloomfield.

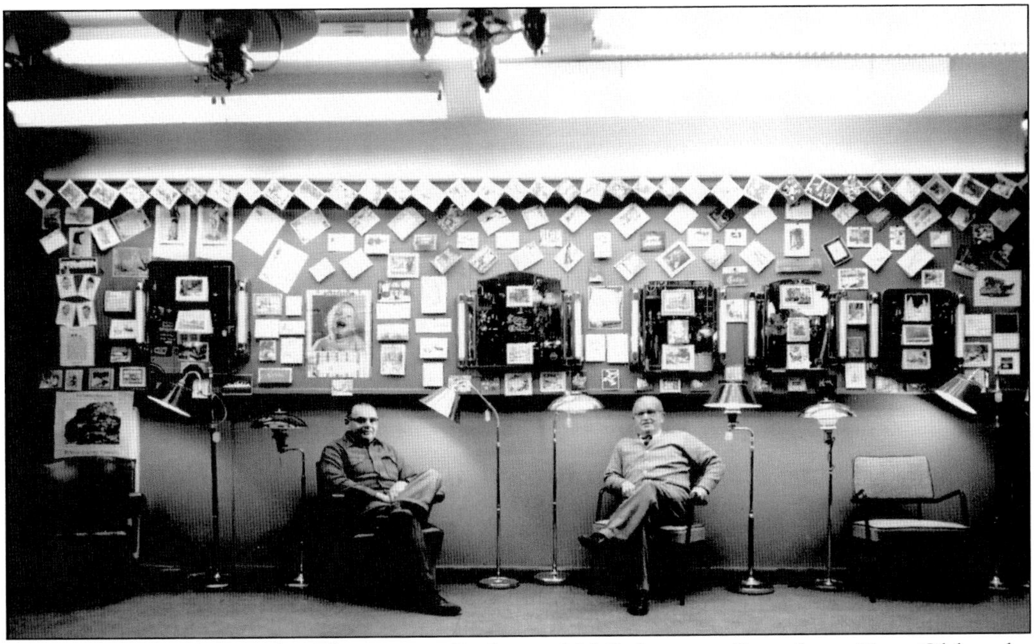

This 1954 view shows Elm Electric, on Richmond Hill Avenue. Seated are Nate Olshansky (left) and Jack Levine.

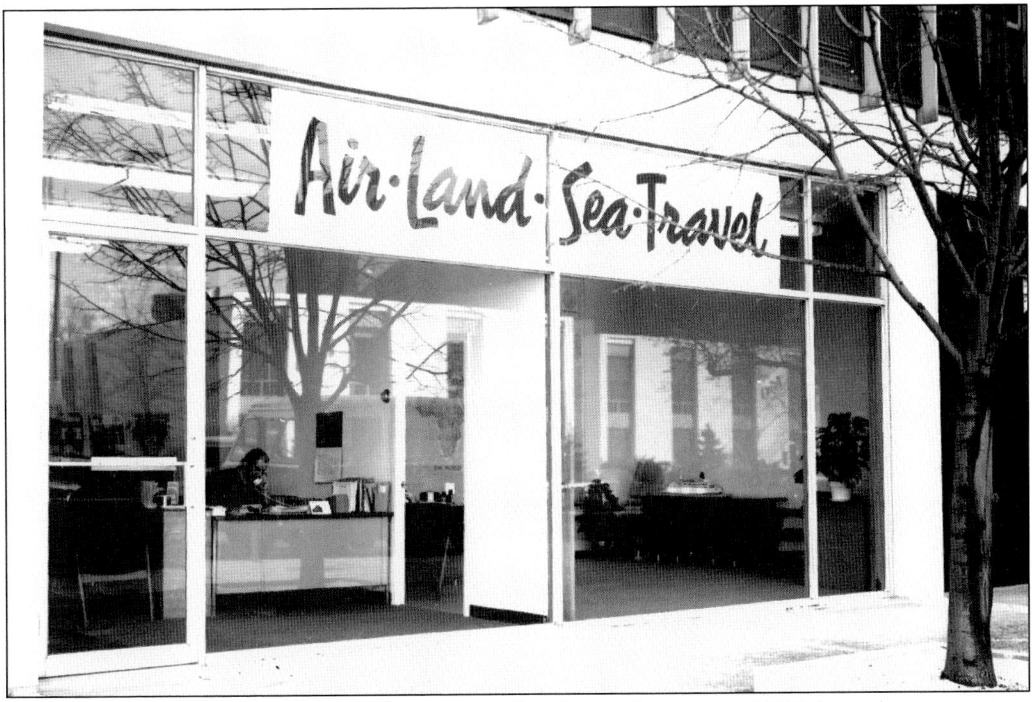

On the off chance that one might have wanted to leave the area in 1968 for a short vacation, there was Air-Land-Sea Travel on Summer Street, owned and operated by Mickey Grogins.

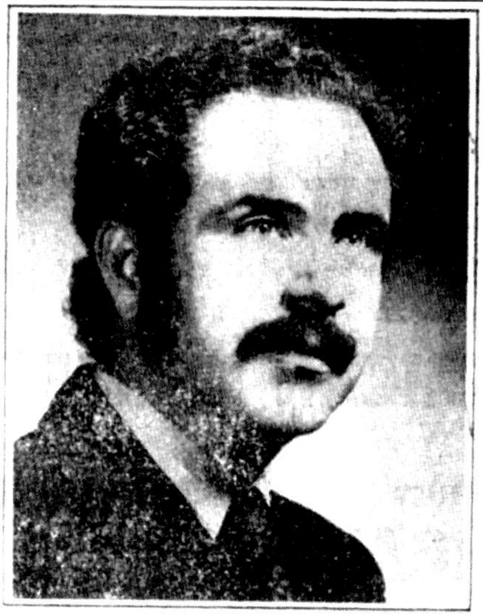

Meet: LESTER SHARLACH

A Director of Stamford's new Liberty National Bank

A native of Stamford, Mr. Sharlach received all of his education in Connecticut. He is a former member of the Stamford Jaycees and the Naval Reserve.

Mr. and Mrs. Sharlach have 3 children—Debra is in Grammar School, Brian in High School, and Jeff attends Northwestern.

Mr. Sharlach is Secretary-Treasurer of Rovens Curtain Shops, President of Rovens of Wilton, and Vice-President of Rovens of Greenwich.

Actively interested in the Boy Scouts of America, he is Committee Chairman of Troop 15 and is on the Executive Board of the Scouts. Mr. Sharlach is also a member of the Stamford Area Commerce and Industry Association, the Stamford Jewish Center, and the Congregation Agudath Sholom.

Lester Sharlach knows Stamford well, and is proud to be part of its new Liberty National Bank, Stamford's bank of today, building for *your* tomorrow.

We cordially invite you to visit our new building and ask about any of our dozens of services, including a full range of regular and special checking accounts.

Liberty National Bank is the modern bank where decisions are made *on the premises*, with friendly and courteous efficiency.

LIBERTY NATIONAL BANK

BANK WITH US...BANK ON US!

51 BANK STREET, STAMFORD

Telephone: 359-4900

Lester Sharlach joined the Board of Directors of Liberty National Bank in 1972.

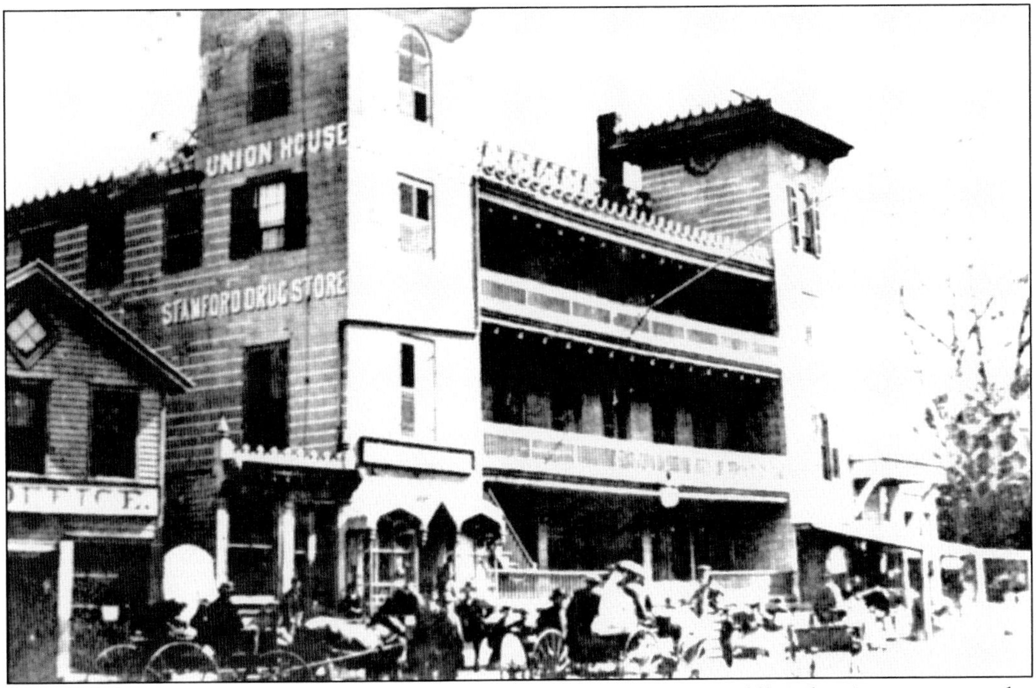

The Union House Hotel was located on Main Street *c.* 1868. Wolff Cohen's store is on the right at the canopy. Cohen occupied this location from 1856 to 1874, when he moved to 7 Park Row. His sons Samuel and Byron Cohen were the first Jewish lawyers in Stamford.

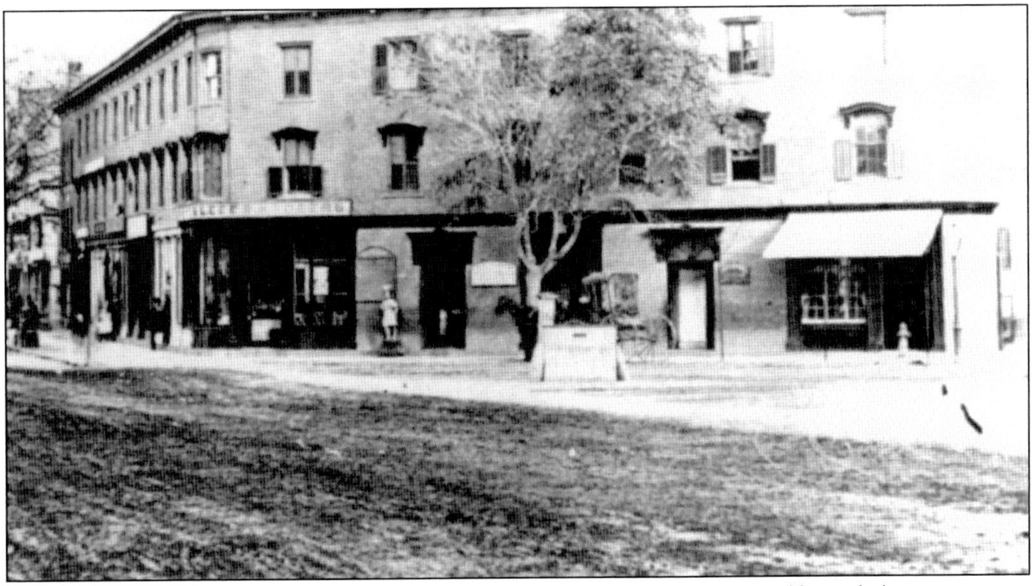

Pictured *c.* 1870 is the Quintard Block, with Jacob Fox's clothing store (far right).

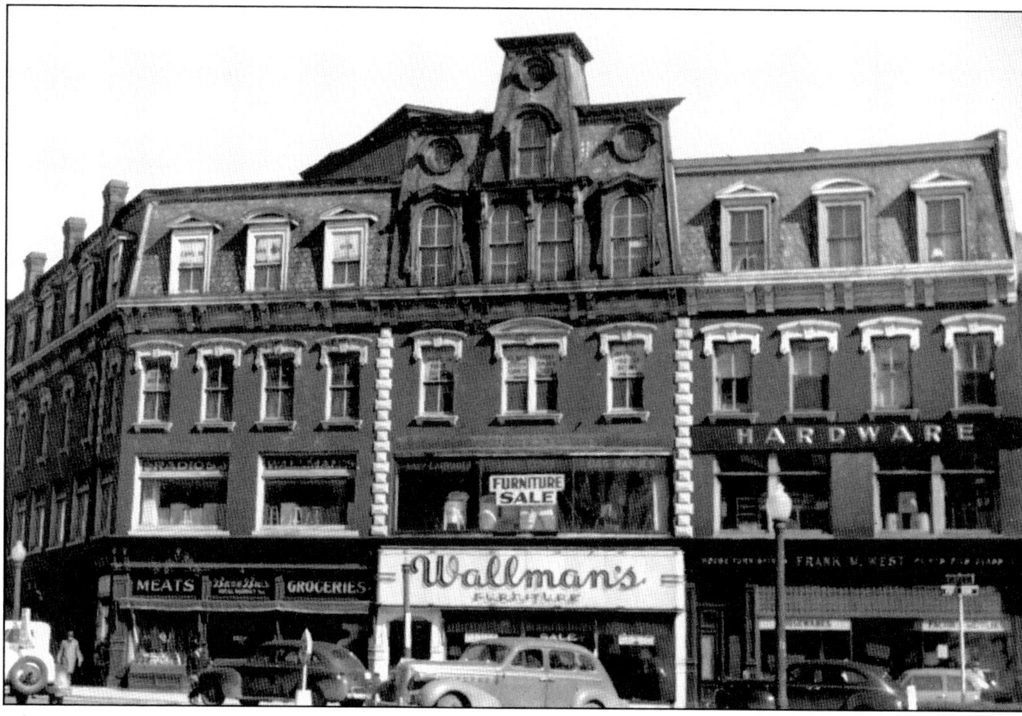

This is a 1930s view of the corner of Atlantic Street and Park Row, which includes Wallman's Furniture (center).

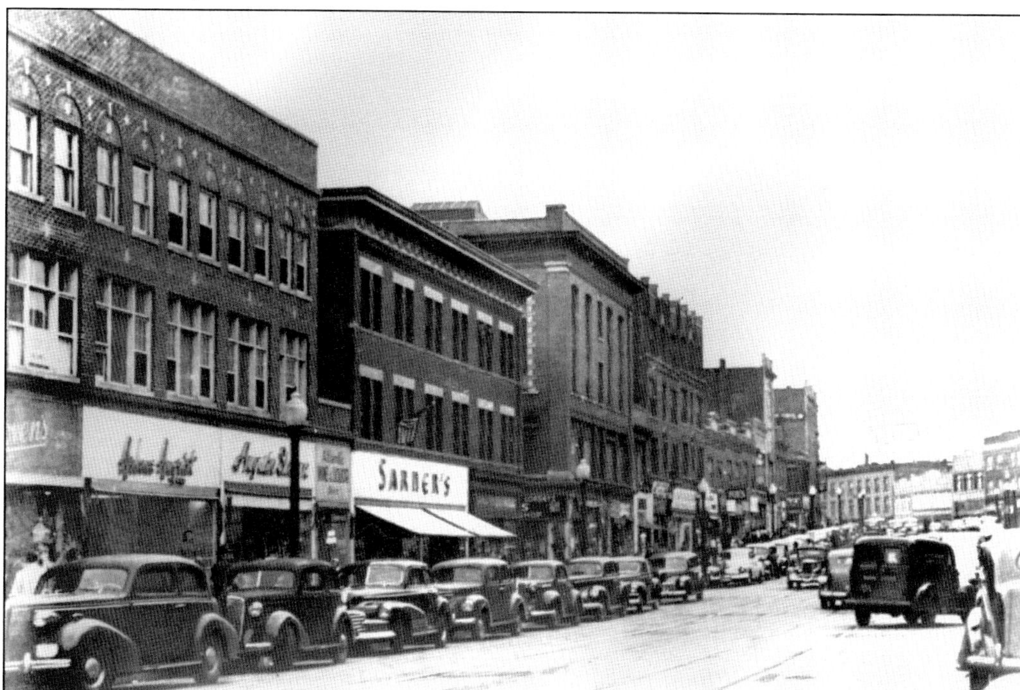

In the early 1940s, Atlantic Street looked like this. Visible (along the left) are Roven's, Arlene August, the Augusta Shop, and Sarner's.

Six

Our Community at Play

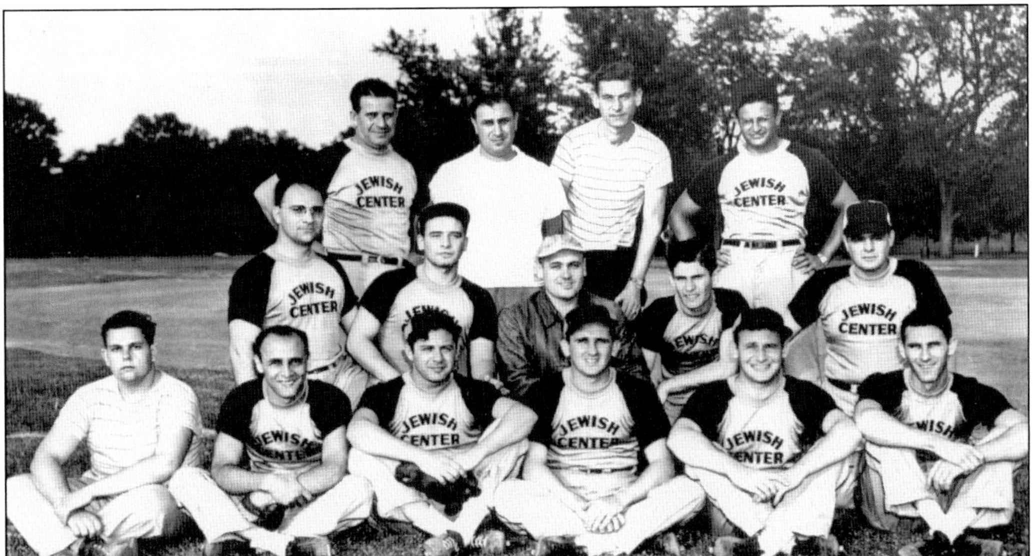

Pictured is the 1949 International League Stamford Jewish Center softball team. From left to right are the following: (front row) Harold Knopf, Jack Gordon, Shelly Leferman, Murray (Murph) Weingrad, Dave Brody, and Allie Alter; (middle row) Irv Peckerman, Gene Plotnick, Walter Bloom, Leo Gold, and Bob Cooper; (back row) Al Roven, Oscar Shulman, Bernie Eskowitz, and Gene Meyers.

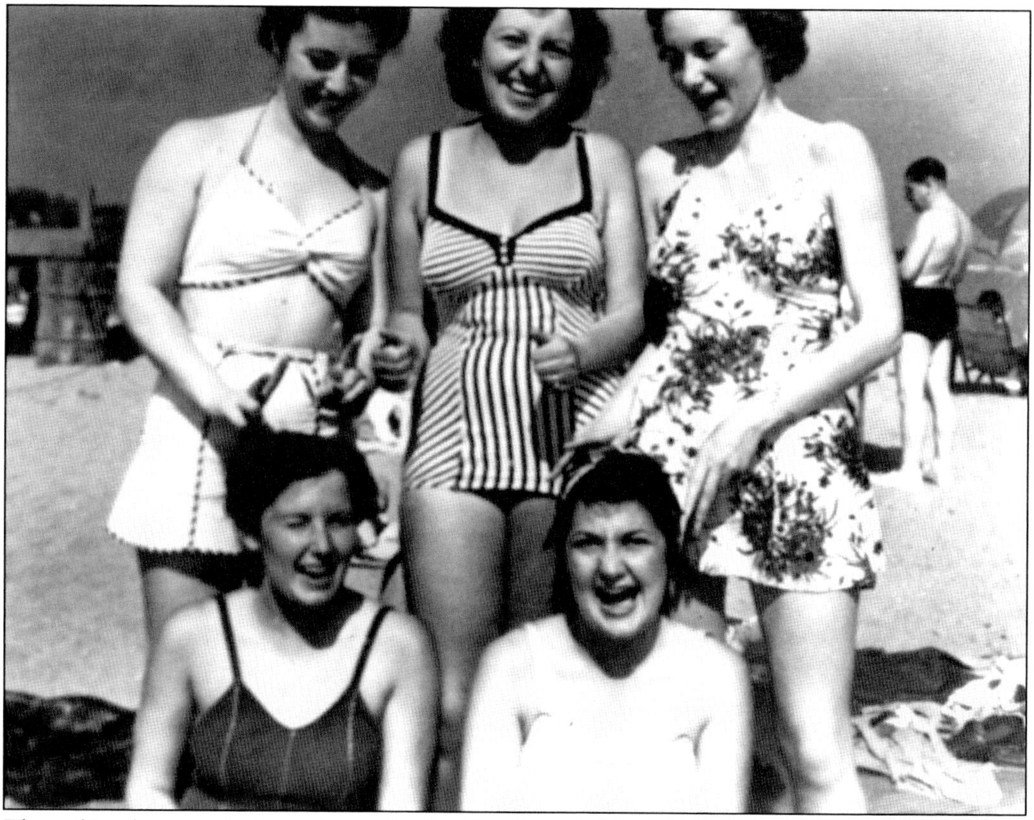

These friends are enjoying a day at Spelke Beach in 1939. From left to right are the following: (front row) Sylvia Gottfried (Schwimer) and Helen Wall (Isaacs); (back row) Edith Anger (Burstein), Pearl Wexler (Bass), and Adele Weisberg (Shulman).

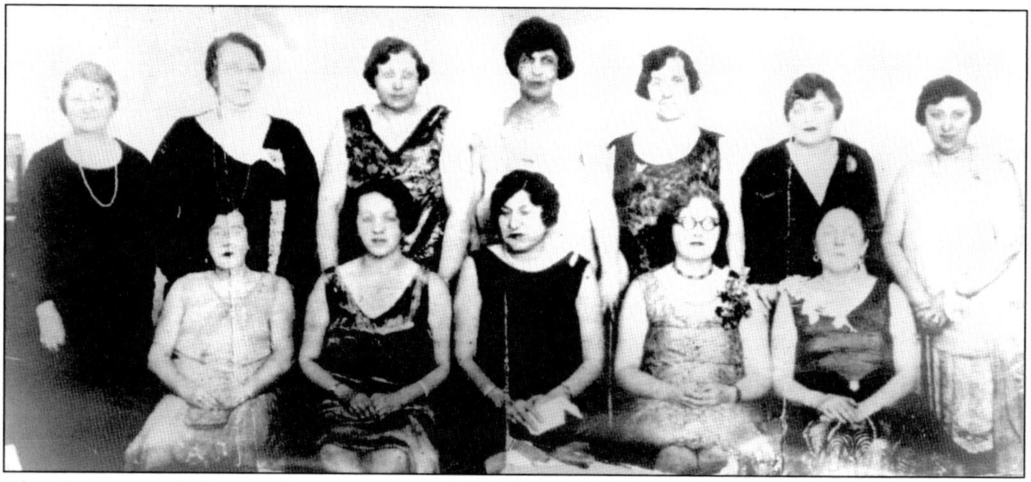

The first annual dinner dance sponsored by the sisterhood of Temple Beth El was held in 1923. Pictured are the women of the organizing committee. They are, from left to right, as follows: (front row) Julie Sosnowitz, Bessie Davidoff, Olga Karp, Lil Fuherman, and Bessie Kweskin; (back row) Celia Dichter, Annie Sosnowitz, Irene Moltasch, Hannah Wallman, Sarah Walter, and Gussie Siegelbaum.

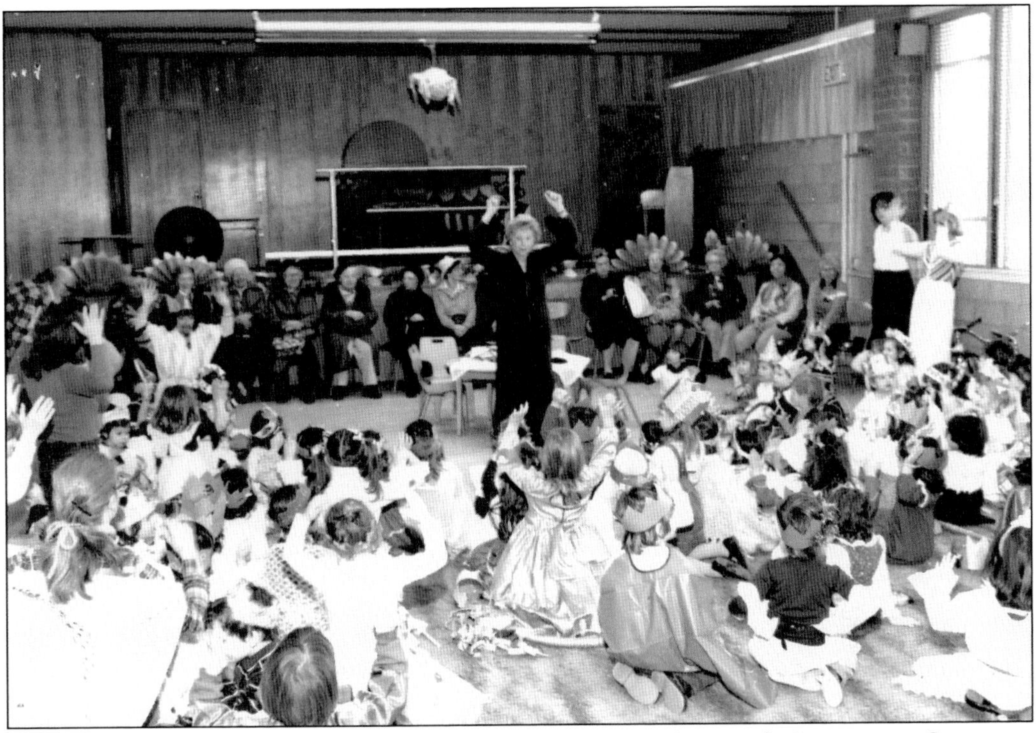

A Purim celebration is being led by Sara Walker (center) at the Jewish Community Center on Prospect Street in 1974.

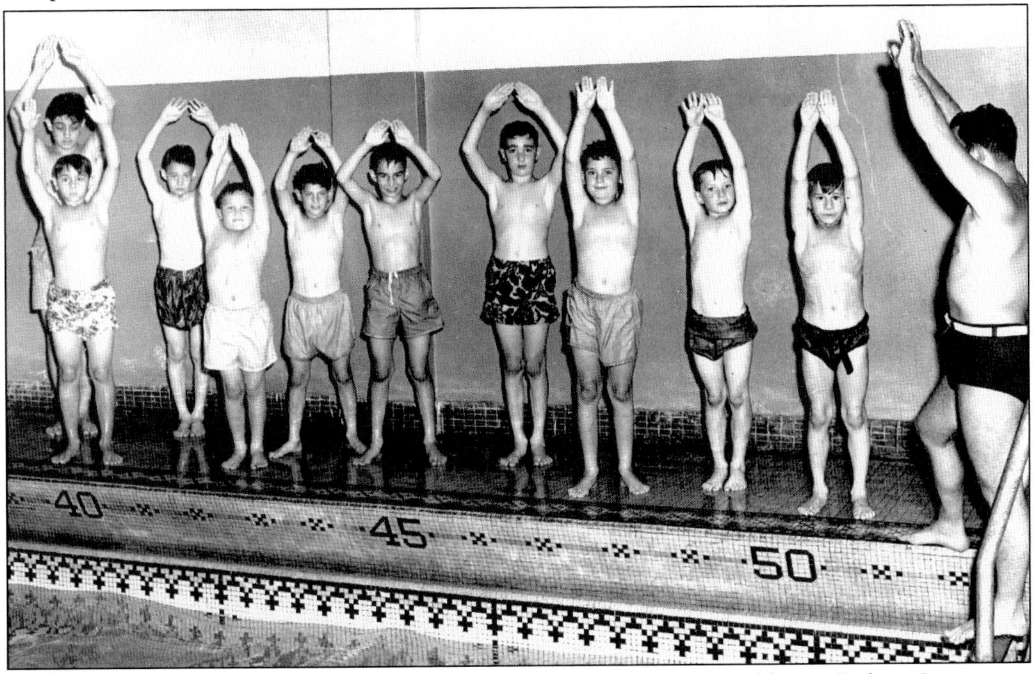

At the pool in 1948 are, from left to right, Marty Schoen, Robert Goldman, Robert Sosnowitz, an unidentified swimmer, Fred Fodiman, Pat DiMuro, Aaron Fodiman, Larry Roven, Ronald Robbins, Irving Goldblum, and coach Murray Goldenberg.

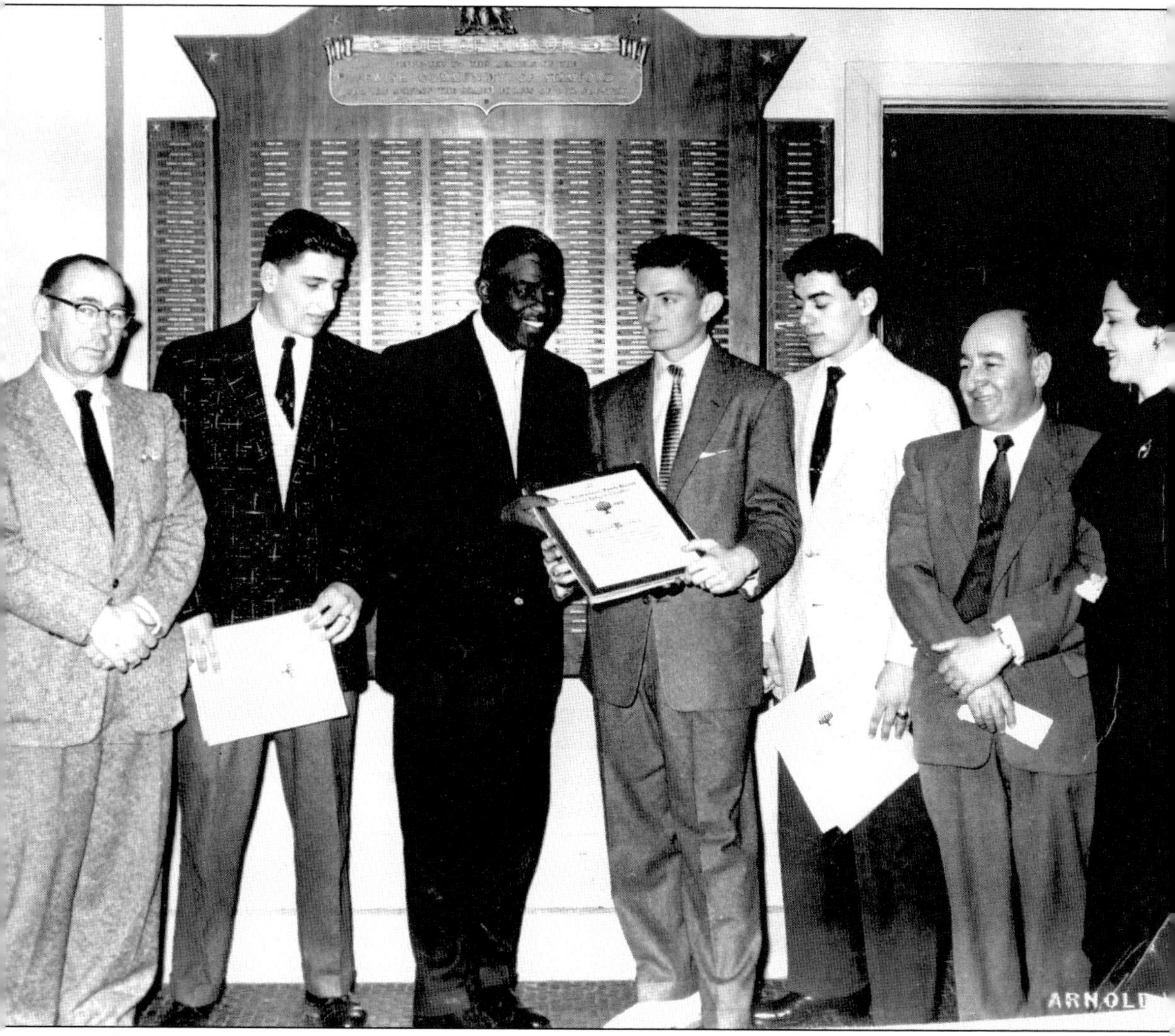

On January 17, 1955, a sports award ceremony was held. From left to right are Robert Nardi, Charles Winski, Jackie Robinson, Skippy Neuwein, Robert Nardi Jr., Abe Hecht, and Doris Wellington.

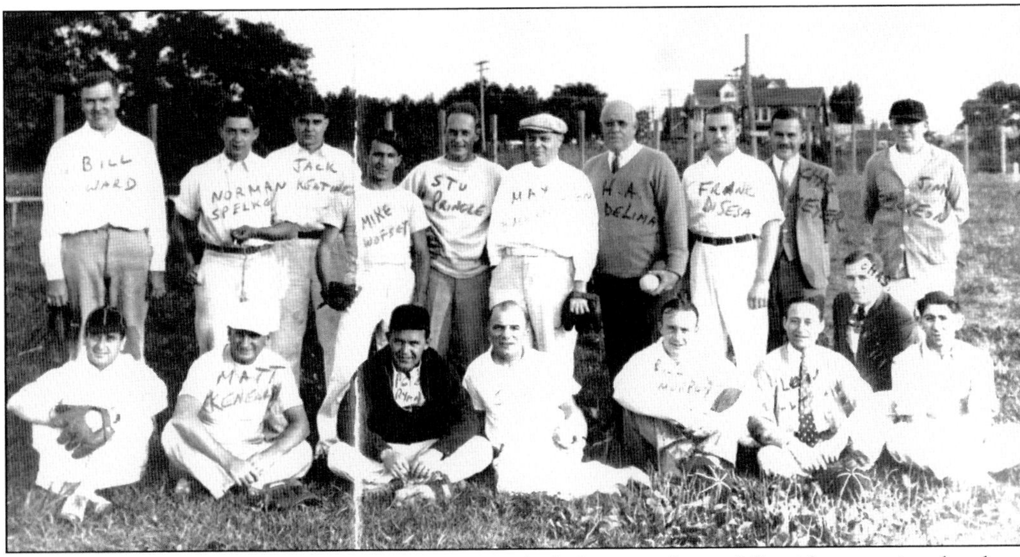

Stamford Lawyers baseball team in 1934 included a number of Jewish men in the legal profession. From left to right are the following: (front row) Barney Plotnick, Matt Kenealy, Pete Ryan, Joe Davidson, Bill Murphy, Lou Altman, Charles Meyer, and Sidney Kweskin; (back row) Bill Ward, Norman Spelke, Jack Keating, Mike Wofsey, Stu Pringle, Max Bernstein, Herbert A. DeLima, Frank DeSesa, Charles Meyer, and Jimmy McKeon.

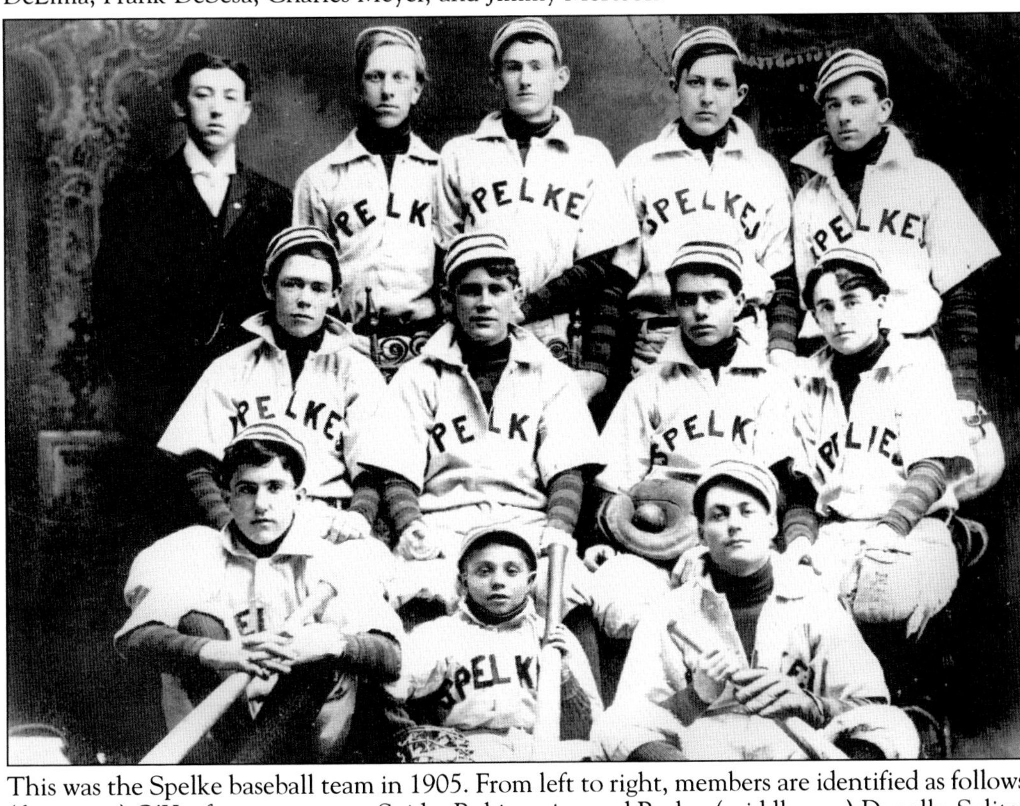

This was the Spelke baseball team in 1905. From left to right, members are identified as follows: (front row) O'Keefe, team mascot Spider Rabinowitz, and Burke; (middle row) Donelly, Saliter, Nichols, and Smith; (back row) manager Abram Spelke, Hoyt, Cuddy, Smith, and Howard.

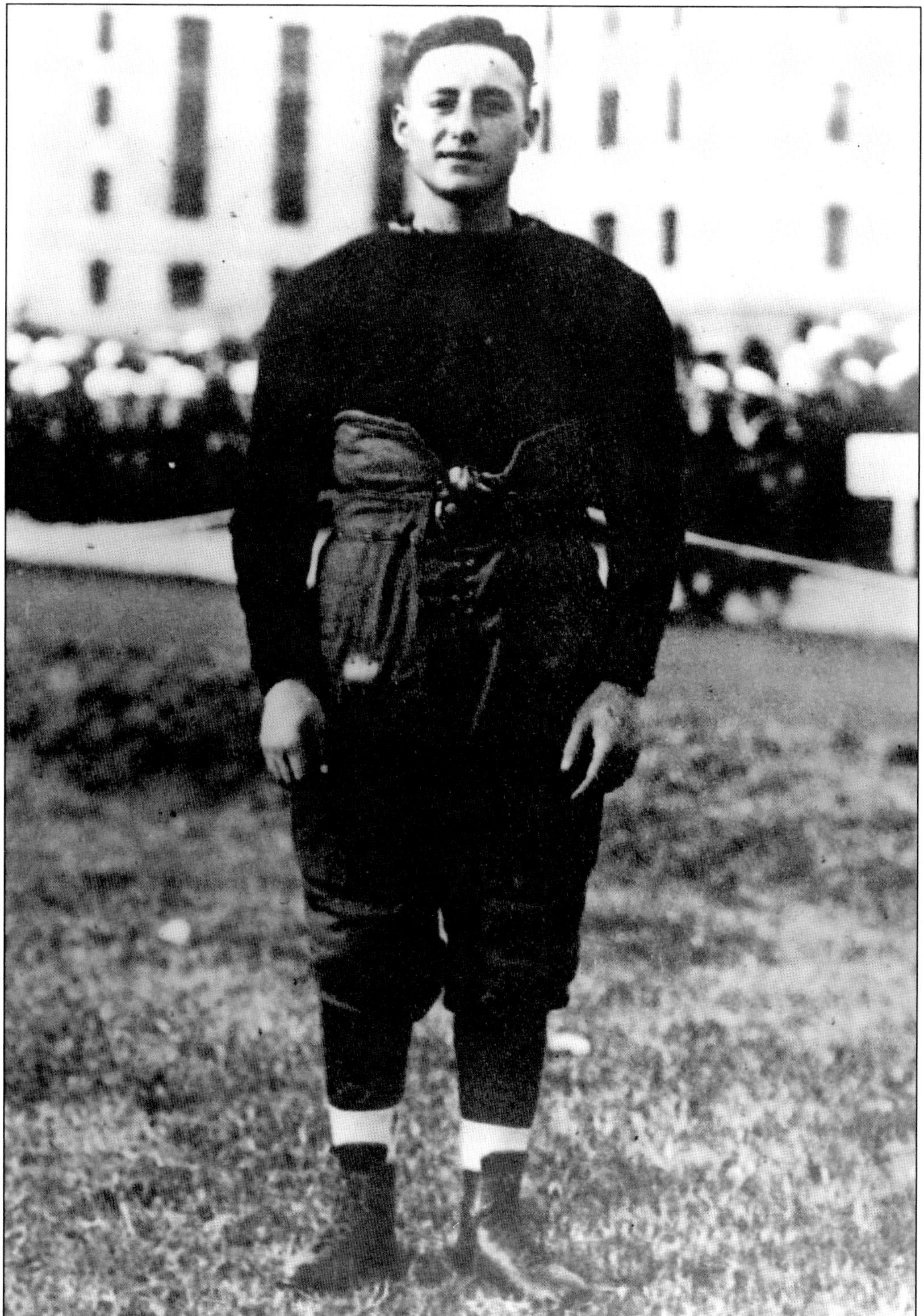

Louis Altman is pictured in his football attire at the Great Lakes Naval Training Station during World War I.

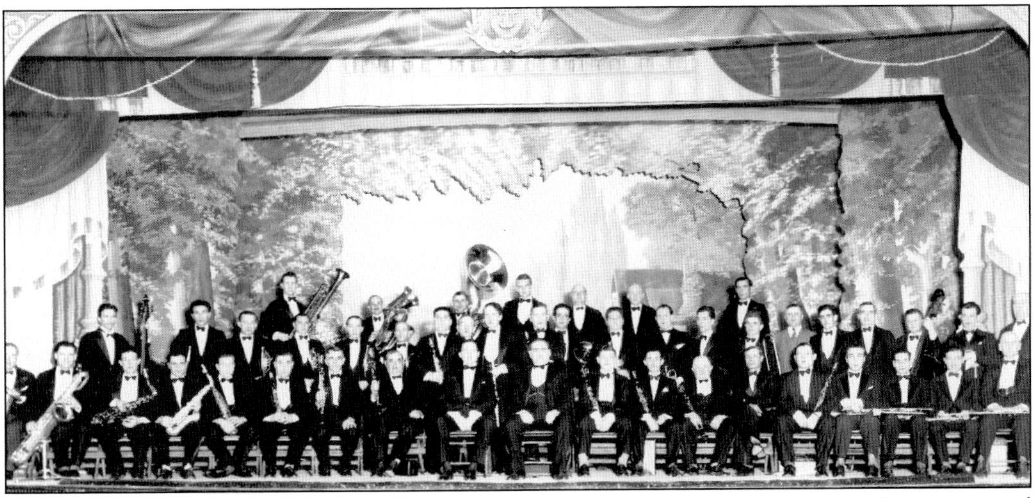

The arts also played a part in the life of the Jewish communities. Members not only participated in the arts including theatrical and musical endeavors but also gave significant support to the arts—and that continues to this day. Among those pictured in this 1936 photograph of Stamford's Works Progress Administration orchestra is George Goldberg (ninth from the right), with his clarinet.

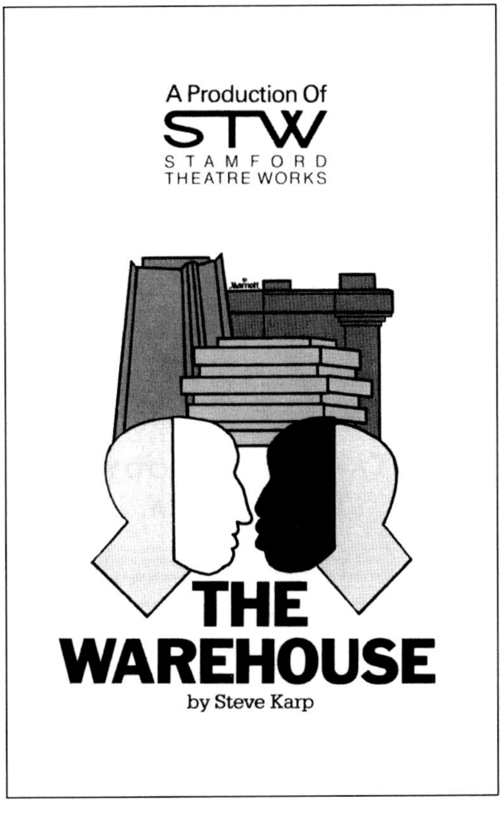

The Warehouse, a play by Steve Karp, is loosely based on his father Mortimer Karp's efforts to continue the family business in Stamford. His three sons did not wish to follow in his footsteps, and in the end it was a longtime employee who bought the business and continued the tradition. Steve Karp is the director of Stamford Theatre Works and just one of the myriad members of the extended Karp family living and working in the area.

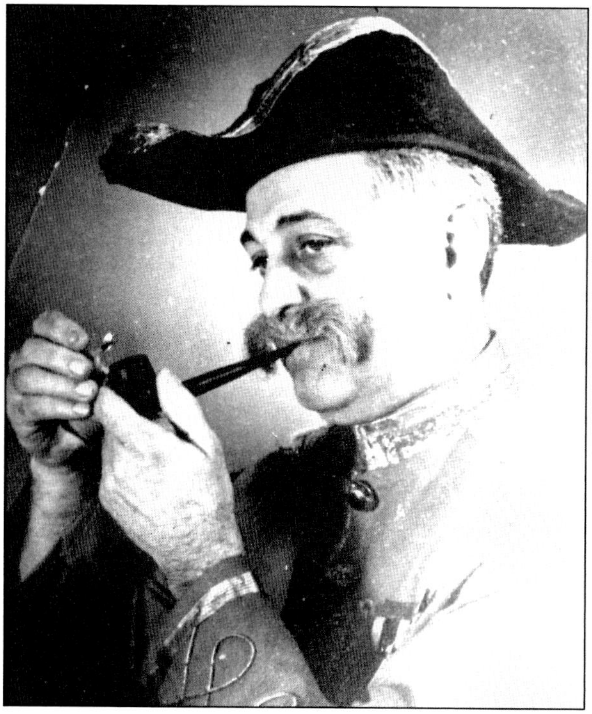

Dr. Bernard Nemoitin plays the role of the admiral in Gilbert and Sullivan's *Pirates of Penzance*. Knowing the lyrics of all Gilbert and Sullivan's light operas surely enhanced Nemoitin's ability as a physician not only to cure his patients but also to entertain them.

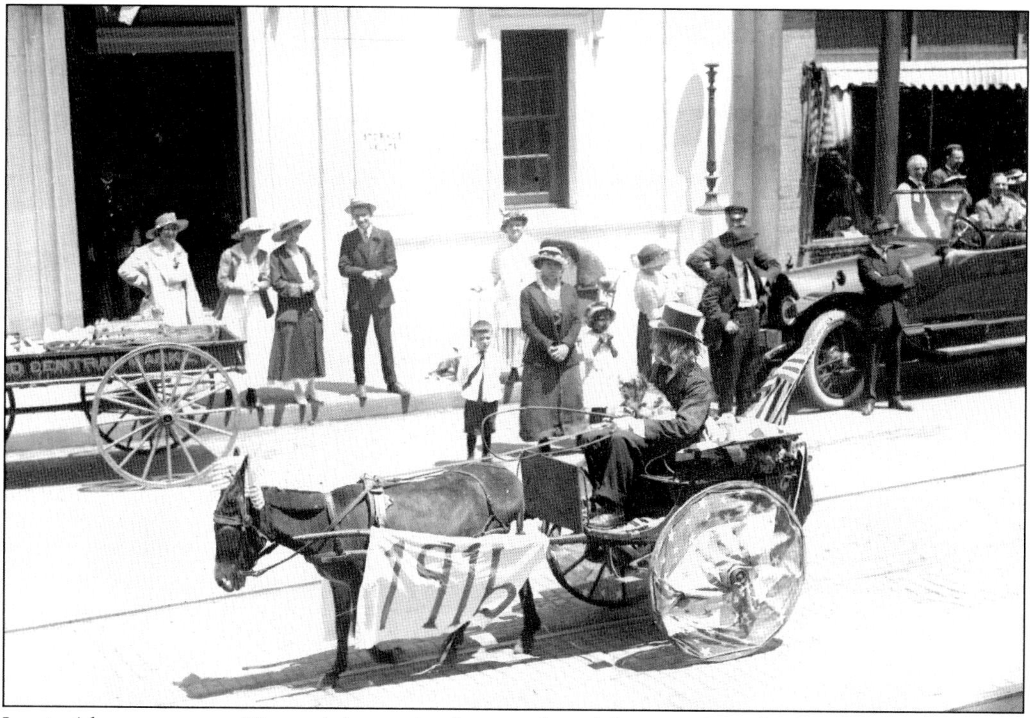

Louis Altman, at age 18, participates in the parade celebrating Stamford's 275th anniversary. Altman served in the Navy during World War I. He became a prominent lawyer and community leader, and was the first commander of Stamford Jewish War Veterans Post No. 142.

Seven

From Generation to Generation

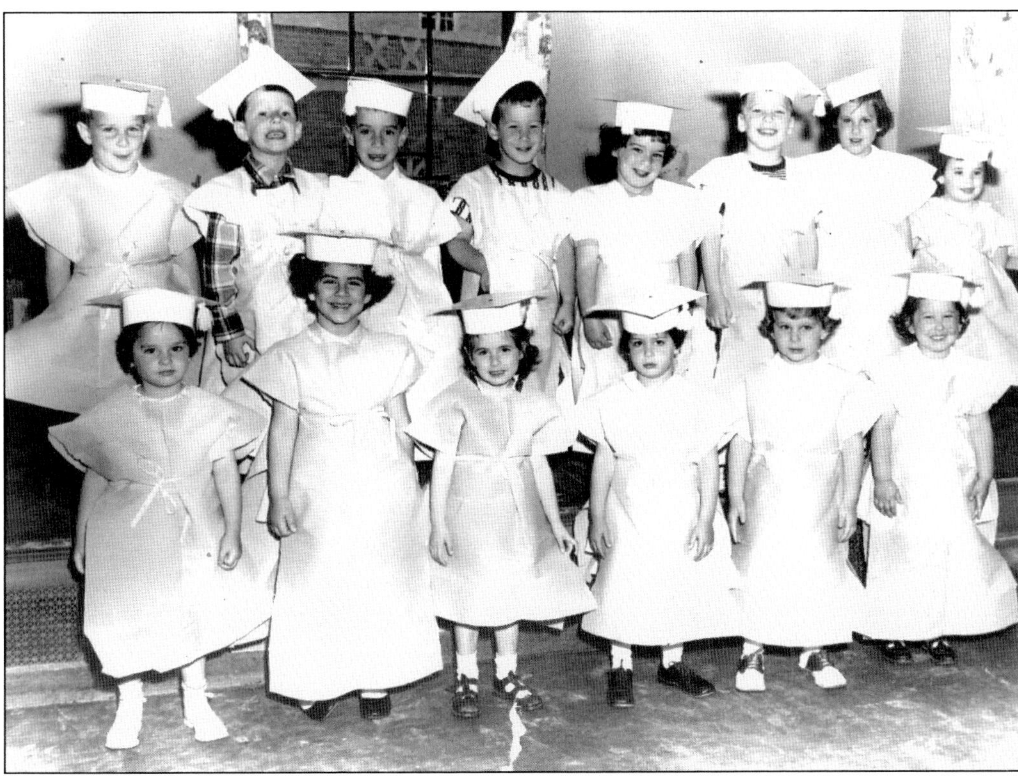

One is never too young to start on the road to educational achievement. In 1951, the nursery school students of the Jewish Community Center participate in the first of many graduations to come.

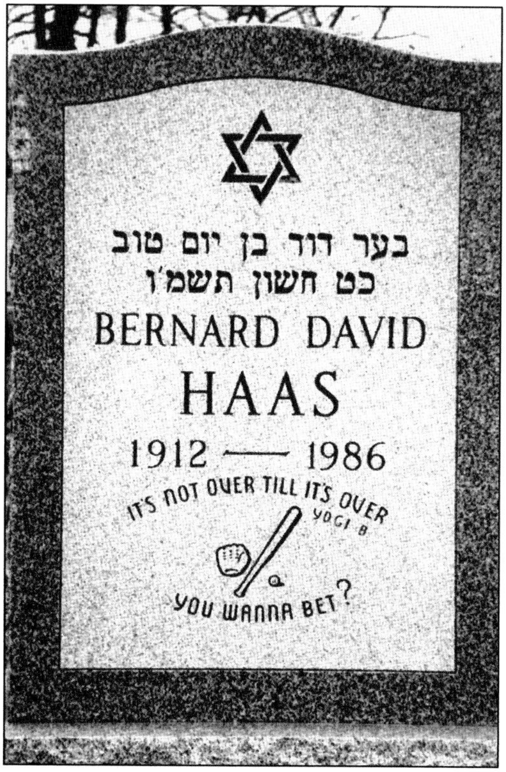

This tombstone of Bernard David Haas is in the Independent Lodge Cemetery in Darien. Bernard David Haas was clearly a man with a sense of humor. Founded in 1903, the Independent Lodge was primarily a mutual aid society, which paid sick and death benefits according to the amount for which the individual and his wife or family were insured. The aim of the organization as stated in the preamble to its constitution was "to create a vast Brotherhood in our community that will embrace and reverently do homage to the spiritual achievements of the glorious past of the Jew, and subscribe to the holy aspirations which illuminate our future national life . . . We assert our unequivocal belief in the national renaissance of Israel saturated with a full realization of these lofty hopes and be flooded with the light of our traditional beacons." The cemetery was established in 1904. In an era when Jews were being held back from purchasing residential property in Darien because of deed restrictions, the existence of a Jewish cemetery was largely ignored.

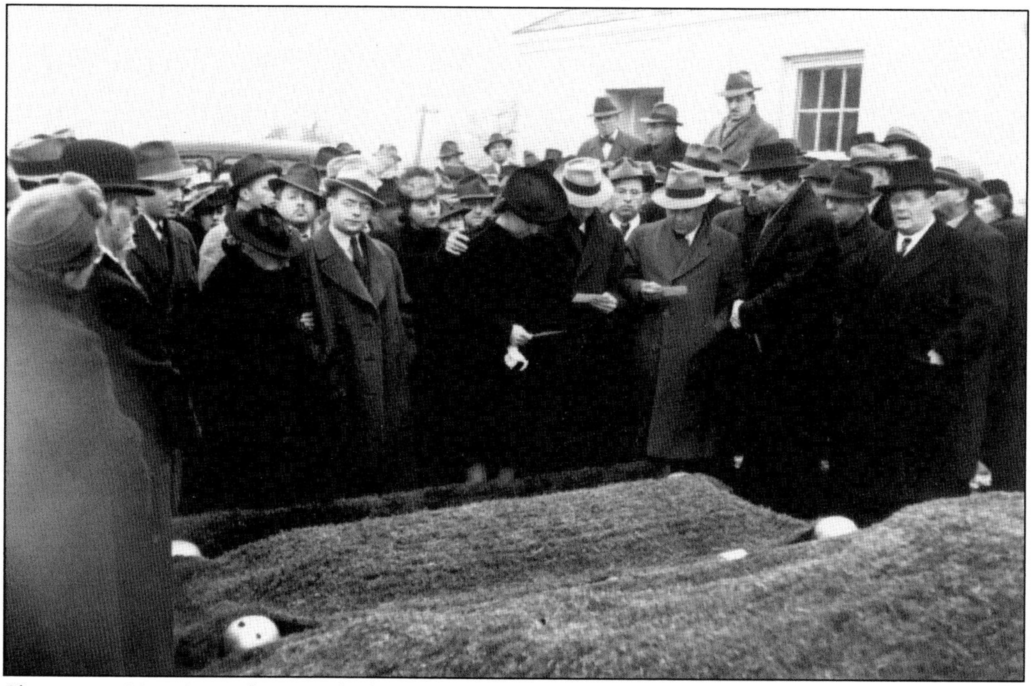

Shown is a 1941 funeral at Agudath Sholom Cemetery. Among those in attendance are Hebrew school principal Rabbi Todes (second man from the left), Rabbi Simon Winograd (second from the right), and Cantor Ephraim Scholsohn (far right).

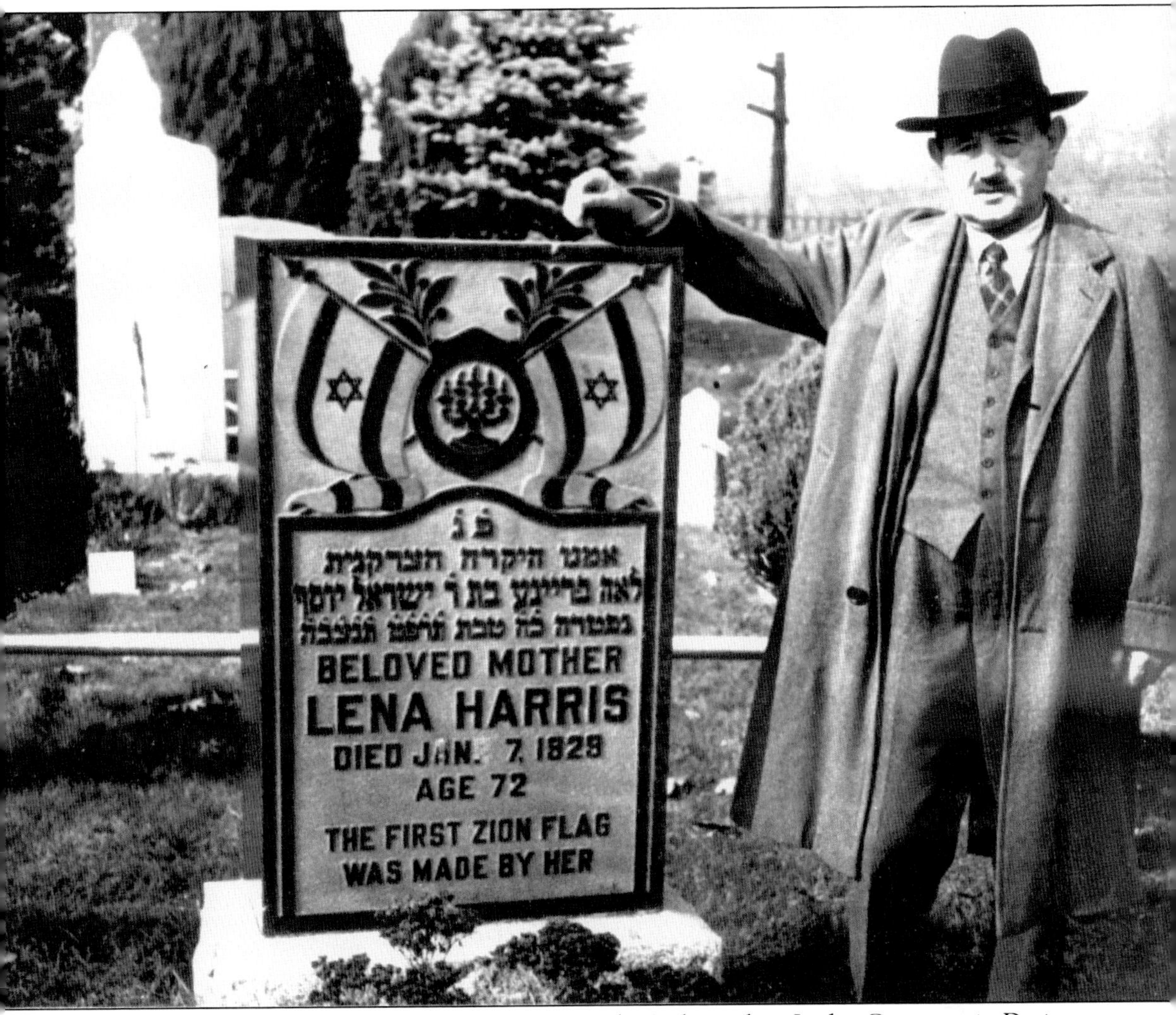

Morris Harris shown at his mother's tombstone in the Independent Lodge Cemetery in Darien. Prior to his coming to Stamford in 1915, Harris lived in New York. It was there in 1897 that he claimed to have designed the first Zionist flag for Hovevei Zion, an organization of which he was a member. He also claimed that his mother, Lena Harris, sewed the first Zion flag in America. Although Jewish encyclopedias credit others for the design, it was probably Harris's flag of Zion that was the first of its kind ever made in the United States.

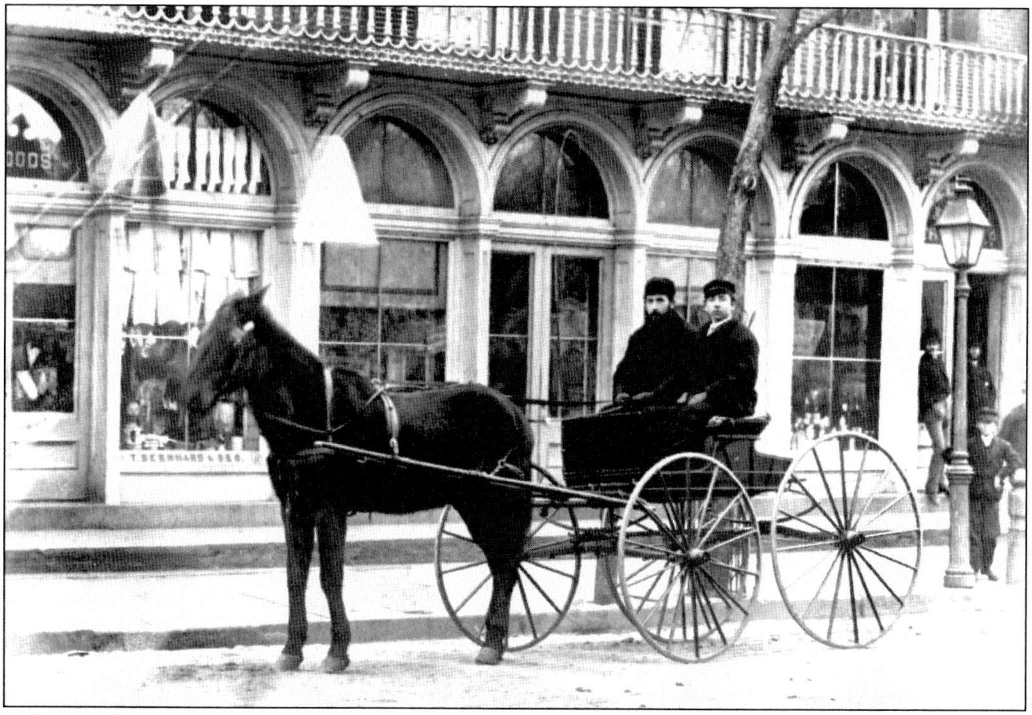

Tobias and Henry Bernhard stop in front of their millinery and fancy goods store in the Seely Block Building in 1869. Henry Bernhard married Rachel Cohen, daughter of Wolfe Cohen, in 1871 and moved to Middletown the following year. He was a successful merchant there and president of the Middletown Board of Trade. His great-grandson, Harry Bernhard, was president of Stamford's Temple Sinai in 1979.

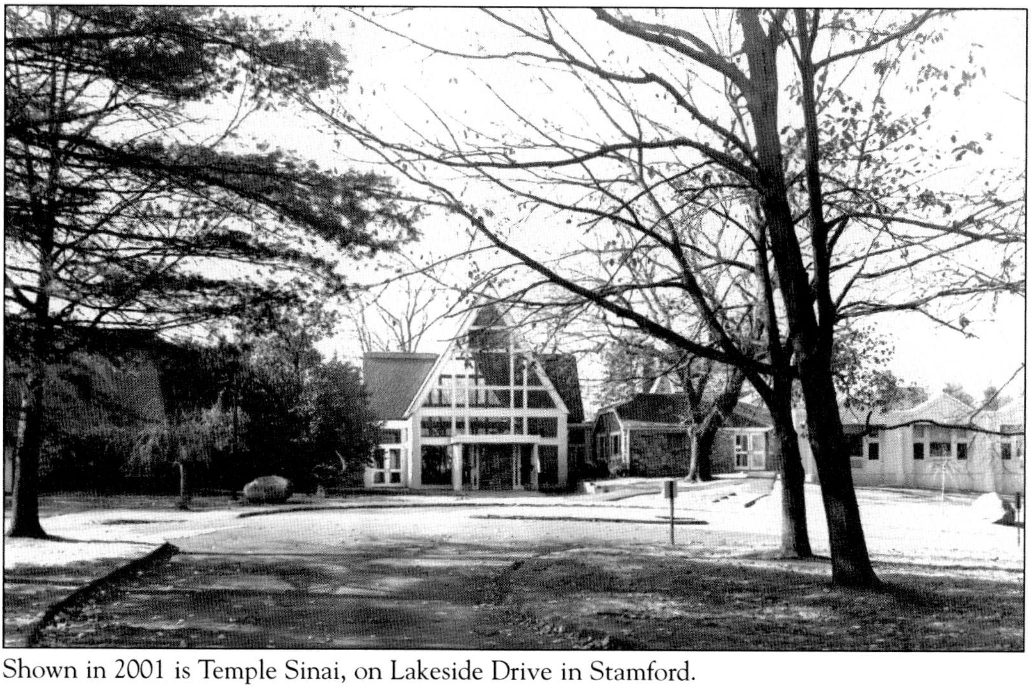

Shown in 2001 is Temple Sinai, on Lakeside Drive in Stamford.

You are cordially invited to attend a

Dinner Dance

to celebrate the

Twentieth Anniversary of

Temple Sinai

Saturday evening, the seventh of December

nineteen hundred and seventy-four

Cocktails at eight o'clock

Lakeside Drive

Stamford, Connecticut

Dress optional
Thirty-five dollars per couple

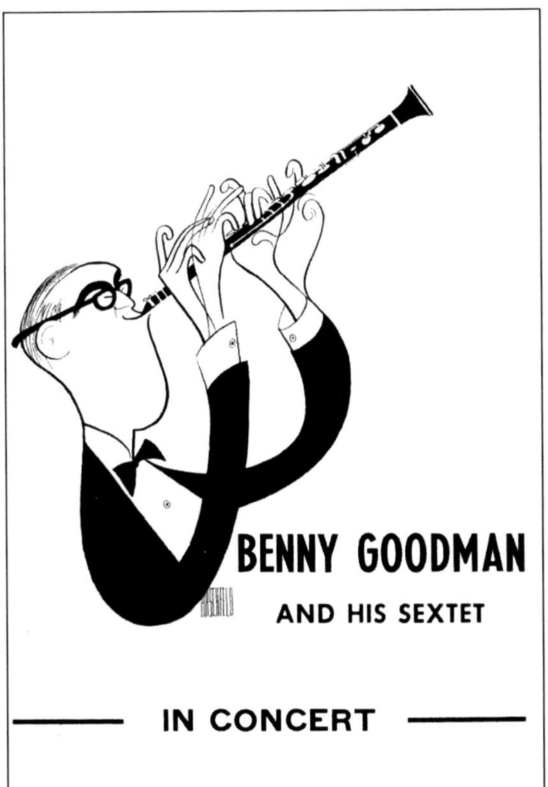

Founded in 1954, Temple Sinai is a congregation based on the principles of American Reform Judaism. It is affiliated with the Union of American Hebrew Congregations. When the congregation was organized in February 1954, services were conducted at 54 Grove Street. The building was purchased from St. John's Lutheran Church. The Lutheran parish voluntarily shared the building with the temple and continued to use the building until its own church on Newfield Avenue was completed. The first president of the Temple Sinai congregation was Harold Sandak. By the fall of 1954, a Sunday morning religious school was established under the direction of Rabbi Robert J. Marx. By 1961, the congregation had purchased 11 acres on Lakeside Drive in North Stamford. The property included a structure for the religious school. In 1964, the sanctuary was completed, followed by a school addition in 1966.

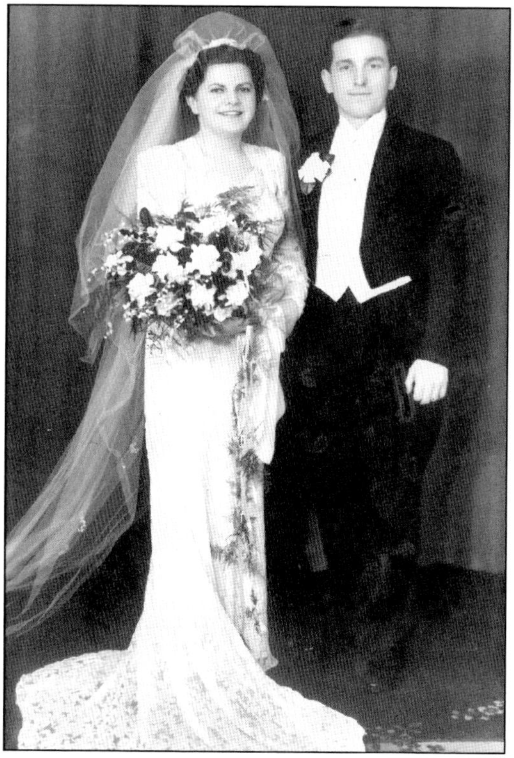

The wedding of Marcia and Henry Lieberman took place on Sunday, January 7, 1940. Cantor Ephraim Fischel Scholsohn officiated.

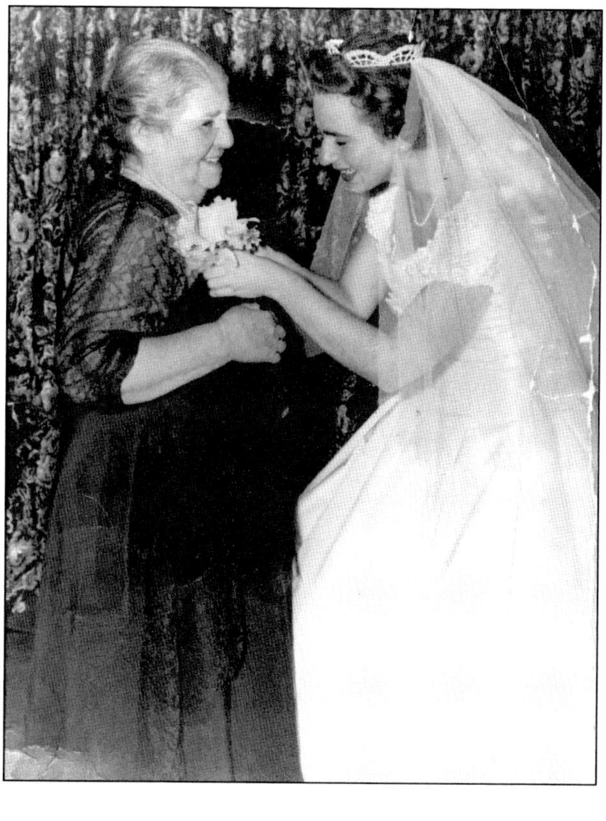

Annley Brenner (Freedman) pins a corsage on her grandmother Minnie Manger, who was Marcia Lieberman's mother and Sen. Joseph Lieberman's grandmother.

Barbara and Arnold Yelin were married in 1952. The owner of Hay Studios, Arnold Yelin is a photographer for the football Giants. He is also a former president of the Jewish Historical Society of Greater Stamford.

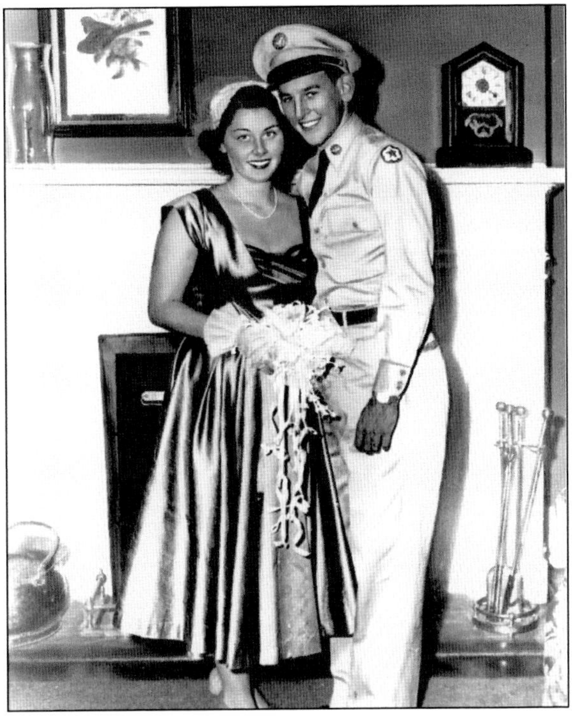

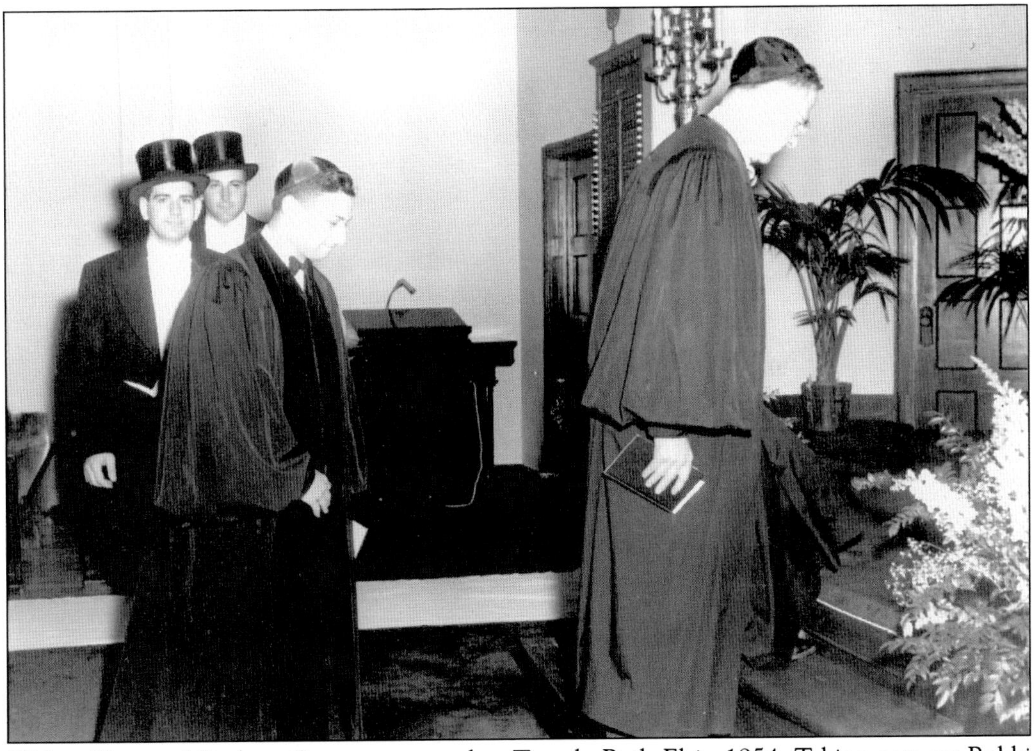

Walter Hotz and Barbara Sarner were wed at Temple Beth El in 1954. Taking part are Rabbi David W. Pearlman of Temple Beth El (right), Rabbi Joseph Ehrenkrantz of Congregation Agudath Sholom (second from the right), Walter Hotz, and George Sarner (rear).

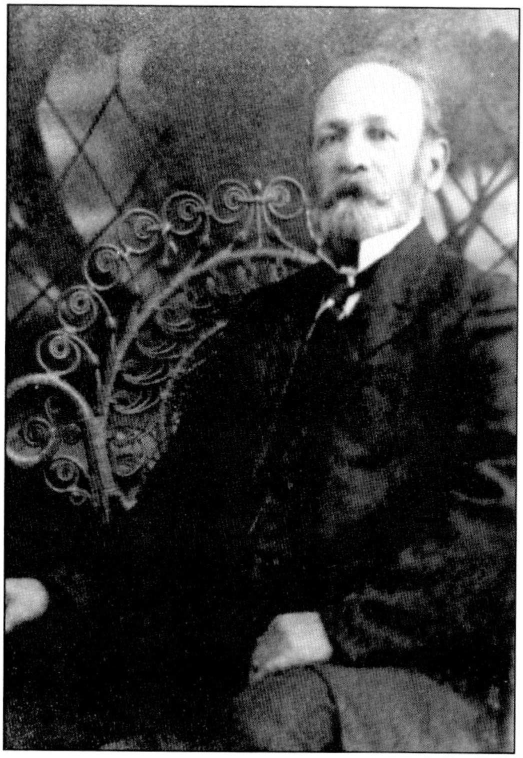

Jacob Rosenblum is thought to have been the earliest eastern European Jewish settler in Stamford. He arrived in 1881 from Sharon, Pennsylvania. He came to America from Kovno Province in Lithuania. In 1898, he was the first kosher butcher of record in Stamford. The first High Holy Day, Minyan, was held in his rooms on Stillwater Avenue in 1887.

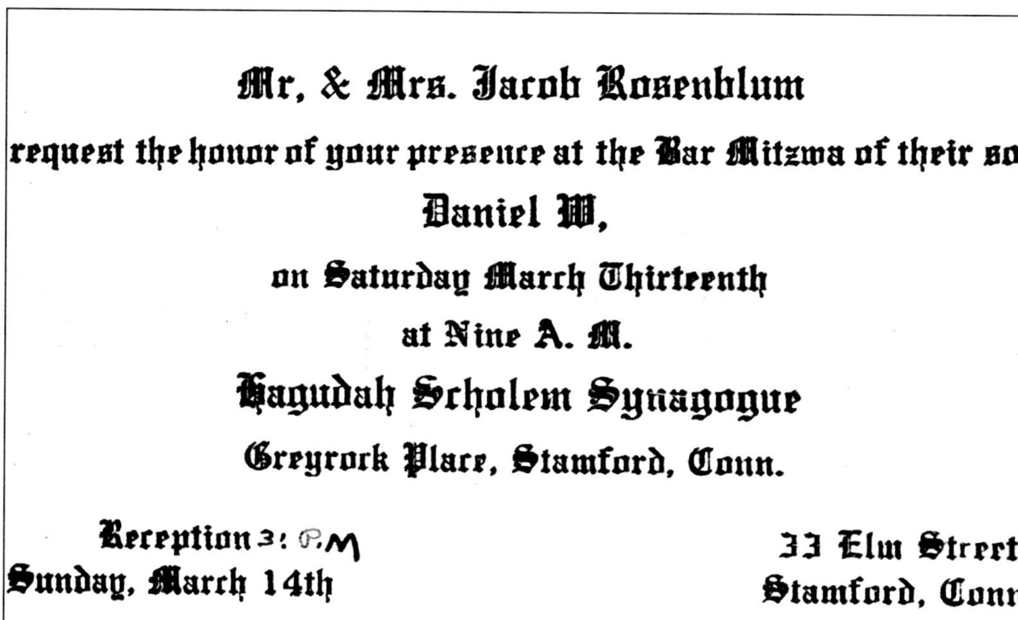

Mr, & Mrs. Jacob Rosenblum

request the honor of your presence at the Bar Mitzwa of their so

Daniel W,

on Saturday March Thirteenth

at Nine A. M.

Hagudah Scholem Synagogue

Greyrock Place, Stamford, Conn.

Reception 3: P.M
Sunday, March 14th

33 Elm Street
Stamford, Conn

This was the invitation to the Bar Mitzvah of Daniel W. Rosenblum, the son of Jacob and Minna Cohn Rosenblum. Minna Cohn was born in Germany (note the spelling of *mitzwa* and the Gothic German font). Daniel Rosenblum was also confirmed at the National Council of Jewish Women's Sabbath School in 1915. The address, 33 Elm Street, has been identified with Jewish residents since at least 1883.

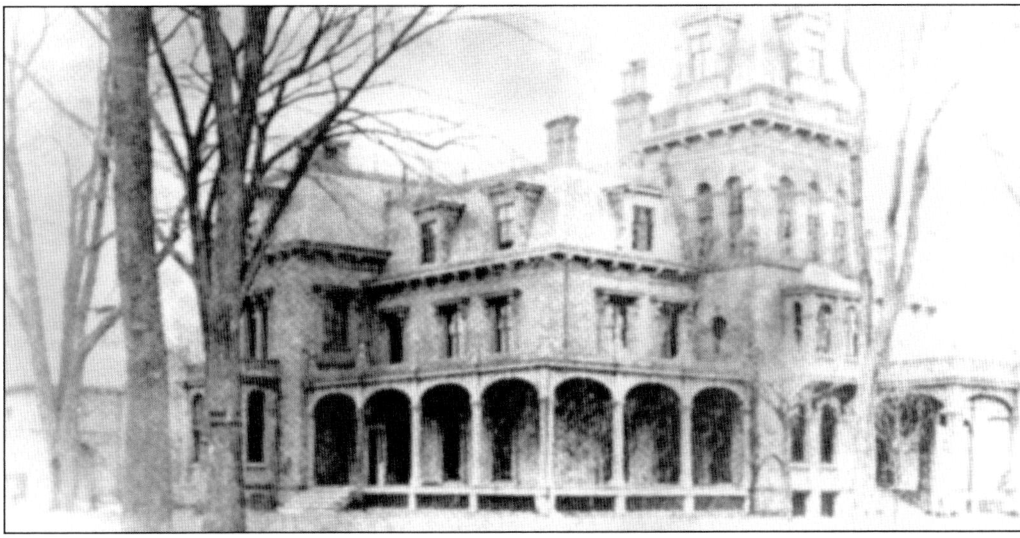

Constructed as a mansion by George Hoyt in 1861, this building served as headquarters for the Suburban Club from 1894 until the Hebrew Institute purchased it in 1916. The building became a center of educational and social activities for the community. It formally ceased to exist in October 1928, when its name was changed to the Stamford Jewish Center. The cornerstone for a new building at 132 Prospect Street was dedicated at that time, and the center was dedicated on January 19, 1930. From 1920 to 1927, the building also served as a place of worship for Temple Beth El.

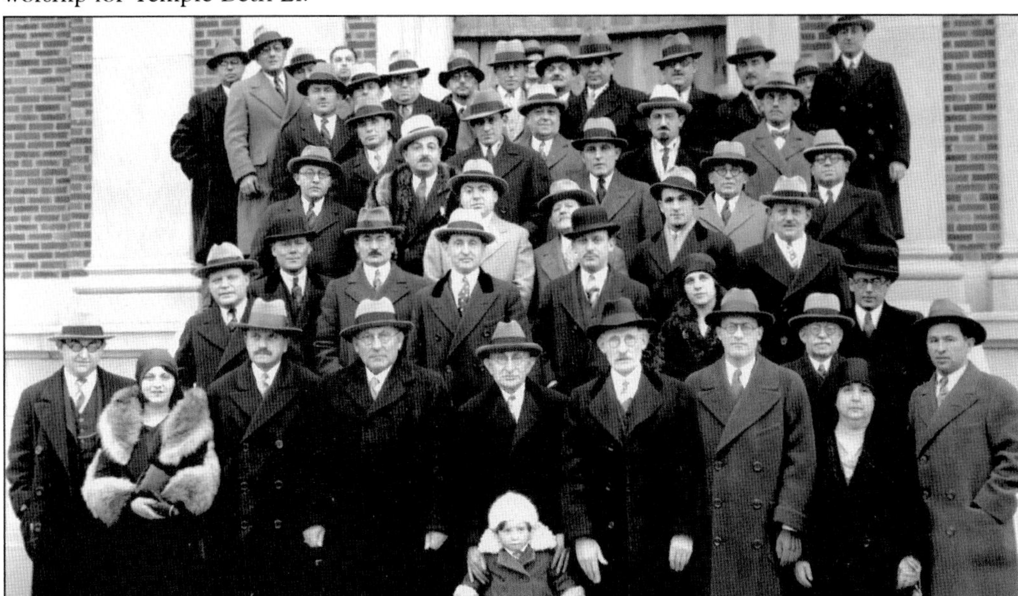

On the steps of the new Jewish Community Center building just before its completion in 1930 are some of the founding members, who include Mr. Fishman, Meyer Wise, Morris Epstein, Hyman Frankel, Mr. Weissman, Noah Adler, Mr. Davidoff. Behind them are Nathan Gold, Mr. Coleman, Mr. Berger, Dr. Harry Levine, Mr. Rosen, Judge Abe Wofsey, Myron Frankel, Morris Lavinsky, Dr. Jack Levinson, Manuel Chausky, Mike Wofsey, Aaron Weissman, Mr. Shulman, Sam Rossenblum, Jake Weisberg, Mr. Shenson, Harry Nevas, and Louis Altman.

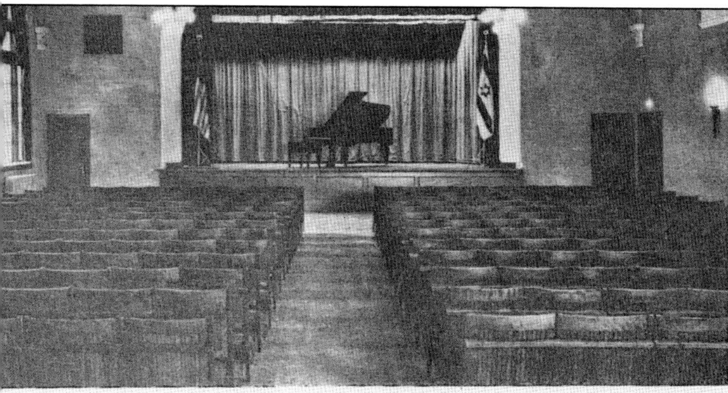

he community attends lectures, concerts and social activities here

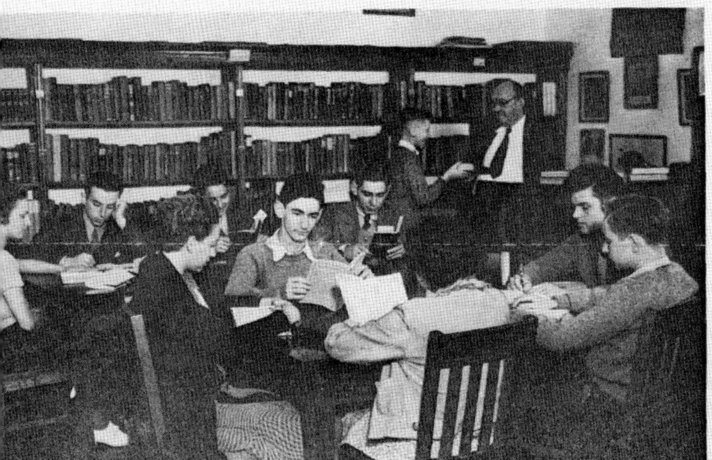

For study and reading this well equipped library is maintained

One can hear many pins drop here.

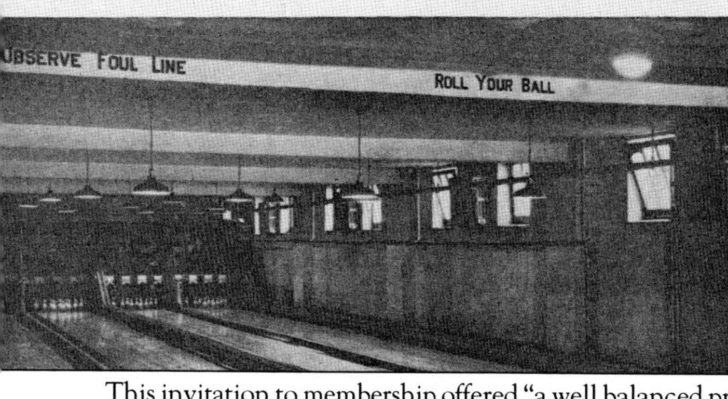

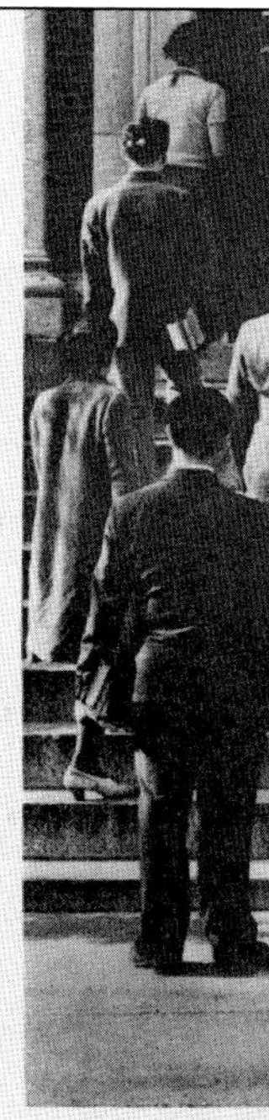

ENTER . . .
THE STAMFC

with the 100,C
every year for Ec
to participate in
Activ:ties for adu

Forums - Ca
Dramatics - Music
Social Events - Jur
Ping Pong - Ga
Adult Organizatic
Zionist Activity

" The Entire Jewish

MEMBER OF S

MEMBER O

This invitation to membership offered "a well balanced program for young and old within modern facilities under trained supervision." The Stamford Jewish Center assured prospective members

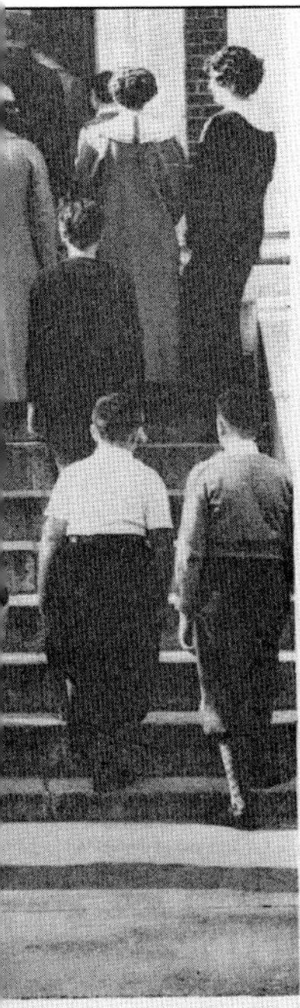

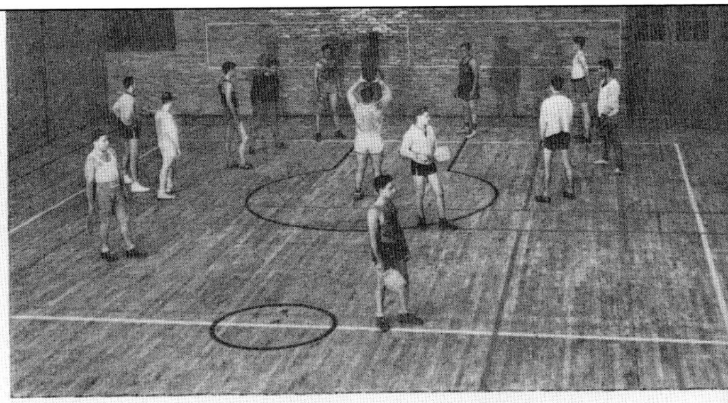

Recreation—that brings health

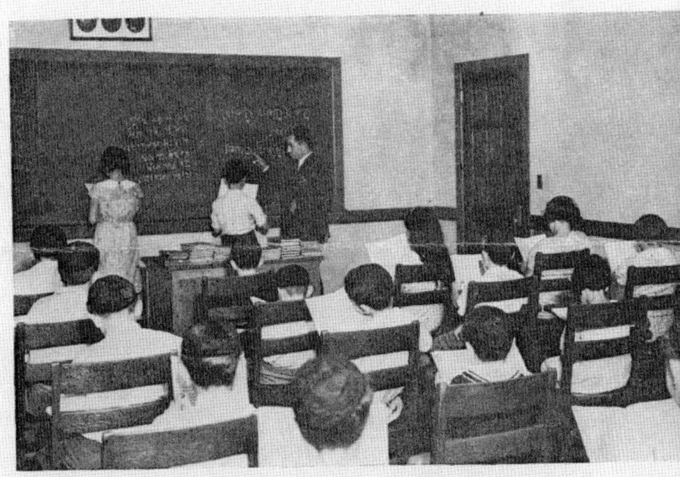

A Hebrew School that assures a Jewish education.

EWISH CENTER

more who come

ı, Health, Recreation

or the many other

children.

- Hebrew Classes

t Exhibits - Swimming

s - Bowling and Billiards

Dances - Guidance

Children's Playhouse

Community Welfare

ity within its Four Walls "

COMMUNITY CHEST

WELFARE BOARD

For vim, v.gor and vitality.

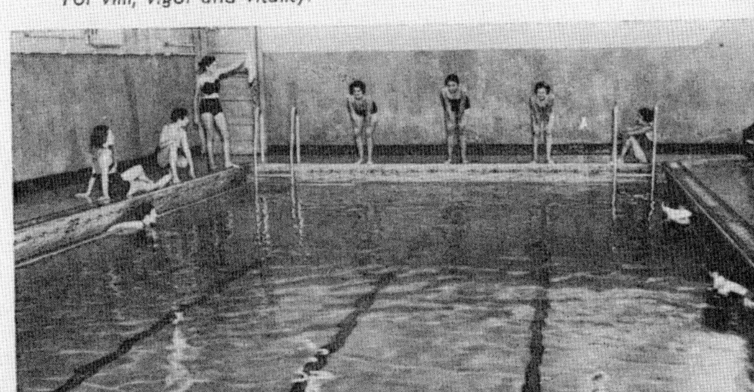

that it "adheres to the highest standards in order to give opportunity to all for every type of self expression and to participate in the life of Stamford's Civic and Jewish Community."

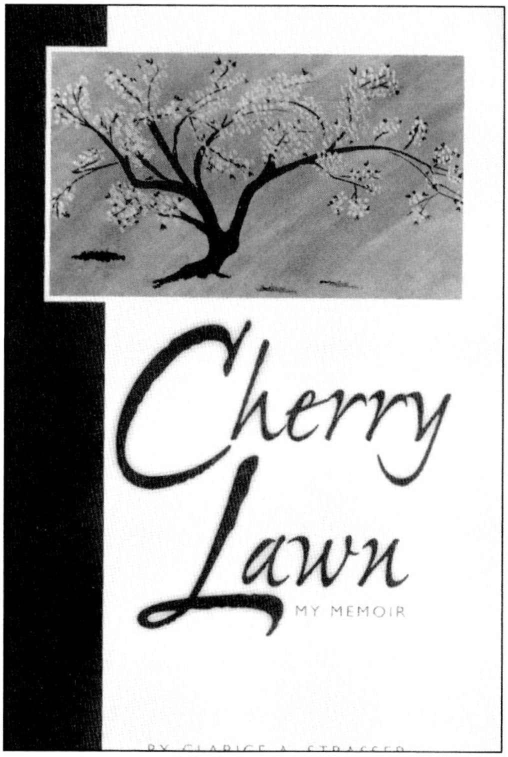

Cherry Lawn School opened in 1915 on the Stein estate in Hillcrest Park in Old Greenwich. The school was started as an effort in private tutoring by Dr. Fred Goldfrank, a New York pediatrician. The first students were Dr. Goldfrank's niece Beatrice, who was stricken with polio and destined never to walk again, her brothers Bob and Harold, and the child of a family friend. The effort was so successful that after four years it was decided that Goldfrank should have his own school. In 1920, an estate was purchased by the Stein and Goldfrank families in Darien and given to the school on a 99-year lease to continue what was no longer just an experiment in educating children. The front lawn of the Hillcrest Park estate had four large cherry trees and, thus, the founders named their school Cherry Lawn. (Information courtesy of Clarice A. Strasser.)

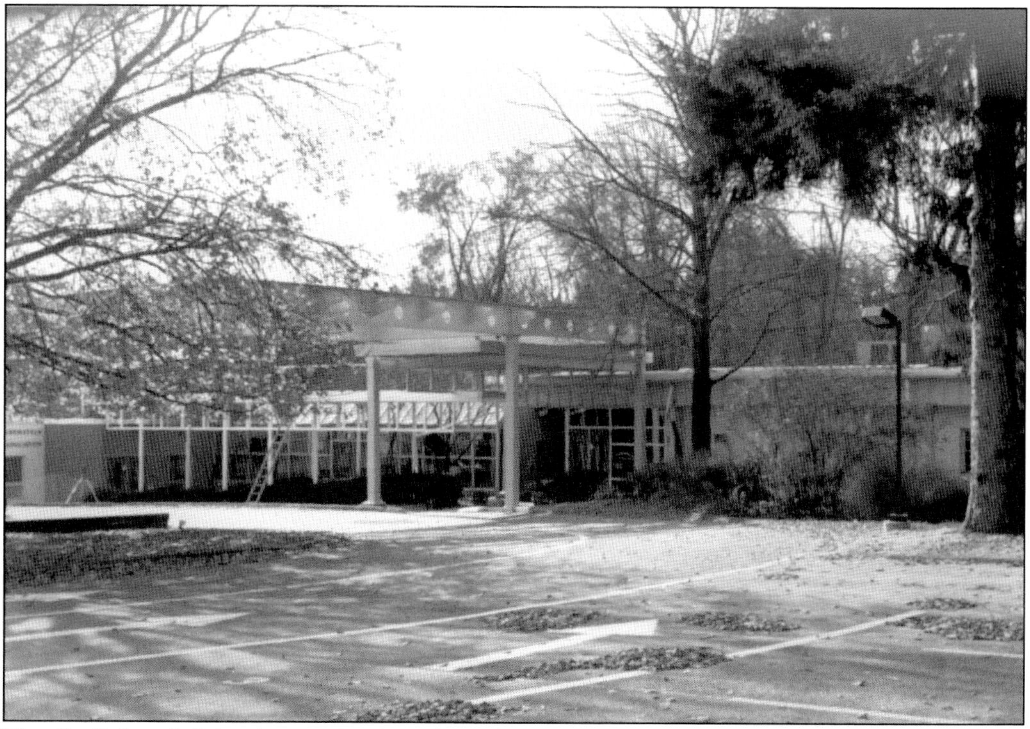

The Bi-Cultural School is at 2186 High Ridge Road in Stamford. Pictured in 2001, it is a private Jewish day school.

Eight

WORTH MENTIONING

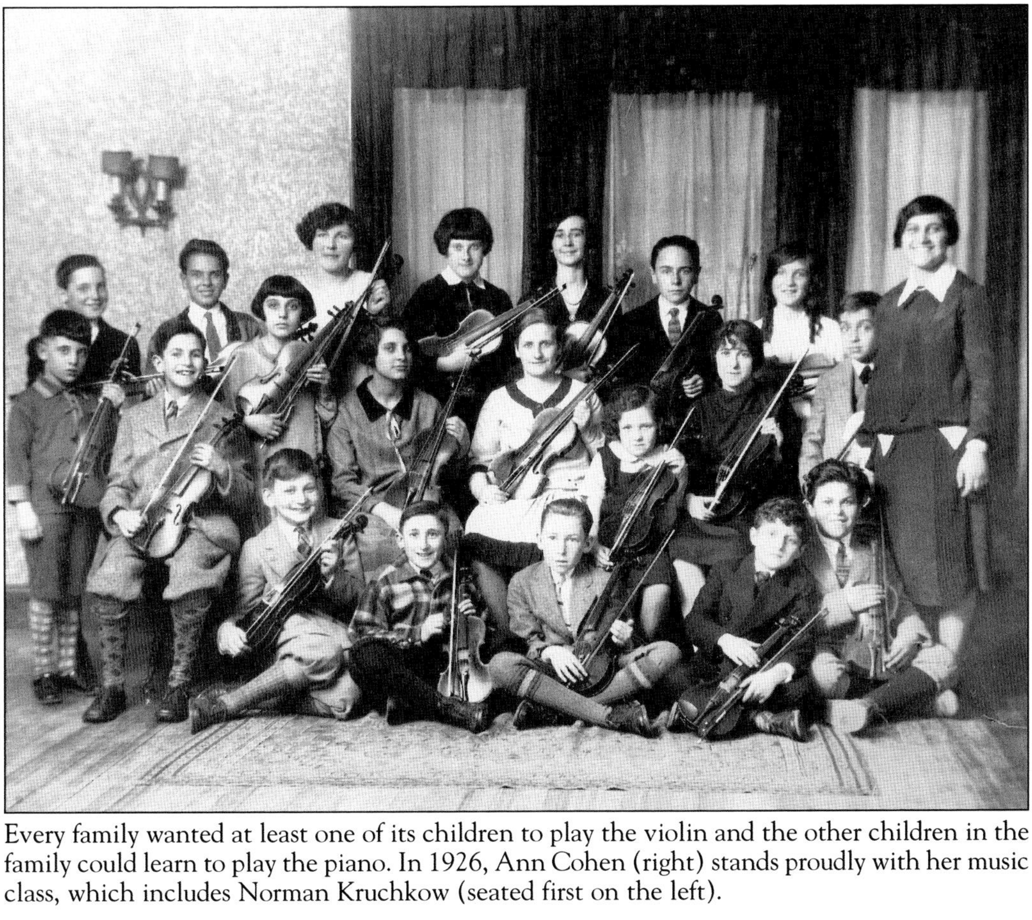

Every family wanted at least one of its children to play the violin and the other children in the family could learn to play the piano. In 1926, Ann Cohen (right) stands proudly with her music class, which includes Norman Kruchkow (seated first on the left).

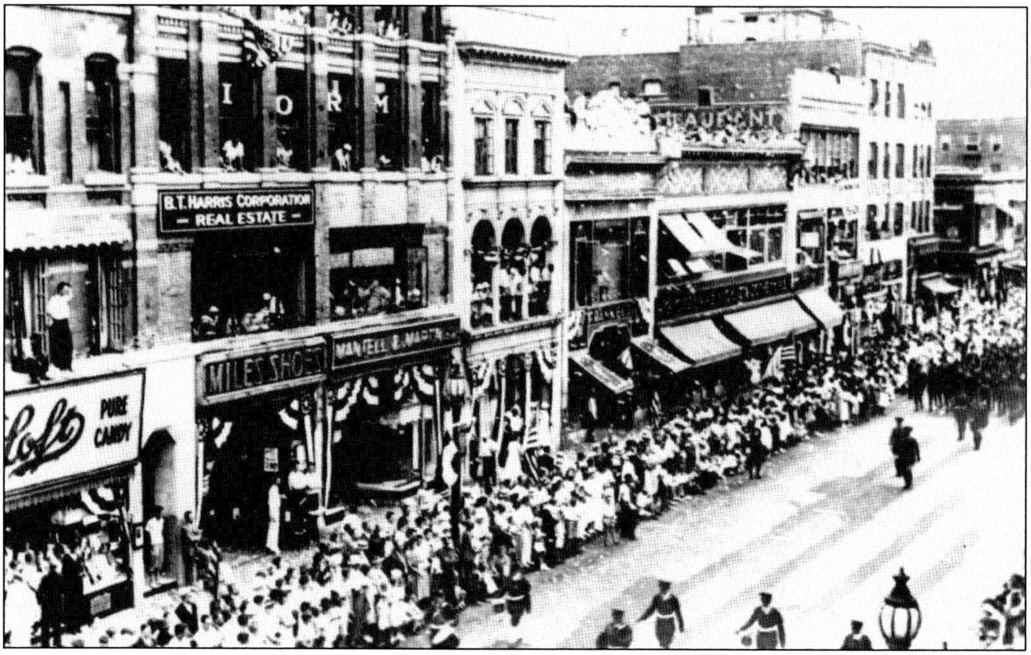

Atlantic Street in 1937 illustrates the number of Jewish merchants in Stamford's main shopping hub. Visible are B.T. Harris Real Estate and Mantell and Martin (left).

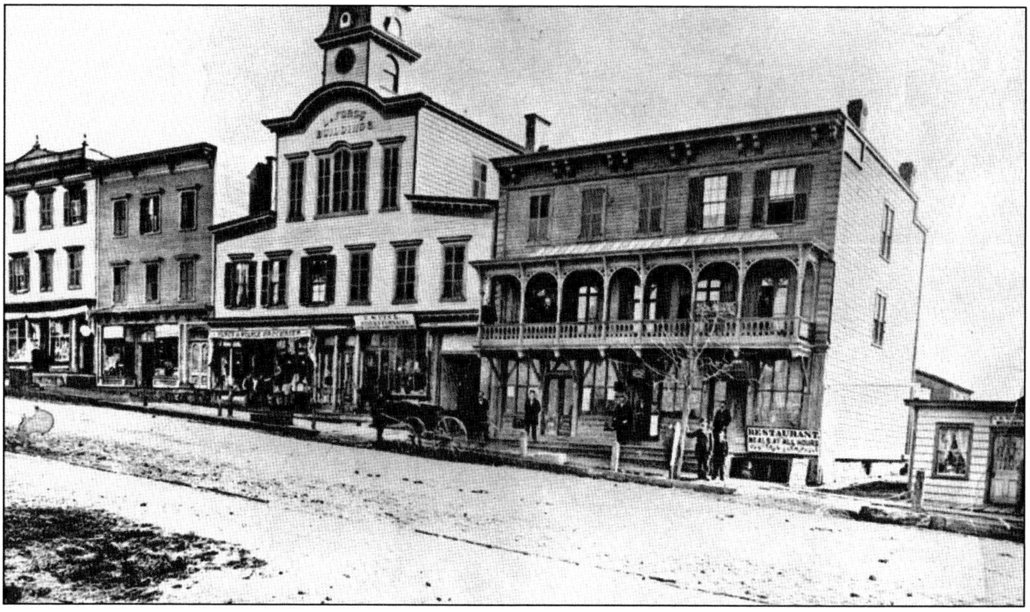
Meyer Cohen operated a grocery and fruiterer in a building (center) on Greenwich Avenue. The Greenwich Town Hall is large building (right). It is the present site of Amogerone Crossway. Taken in 1880, this photograph was reproduced from the collections of the Historical Society of the Town of Greenwich.

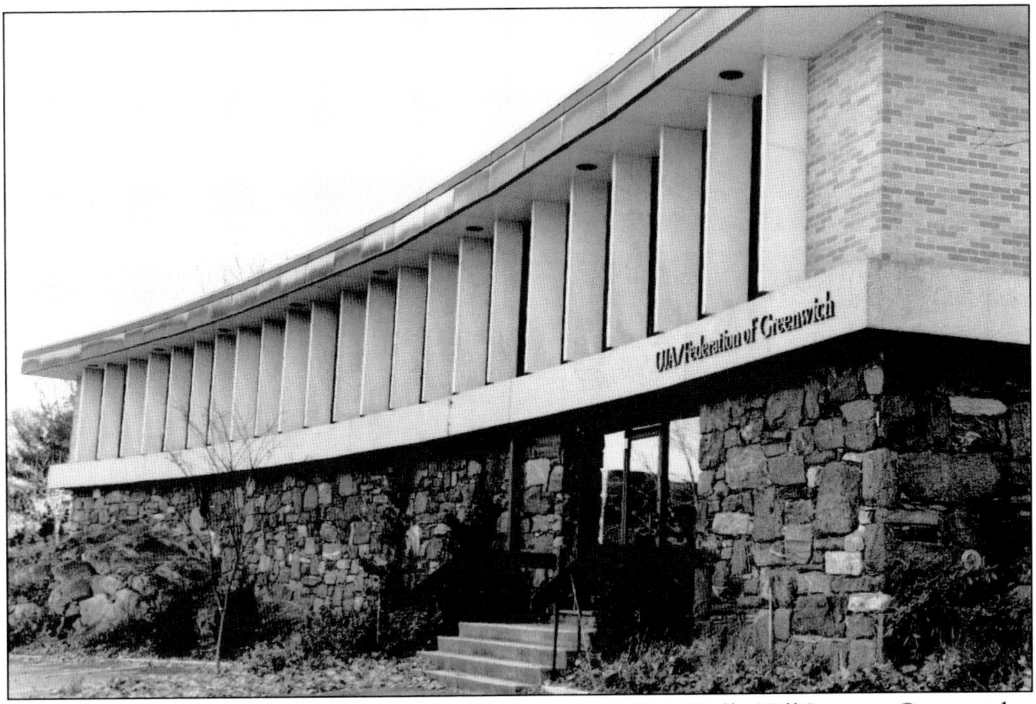

The United Jewish Appeal Federation building stands at One Holly Hill Lane in Greenwich.

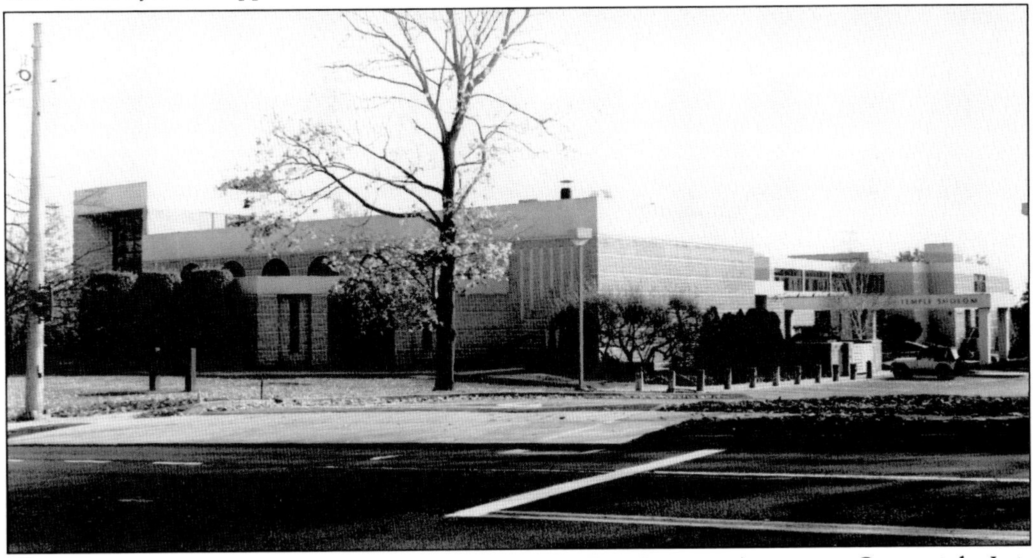

This is the current home of Temple Sholom, at 300 East Putnam Avenue in Greenwich. It is the third structure that has housed the congregation. In 1915, 10 Jewish families—professionals and shopkeepers who lived and worked in Greenwich—decided the time had come to create a spiritual home of their own. They rented Abrams Hall on Greenwich Avenue where they conducted High Holiday services and arranged for the Hebrew education of their children. In 1919, the group was officially incorporated as the Greenwich Hebrew Institute and, by 1924, had purchased a building at 23 East Elm Street. The founding members were Mayer M. Bennett, Samuel Bennett, Mayer H. Cohen, Jacob Dworkind, Harry Friedlander, Marie and Nathan Kletz, Philip Marks, Joseph Miller, Sarah Tunick, and I.J. Weiss.

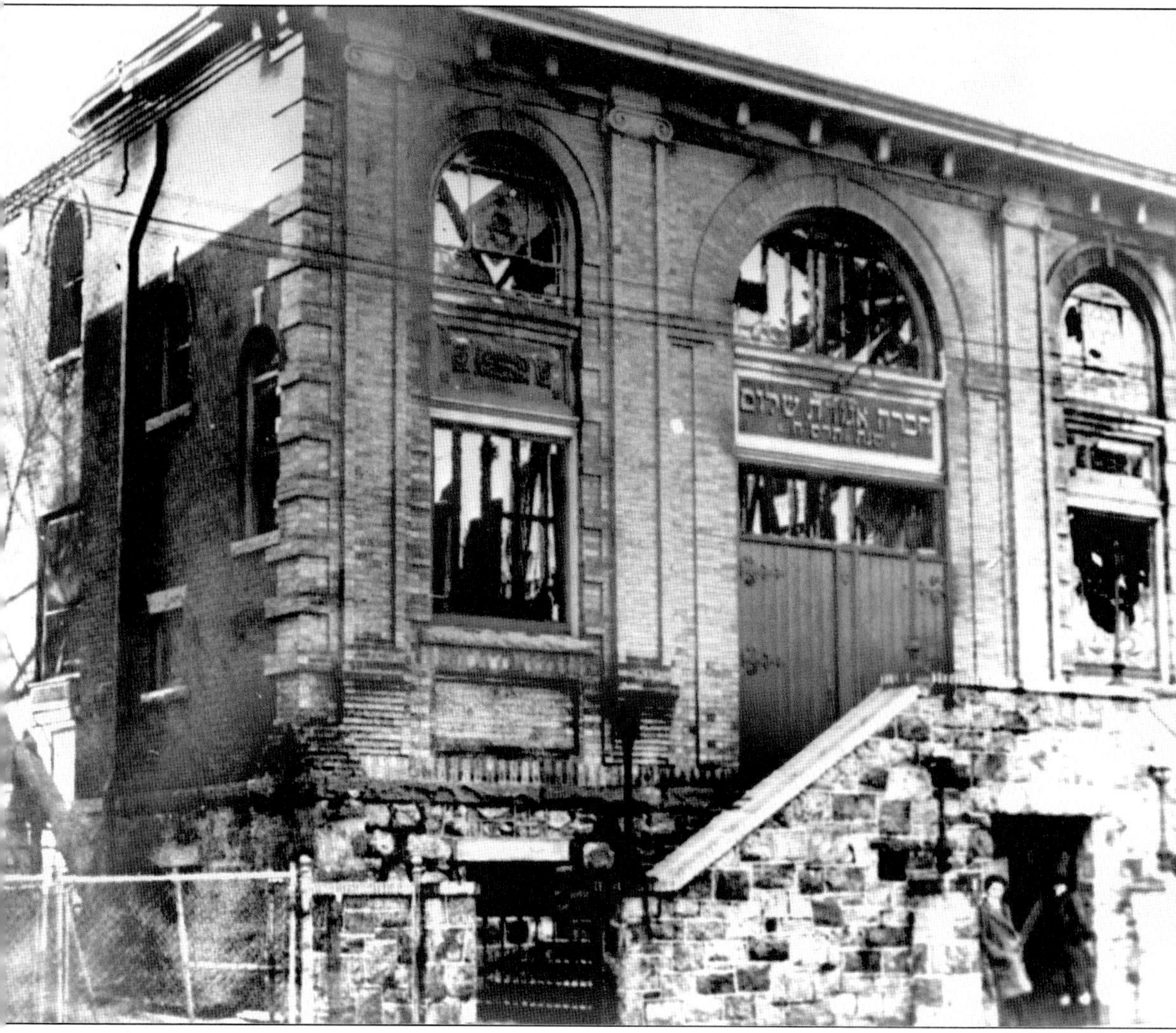

The first home of Congregation Agudath Sholom, on the south side of Grey Rock Place, was destroyed by fire in 1932. Agudath Sholom is the oldest organized Jewish congregation in Stamford.

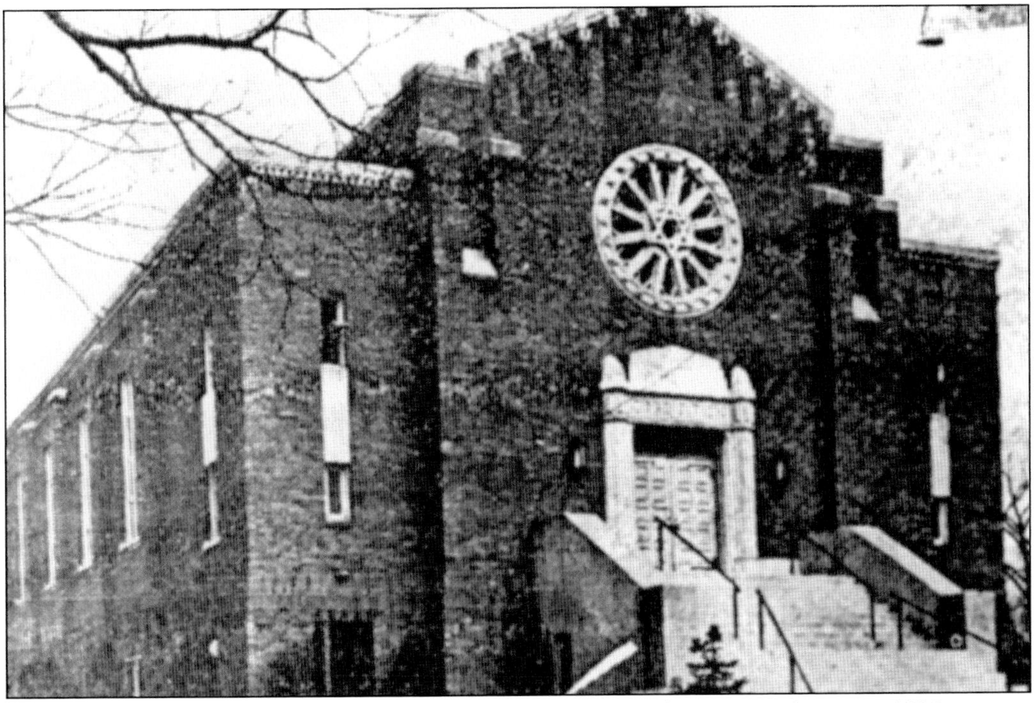

The second home of Congregation Agudath Sholom opened on Grove Street in 1938.

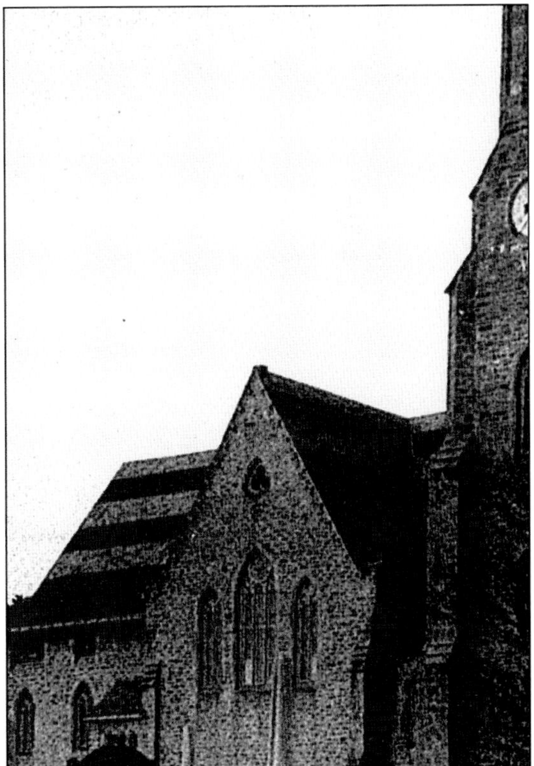

Shown is the Second Congregational Church, designed by Leopold Eidlitz in 1856 and located on the Post Road in Greenwich.

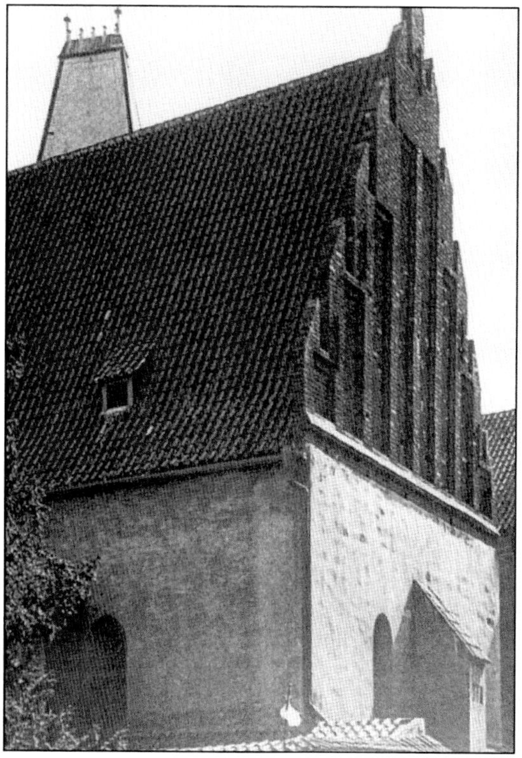

Leopold Eidlitz, a Jewish architect who was born in Prague, designed the church in 1856. The strong architectural influence of Prague's Altneuschul can clearly be seen in the church design.

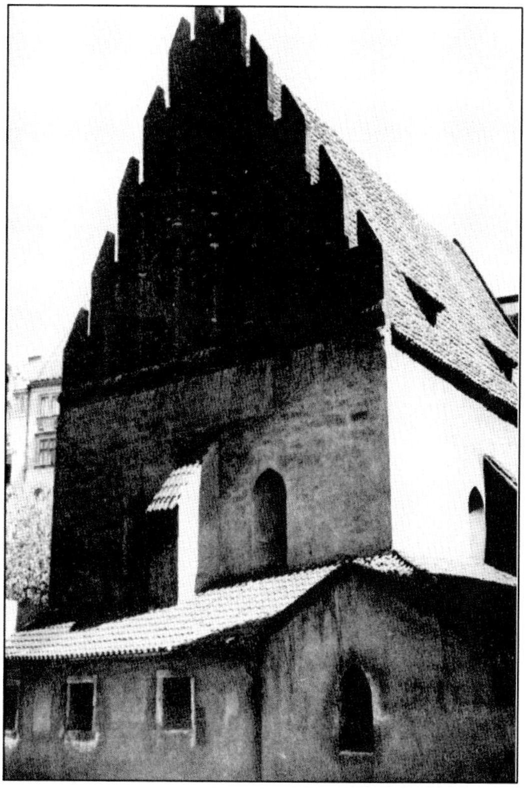

The Altneuschul in Prague dates from the 13th century. Its architecture inspired the 33-year-old Leopold Edlitz, a noted synagogue and commercial architect.

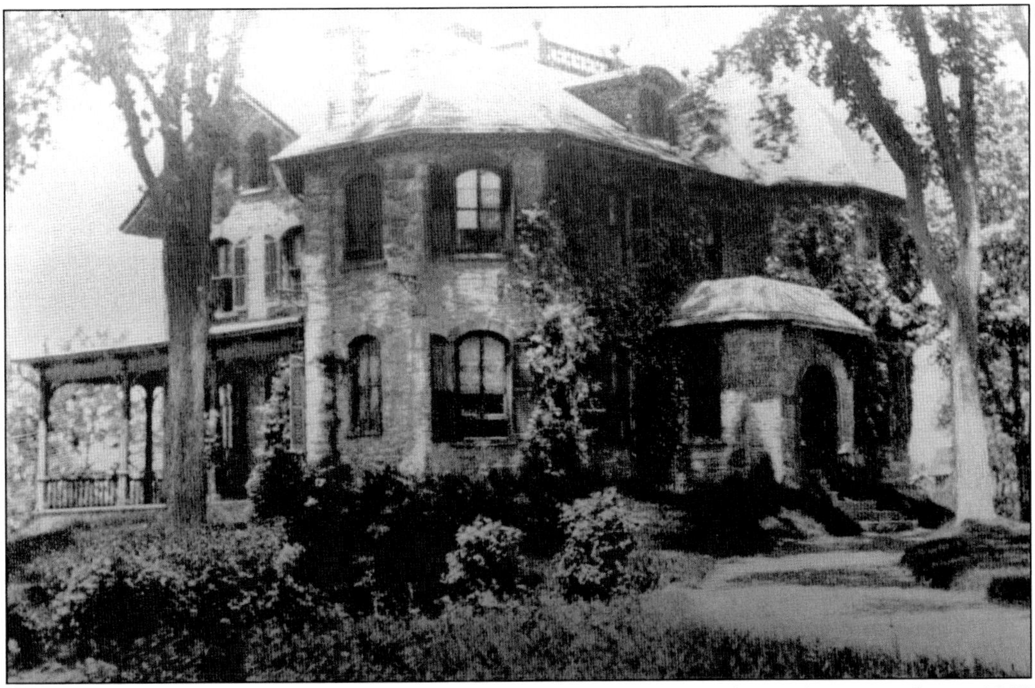

Shown is the Dr. John Lord House on Strawberry Hill. Robert Weeks Nathan rented it in 1867 for his family. In 1868, Nathan's brother Benjamin Nathan rented the house for six months for $1,500 as a country retreat away from his New York City brownstone mansion, at 12 West 23rd Street. In 1939, his daughter Frances Nathan Wolff wrote in her autobiography that "it was there in Stamford, Connecticut that I spent the happiest year of my life." She was referring to her stay at the Lord House on Strawberry Hill in 1868.

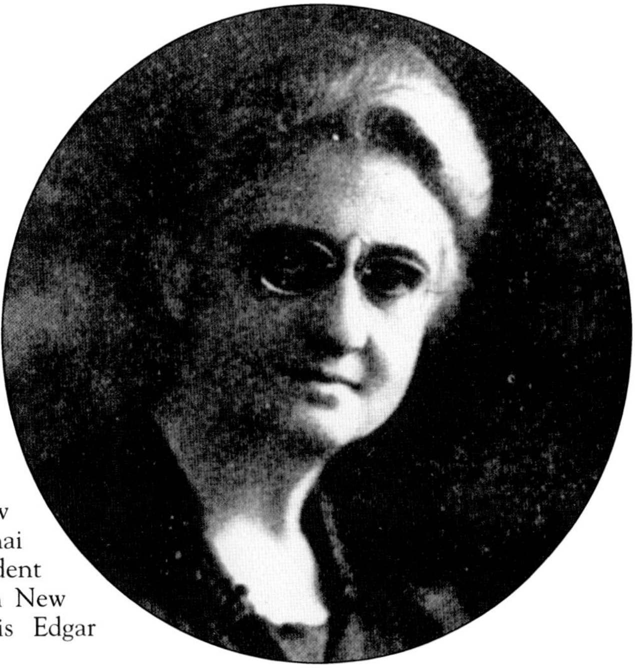

Frances Nathan Wolff was born in 1856. She was the daughter of Benjamin Nathan, a stockbroker and secretary of the New York Stock Exchange. Benjamin Nathan was the grandnephew of Rabbi Gershom Mendes Seixas, known as the "Patriot Rabbi of the American Revolution" and a founder of the Jews Hospital in New York City, now called Mount Sinai Hospital. Nathan was also a president of Congregation Shearith Israel in New York City. His great-grandson is Edgar Cullman of Stamford.

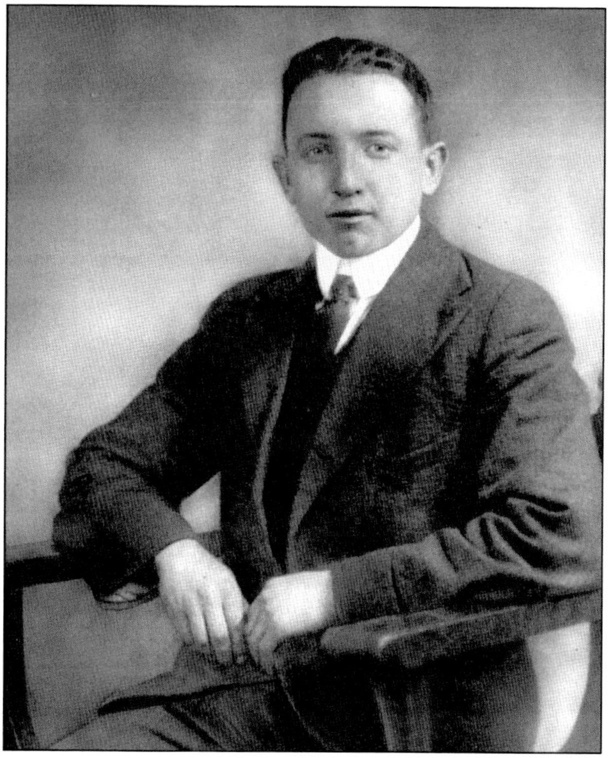

Born in 1897, Samuel N. Tresser was the son of Mr. and Mrs. Morris Tresser of 83 Hawthorn Street. On August 24, 1918, he was killed in action south of Fismes, France.

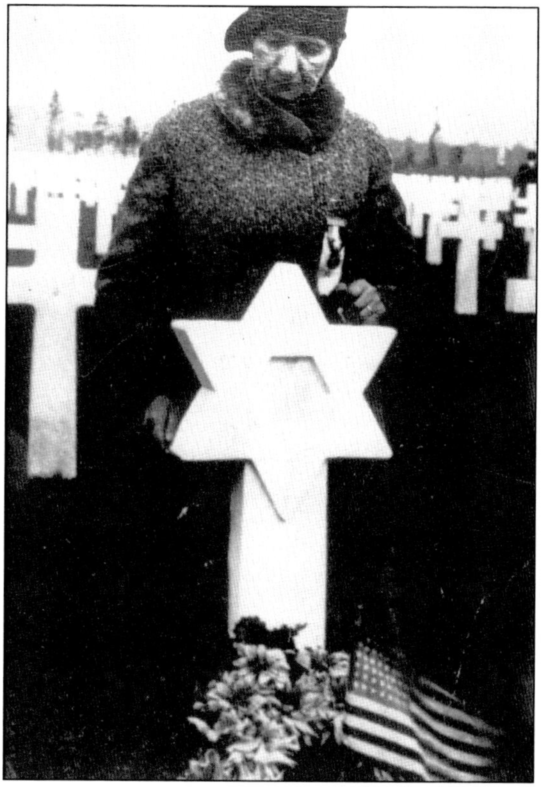

Mrs. Morris Tresser is shown at the grave site of her son Samuel Tresser in 1925. She was a member of the Gold Star Mothers, whose sons were killed in action. The government paid for the trip to France so that these mothers could visit their son's grave.

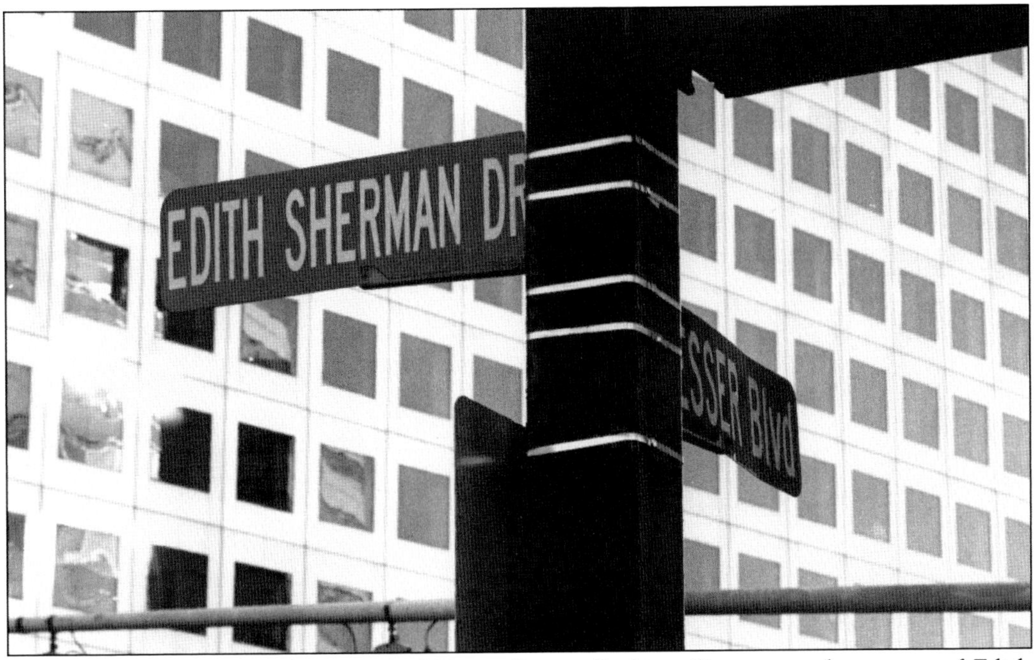

This is the entrance to the Stamford Town Center Parking Garage, at the corner of Edith Sherman Drive and Tresser Boulevard. The boulevard was named in honor of Samuel Tresser in 1973. As head of the Urban Redevelopment Corporation, Edith Sherman was instrumental in the development of the mall.

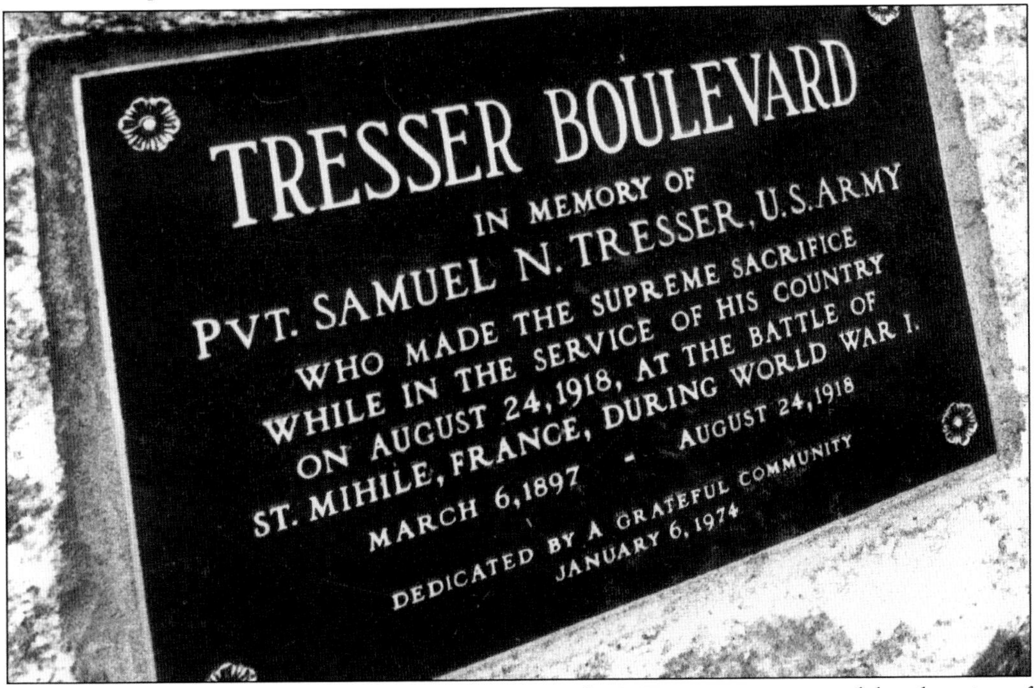

A plaque dedicated to the memory of Pvt. Samuel N. Tresser, was erected by the city of Stamford in January 1974. It is now located at the southwest corner of Washington and Tresser Boulevards.

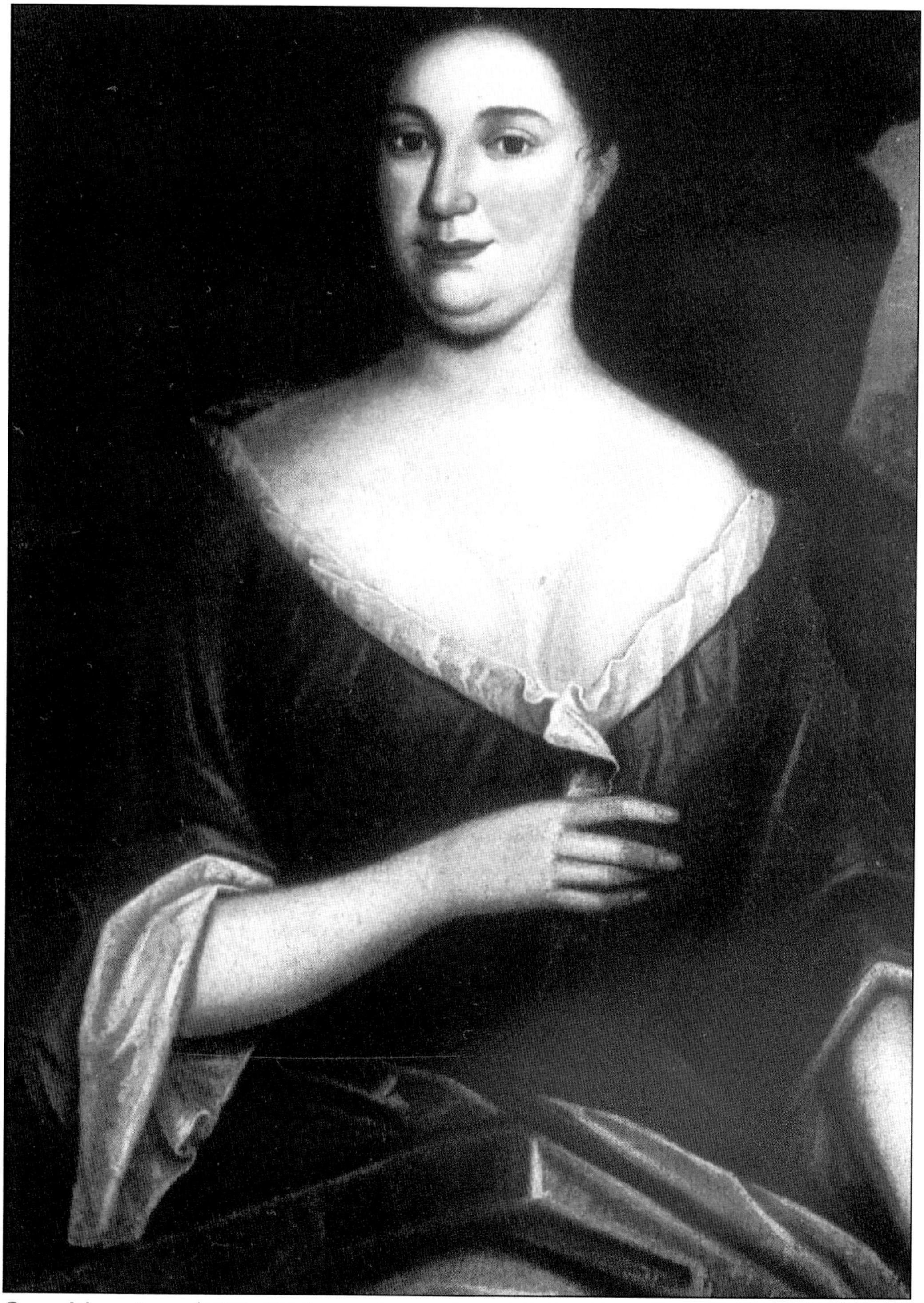

Grace Mears Levy (1694–1740) was the mother of Esther Levy Hart of Stamford and the grandmother of the first Jewish children born in Stamford. Her second husband was David Hays Sr., who in 1735 owned what is now known as the Bush-Holley House in Greenwich.

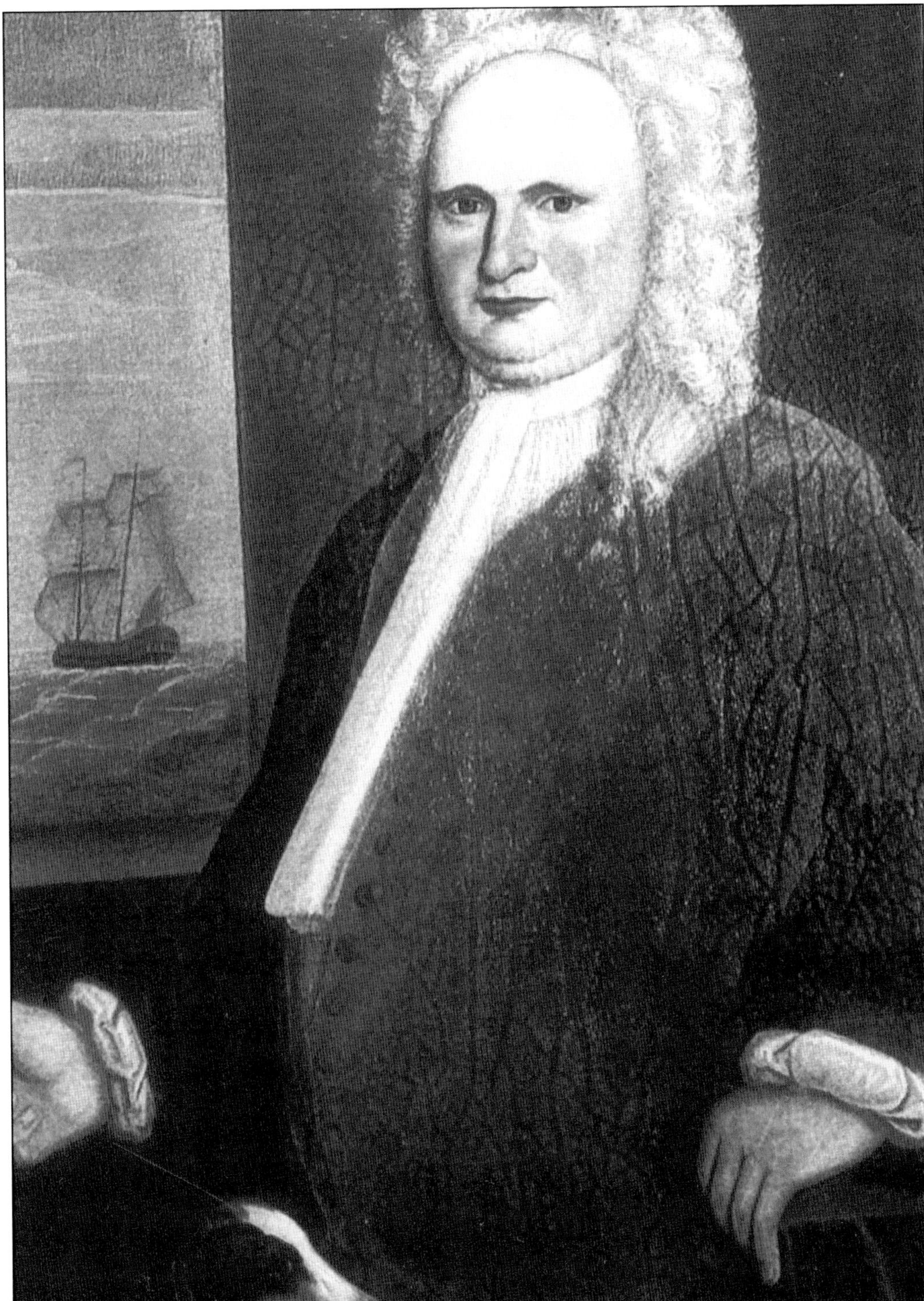

Moses Levy (1665–1728) was listed in the 1698 town records in connection with the purchase of a slave from Mary Turney. Levy was a New York merchant and shipowner. He was the grandfather of Moses, Samuel, and Miriam Hart, the first Jewish children born in Stamford.

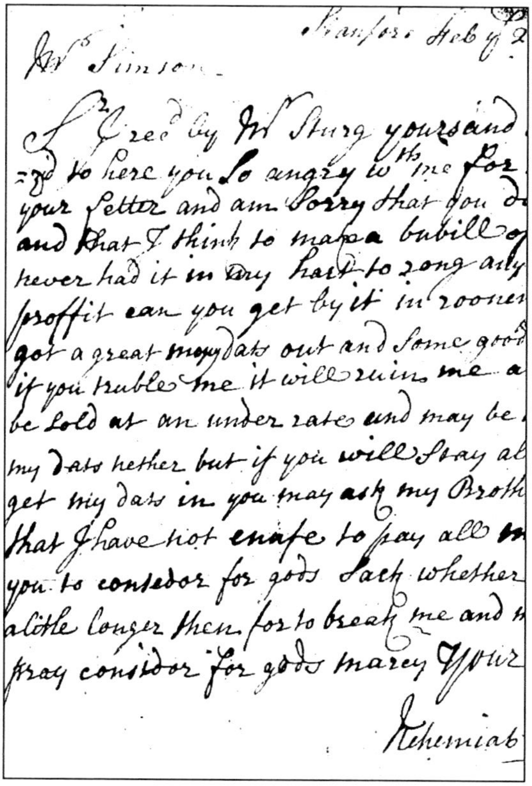

Stanfor Feb y 2

Mr Simson –

Sr I recd by Mr Sturg yours and
to here you So angry wth me for
your Letter and am Sorry that you d
and that I think to mak a bubill of
never had it in my hart to wrong any
proffit can you get by it in zooner
got a great mony dats out and Some good
if you truble me it will ruin me a
be Sold at an under rate and may be
my dats nether but if you will Stay a
get my dats in you may ask my Broth
that I have not enafe to pay all m
you to consedor for gods Sack whether
a litle longer then for to break me and m
pray considor for gods marcy Your

Nehemiah

Nehemiah Marks, an early Stamford merchant, was being dunned by Nathan Simson, his co-religionist and supplier in New York in 1720. Simson sent Marks two collection letters. Marks responded on February 23, 1721, to the first letter:

Mr. Simson –
Sir I received by Mr. Sturg yours and am more surprised to hear you so angry with me for not answering your letter and am sorry that you do call me unwilling and that I think to make a bubill of God knows I never had it in my heart to wrong any man. What profit can you get by it in zooning me for I have a great many debts out and some goods by me, so that if you trouble me it will ruin me and my goods must be sold at an under rate and may not be enough to pay my debts either but if you will stay a little longer I can get my debts in. You may ask my brother whether he thinks that I have not enough to pay all my debts. So I desire you to consider for god's sake whether it is best to stay a little longer than for to break me and make a beggar of me. Pray consider for Gods mercy.
Your Humble Servant

Nehemiah Marks

This is Marks's June 30, 1721 response to the second letter, received via Andris Trube, a Jewish merchant from Fairfield:

Mr. Simson –
Sir – This is to let you know that I received yours by Mr. Trube and am sorry that I have not made payment in the time but I will send you by the first boat an hundred bushel wheat. I pray you to get a good market as you can I will more very quickly it now very near harvest. I hope to pay you this Fall. If you know any one that will buy six thousand foot of 2 inch oak plank I will send them to you. I thank you for your kindness in being so kind as to send me word. God knows my heart. I mean nothing but honesty and pay every man his own but the last years crop failing is the case that I have not paid my debts in time. I live as near as any man can live and spend no money but for my just necessity. That you had not fear but I pay you very honestly. Tis is all for the present— — —
Sir your humble servant
please to write an answer about the plank
Nehemiah Marks

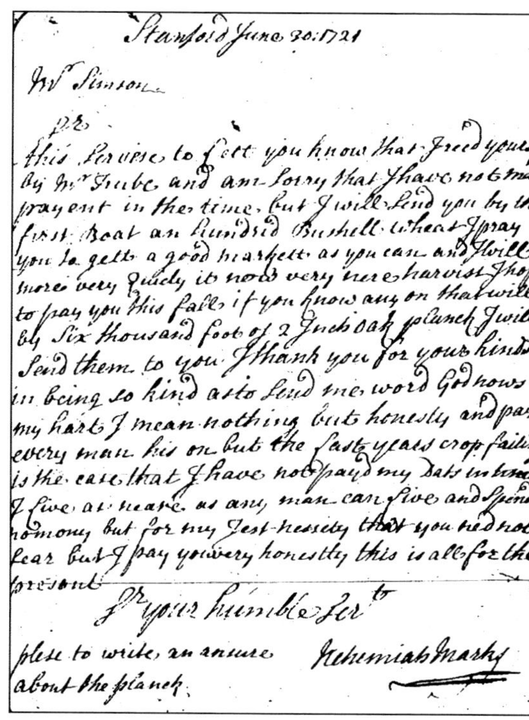

Stanford June 30:1721

Mr Simson

Sr

this Servse to lett you know that I recd yours
by Mr Trube and am Sorry that I have not ma
payment in the time but I will Send you by the
first Boat an hundred Bushell wheat I pray
you to gett a good markett as you can and I will
more very Quickly it now very near harvist I hop
to pay you this fall, if you know any on that will
by Six thousand foot of 2 Inch oak planck I will
Send them to you I thank you for your kindn
in being so kind as to Send me word God nows
my hart I mean nothing but honesty and pay
every man his on but the last years crop failing
is the case that I have not payd my dats in time
I live as neare as any man can live and Spend
no mony but for my Jest-nessity that you ned not
fear but I pay you very honestly this is all for the
present

Sr your humble Sert

plese to write an anser
about the planck

Nehemiah Marks

Segar (cigar) Factory on Main Street was owned by A. Benas from 1865 to 1868.

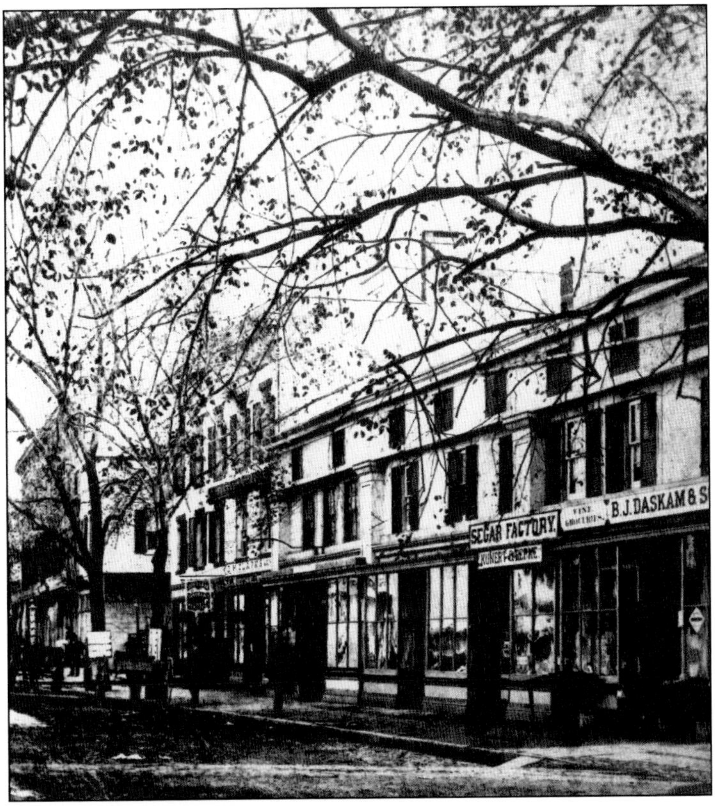

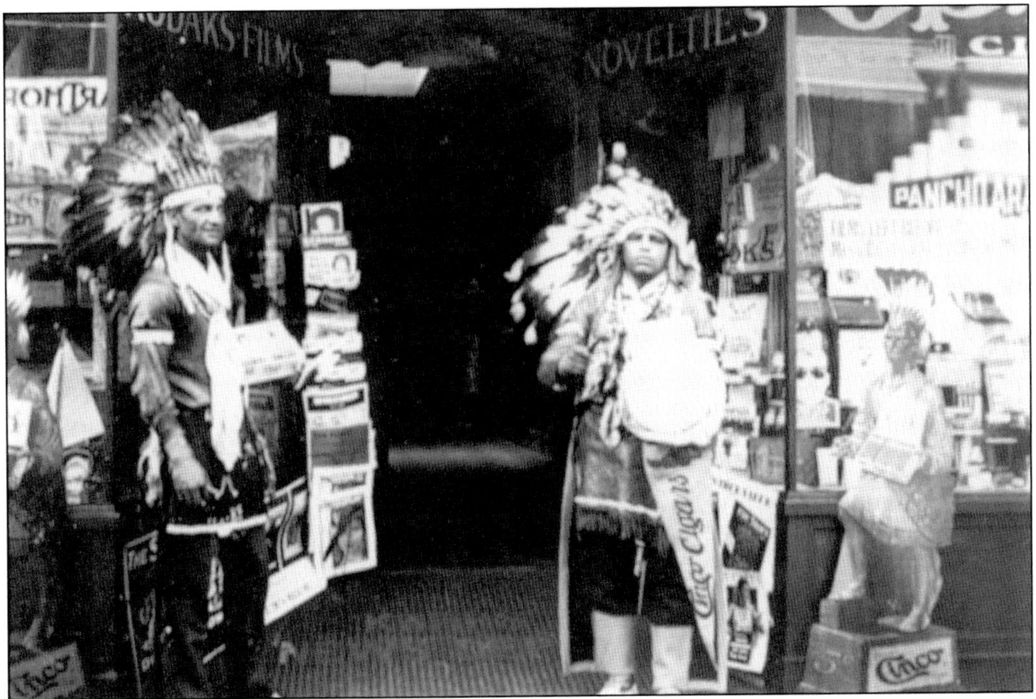

Harry Karp, dressed as a cigar store Indian, poses with a cigar store Indian in front of his store.

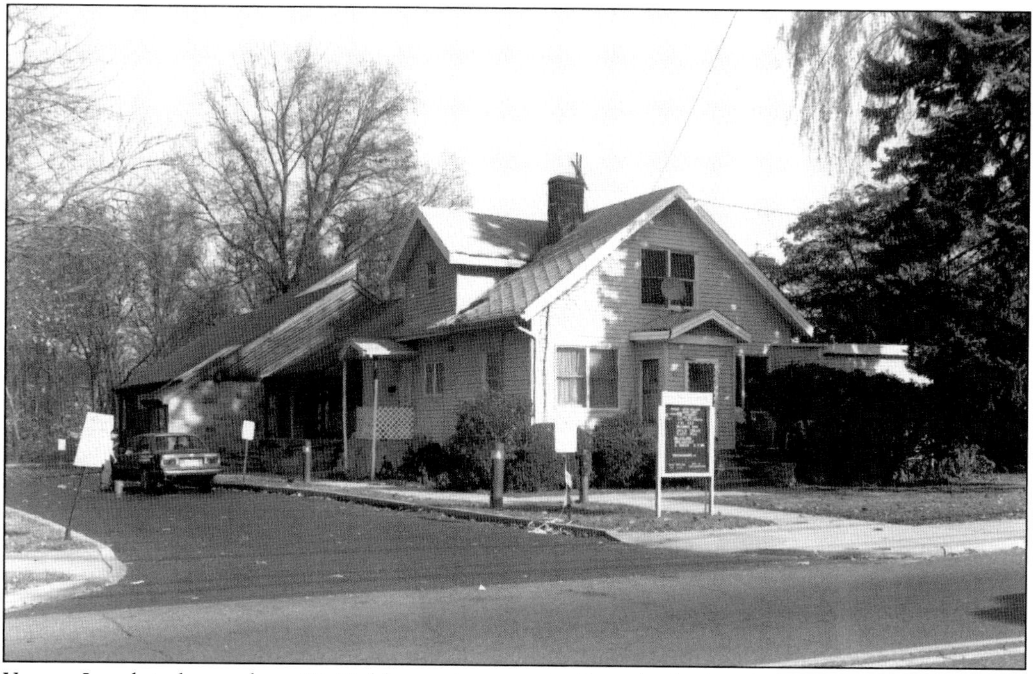

Young Israel is located at 69 Oaklawn Avenue in Stamford. A relatively new arrival, this Modern Orthodox congregation turned 18 in 2002.

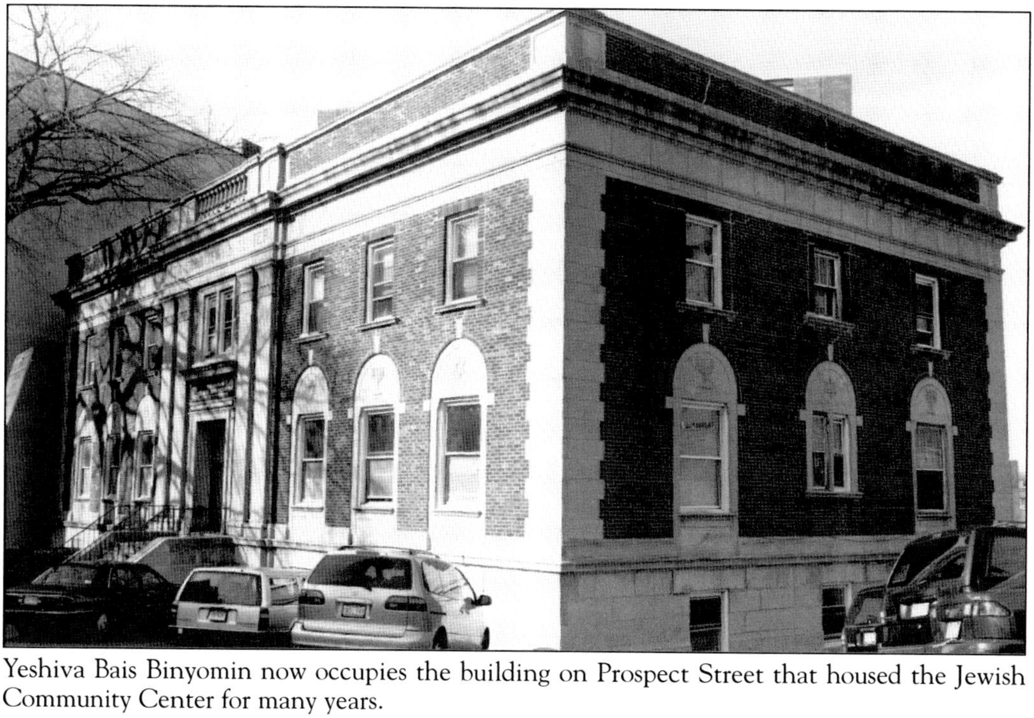

Yeshiva Bais Binyomin now occupies the building on Prospect Street that housed the Jewish Community Center for many years.

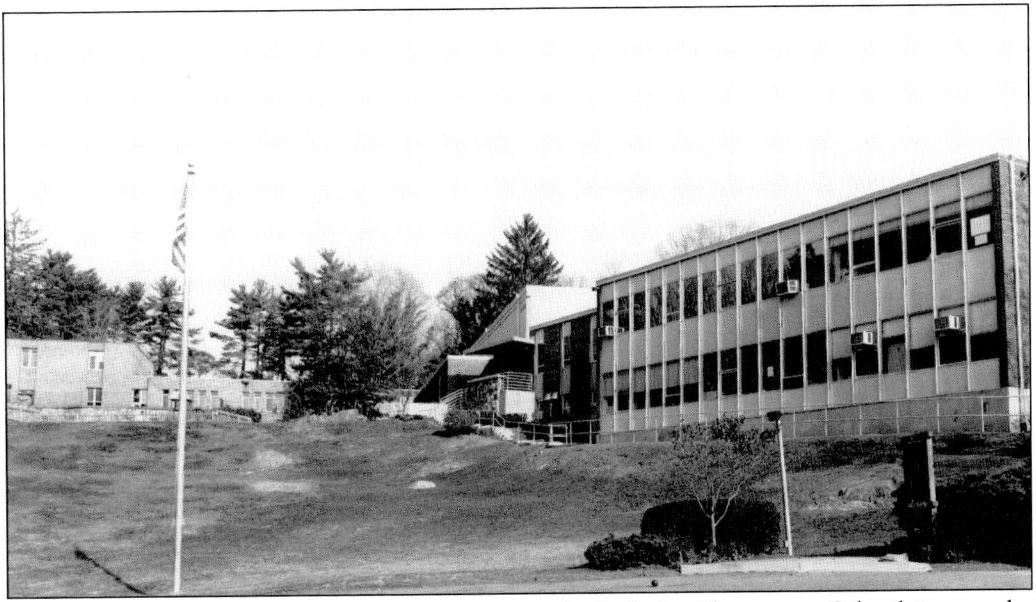

Located on Stanwich Road, the former Greenwich Catholic Elementary School is now the home of the Greenwich Reform Synagogue.

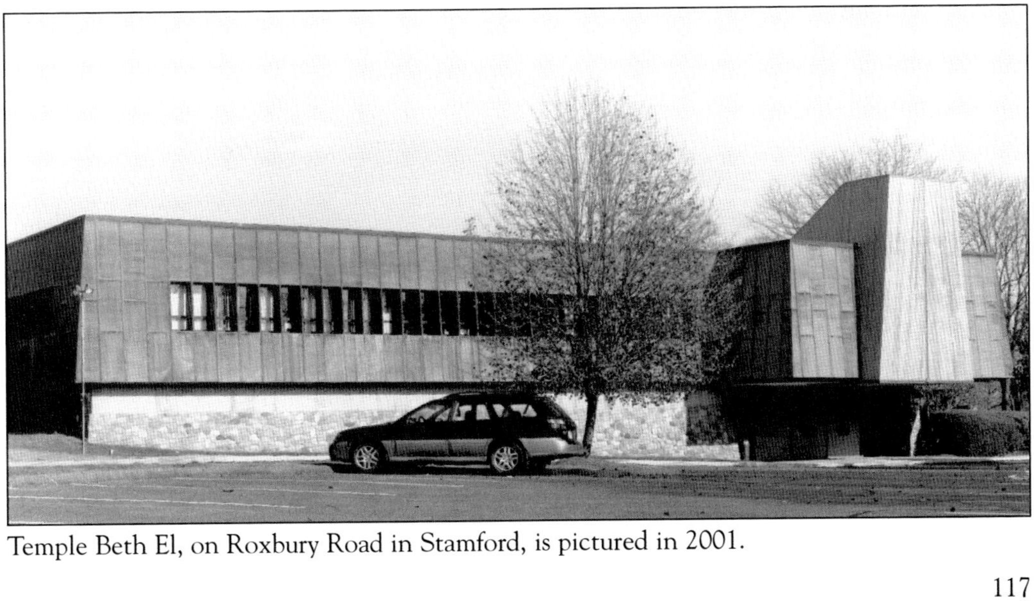

Temple Beth El, on Roxbury Road in Stamford, is pictured in 2001.

Humanity: Arthur Szyk's View of the World

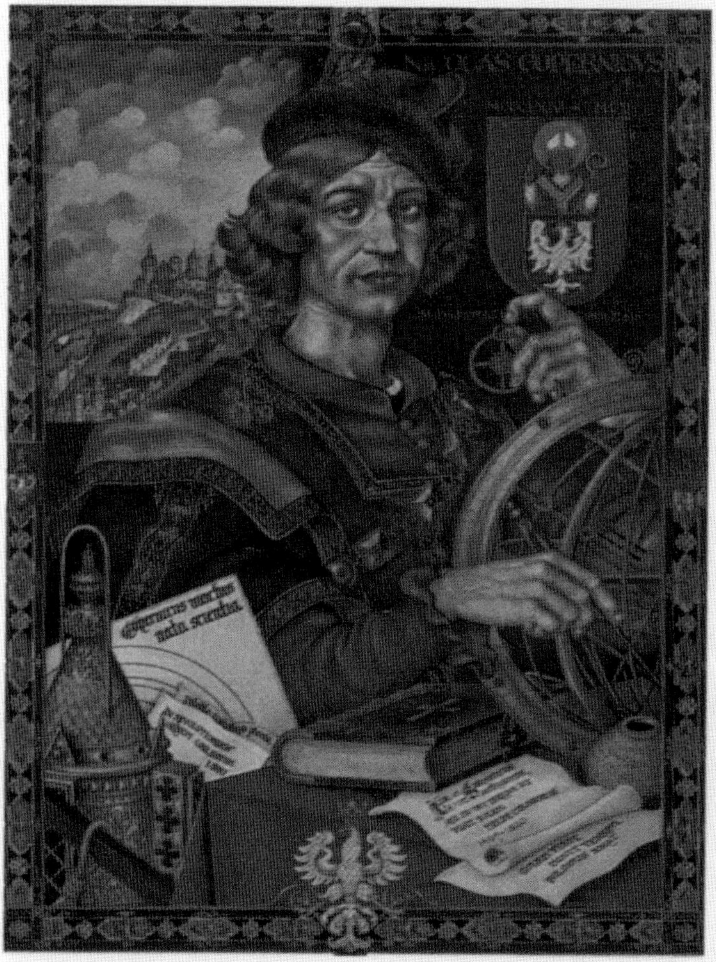

The New Canaan Historical Society exhibited the work of the late Arthur Szyk, a former resident of the town. Cochaired by Bette J. Chachkes and Geraldine Wolff Snyder, the exhibit highlighted more than 100 works of art that reflect the diverse media and styles that Szyk used. "He created biting political cartoons and memorable magazine covers that reflected his editorial assessments of world leaders and contemporary events. . . . He devoted his life to his artwork through which he could communicate his hopes and desires for justice, mortality and security." (Excerpt from New Canaan Historical Society brochure, July 17 to July 28, 2000.)

Considered to be one of the finest books published in the 20th century *The Haggadah*, executed by Arthur Szyk and edited by Cecil Roth, was published in London.

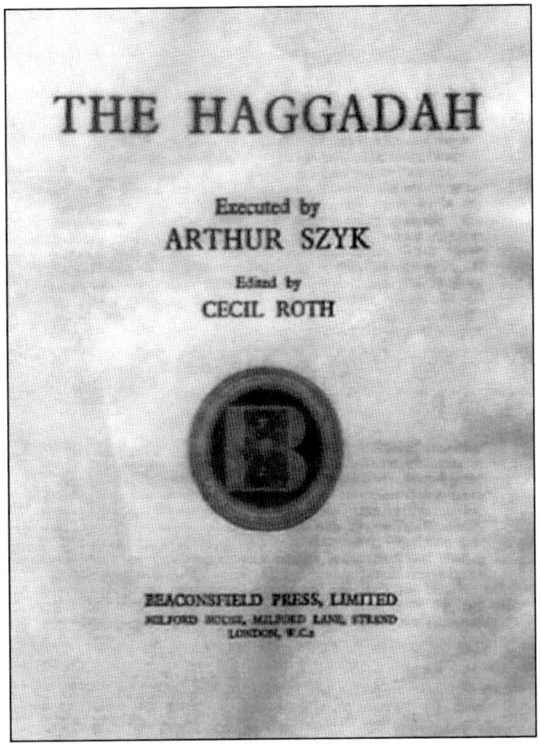

THE HAGGADAH

Executed by
ARTHUR SZYK

Edited by
CECIL ROTH

BEACONSFIELD PRESS, LIMITED
MILFORD HOUSE, MILFORD LANE, STRAND
LONDON, W.C.2

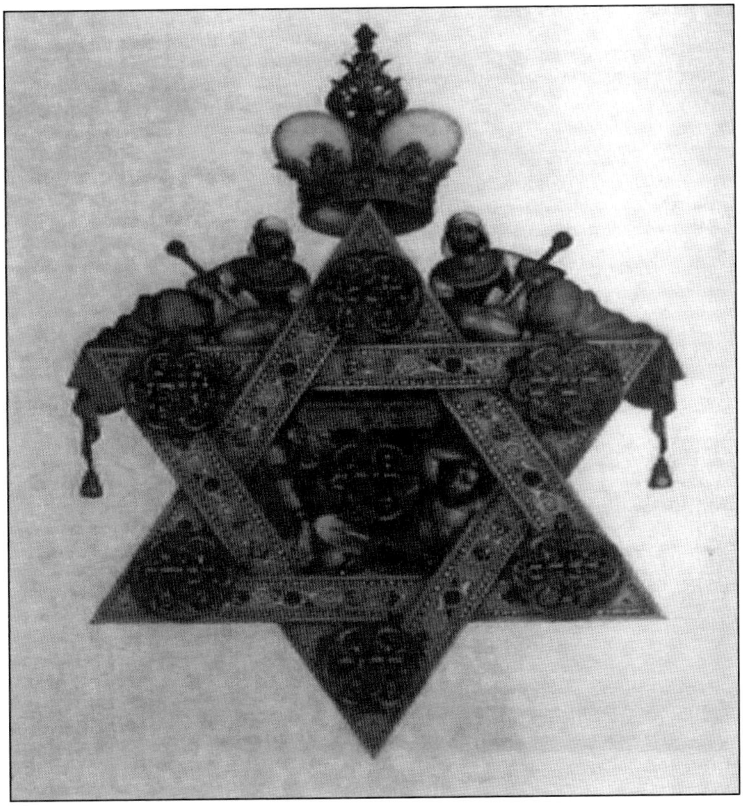

An illustration from the Szyk *Haggadah* represents the Israelites as free men.

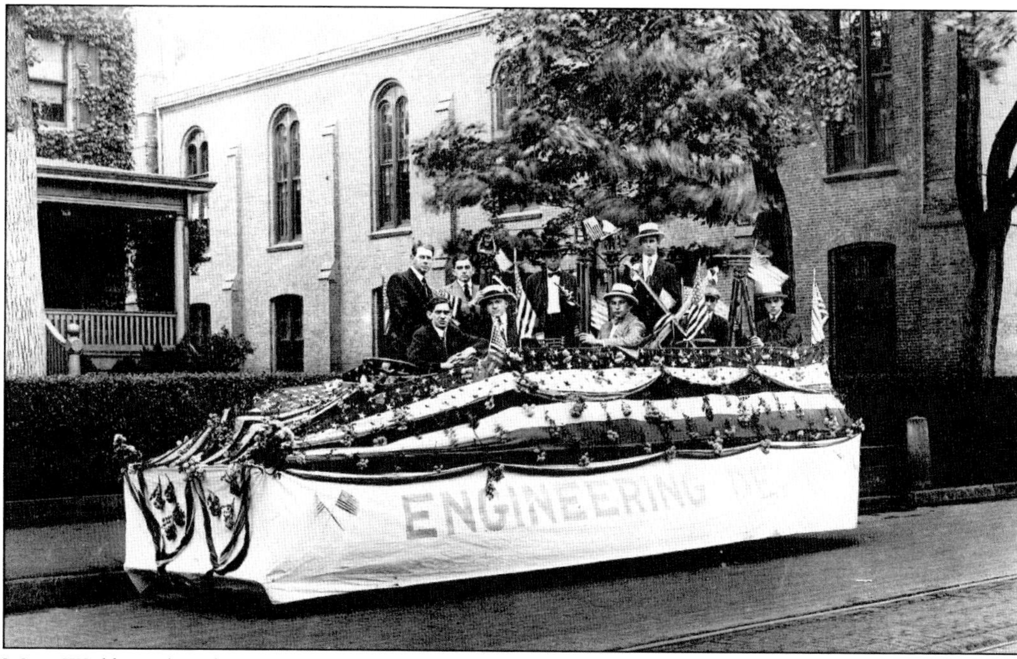

Max Wolfson (at the center of a float, wearing a white hat and holding a tripod) became director of the City of Stamford Engineering Department in 1962. This photograph was taken c. 1920.

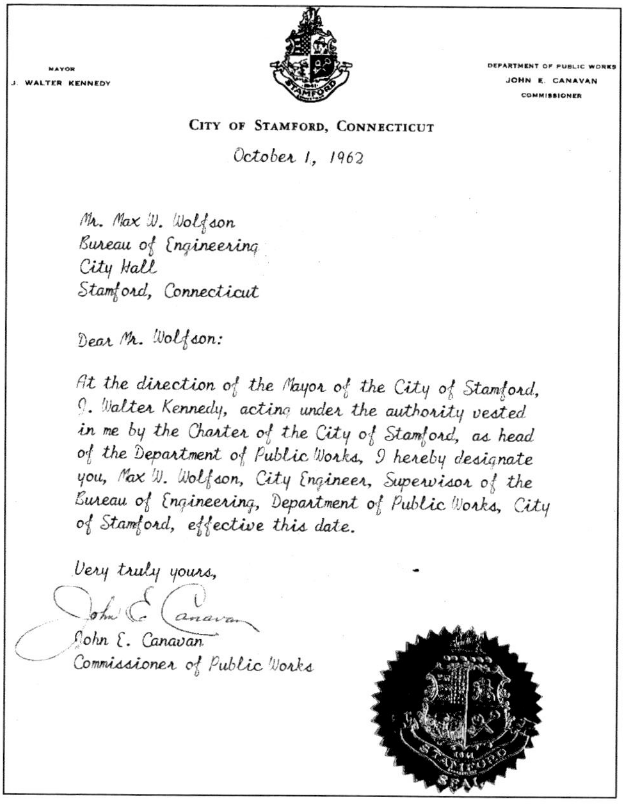

MAYOR
J. WALTER KENNEDY

DEPARTMENT OF PUBLIC WORKS
JOHN E. CANAVAN
COMMISSIONER

CITY OF STAMFORD, CONNECTICUT

October 1, 1962

Mr. Max W. Wolfson
Bureau of Engineering
City Hall
Stamford, Connecticut

Dear Mr. Wolfson:

At the direction of the Mayor of the City of Stamford, J. Walter Kennedy, acting under the authority vested in me by the Charter of the City of Stamford, as head of the Department of Public Works, I hereby designate you, Max W. Wolfson, City Engineer, Supervisor of the Bureau of Engineering, Department of Public Works, City of Stamford, effective this date.

Very truly yours,

John E. Canavan

John E. Canavan
Commissioner of Public Works

STAMFORD SEAL

This is the letter of appointment from John E. Canavan designating Max Wolfson supervisor of the City of Stamford Bureau of Engineering.

This proclamation designates May 16, 1976, Martin Manaly Day.

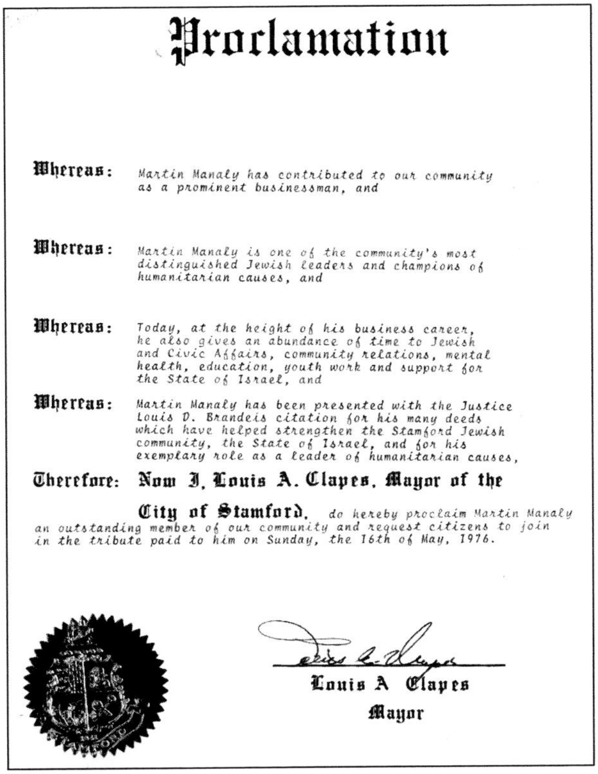

Proclamation

Whereas: Martin Manaly has contributed to our community as a prominent businessman, and

Whereas: Martin Manaly is one of the community's most distinguished Jewish leaders and champions of humanitarian causes, and

Whereas: Today, at the height of his business career, he also gives an abundance of time to Jewish and Civic Affairs, community relations, mental health, education, youth work and support for the State of Israel, and

Whereas: Martin Manaly has been presented with the Justice Louis D. Brandeis citation for his many deeds which have helped strengthen the Stamford Jewish community, the State of Israel, and for his exemplary role as a leader of humanitarian causes,

Therefore: **Now I, Louis A. Clapes, Mayor of the City of Stamford,** do hereby proclaim Martin Manaly an outstanding member of our community and request citizens to join in the tribute paid to him on Sunday, the 16th of May, 1976.

Louis A Clapes
Mayor

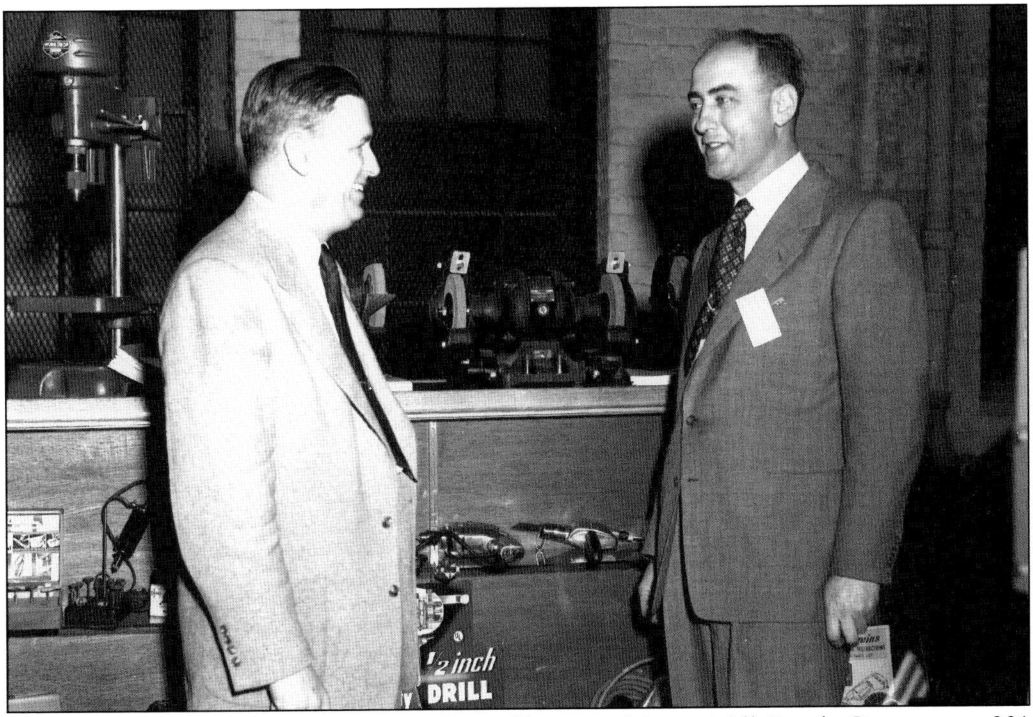

Martin Manaly (right) is shown at his place of business, Martin Mill Supply Company, at 201 Summer Street.

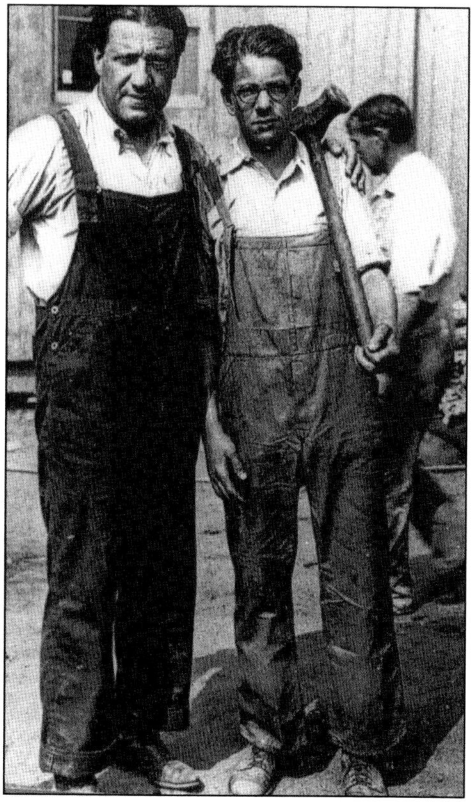

Rabbi Stephen S. Wise (left) and his son James Waterman Wise work at the Luders Shipyard in Stamford during World War I. To assist the war effort, they spent their summer vacation working at the shipyard.

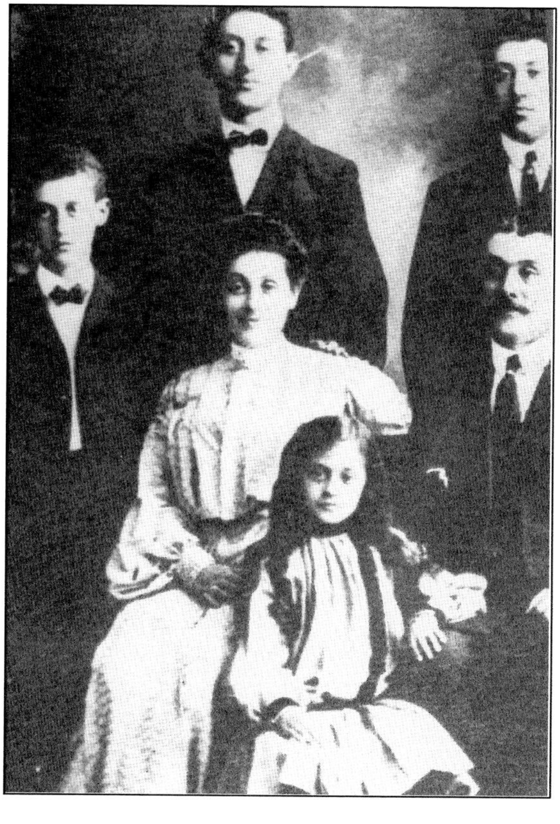

Shown are members of the Spelke family of Stamford in 1908. Counterclockwise from the front they are Mary, Sarah, Max, Morris, Abram, and Louis Spelke.

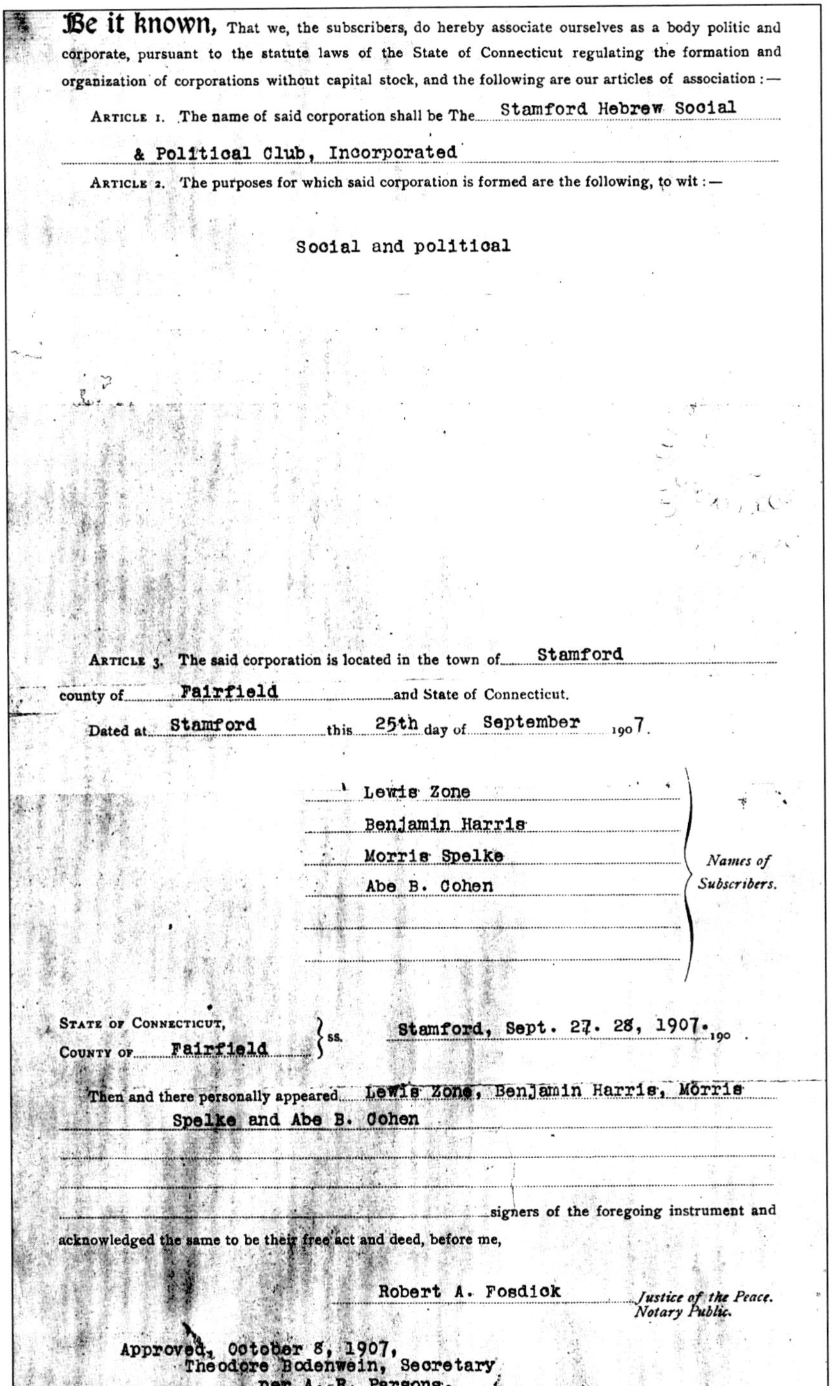

Be it known, That we, the subscribers, do hereby associate ourselves as a body politic and corporate, pursuant to the statute laws of the State of Connecticut regulating the formation and organization of corporations without capital stock, and the following are our articles of association: —

ARTICLE 1. The name of said corporation shall be The Stamford Hebrew Social & Political Club, Incorporated

ARTICLE 2. The purposes for which said corporation is formed are the following, to wit: —

Social and political

ARTICLE 3. The said corporation is located in the town of Stamford county of Fairfield and State of Connecticut.

Dated at Stamford this 25th day of September 1907.

Lewis Zone
Benjamin Harris
Morris Spelke
Abe B. Cohen
} *Names of Subscribers.*

STATE OF CONNECTICUT, COUNTY OF Fairfield } ss. Stamford, Sept. 27. 28, 1907.

Then and there personally appeared Lewis Zone, Benjamin Harris, Morris Spelke and Abe B. Cohen signers of the foregoing instrument and acknowledged the same to be their free act and deed, before me,

Robert A. Fosdick *Justice of the Peace. Notary Public.*

Approved, October 8, 1907,
Theodore Bodenwein, Secretary
per A. R. Parsons.

This 1907 document is the certificate of incorporation of the Stamford Hebrew Social and Political Club. Jewish political clubs were criticized for being too parochial by the Anti-defamation League of B'nai B'rith in 1915 and, by World War I, they had gone out of existence. The Stamford Group was thought to be a Republican Club. Morris Spelke was one of the original club incorporators.

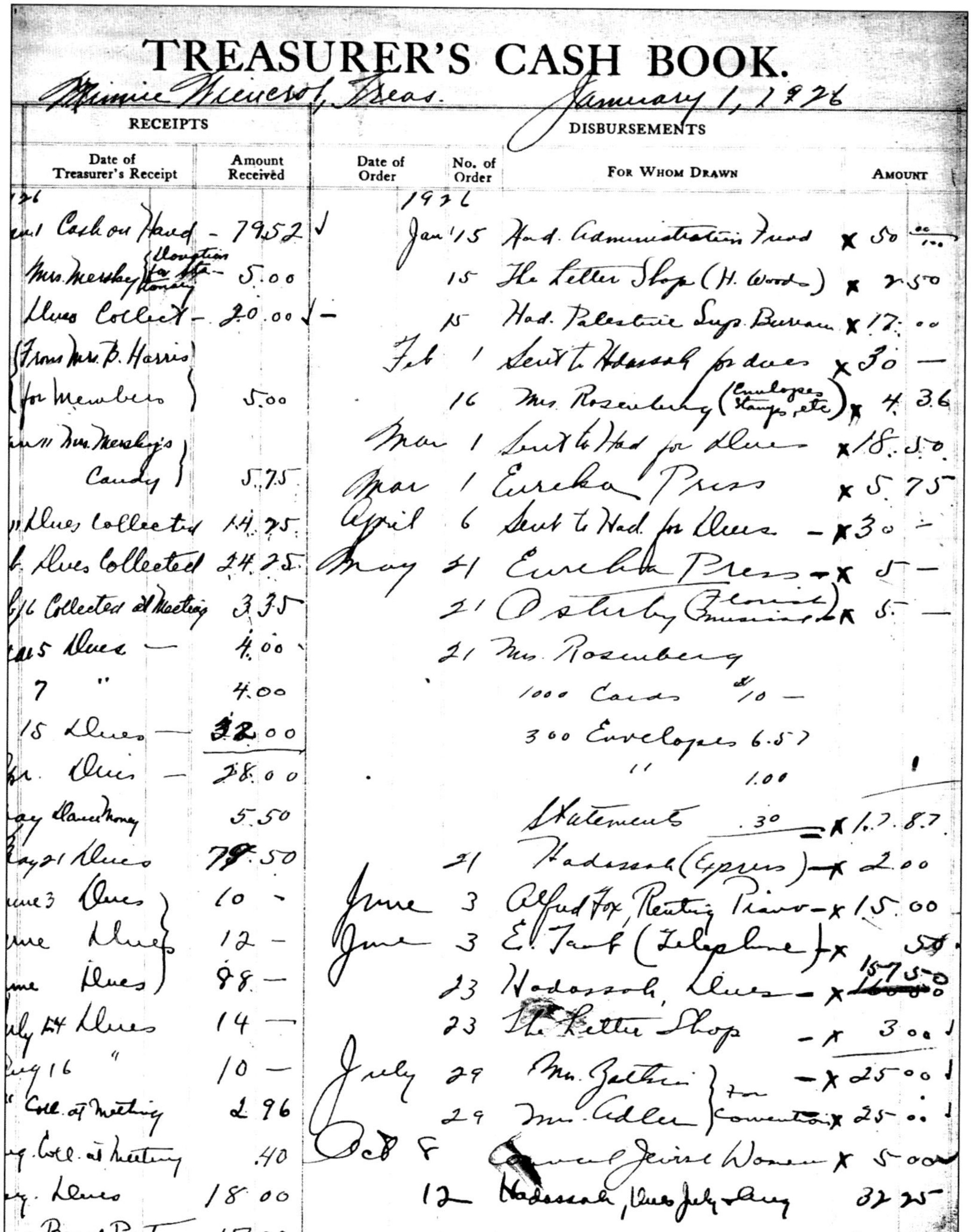

TREASURER'S CASH BOOK.

[illegible], Treas. January 1, 1926

RECEIPTS: Date of Treasurer's Receipt	Amount Received	DISBURSEMENTS: Date of Order	No. of Order	For Whom Drawn	Amount
[illegible]26		1926			
[illegible] Cash on Hand	79.52	Jan	15	Had. Administration Fund	50.00
Mrs. Mersky (Donation for [illegible] money)	5.00		15	The Letter Shop (H. Woods)	2.50
Dues Collect[illegible]	20.00		15	Had. Palestine Sup. Bureau	17.00
(From Mrs. B. Harris		Feb	1	Sent to Hadassah for dues	30 —
for Members)	5.00		16	Mrs. Rosenberg (Envelopes, Stamps, etc)	4.36
[illegible] Mrs. Mersky's		Mar	1	Sent to Had for Dues	18.50
Candy	5.75	Mar	1	Eureka Press	5.75
[illegible] Dues Collected	14.75	April	6	Sent to Had. for Dues	30 —
[illegible] Dues Collected	24.25	May	21	Eureka Press	5 —
[illegible]/16 Collected at Meeting	3.35		21	[illegible] (Florist)	5 —
[illegible]5 Dues	4.00		21	Mrs. Rosenberg	
7 "	4.00			1000 Cards $10 —	
15 Dues	32.00			300 Envelopes 6.57	
[illegible] Dues	28.00			" 1.00	
[illegible] Dance Money	5.50			Statements .30	17.87
May 21 Dues	79.50		21	Hadassah (Express)	2.00
June 3 Dues	10 —	June	3	Alfred Fox, Renting Piano	15.00
June Dues	12 —	June	3	E. [illegible] (Telephone)	.50
June Dues	8 —		23	Hadassah, Dues	157.50
July 4 Dues	14 —		23	The Letter Shop	3.00
Aug 16 "	10 —	July	29	Mrs. [illegible] for Convention	25.00
" Coll. at Meeting	2.96		29	Mrs. Adler	25.00
[illegible] Coll. at Meeting	.40	Oct	8	Council Jewish Women	5.00
[illegible] Dues	18.00		12	Hadassah, Dues July & Aug	32.25
[illegible] Bead Party	17.00				

This is a page from the treasurer's 1926 cashbook of the Stamford Branch of Hadassah.

Jewish communities have both a parochial and universal perspective. A branch of Hadassah, the Women's Zionist Organization is an integral part of Jewish communities. The Stamford branch of Hadassah was named for Gladys Zales.

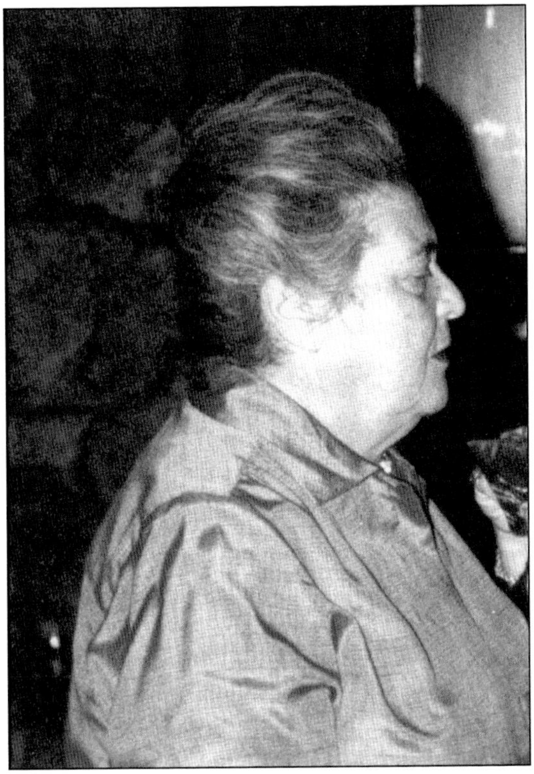

PRESIDENT'S MESSAGE:

On May 14, 1948 my relatives and their Zionist friends gathered at an uncle's home for a spontaneous celebration in honor of the creation of the State of Israel. It was a profoundly personal evening, bursting with tears, laughter, toasts, religious fervor, even dancing. Watching, I never dreamed that one day I would have a chance to express love and hope for this new land through social action in Hadassah.

I have never forgotten the mood of that evening, overshadowed as it was by a sense of foreboding. In the quarter-century that followed, Israelis have known a constant state of war or no-war, but never peace. Yet they have not just survived, but prevailed. They have made major contributions in bio-medicine, agriculture, social services and aerodynamics, to mention a few. And most importantly, they have, with our help, provided a homeland where crumbling Jewish communities around the world could prosper unpersecuted.

Perhaps in the next decade our children will gather with relatives and friends to celebrate the in-gathering of *all* oppressed Jews who wish to emigrate to Israel. We will rejoice in their new freedom. Will there be medical services, schools, rehabilitation for these newcomers? If we will it!

Ruth Zales

In 1972, Ruth Zales, daughter-in-law of Gladys Zales and president of the Greenwich Chapter of Hadassah, sent this message to her fellow members.

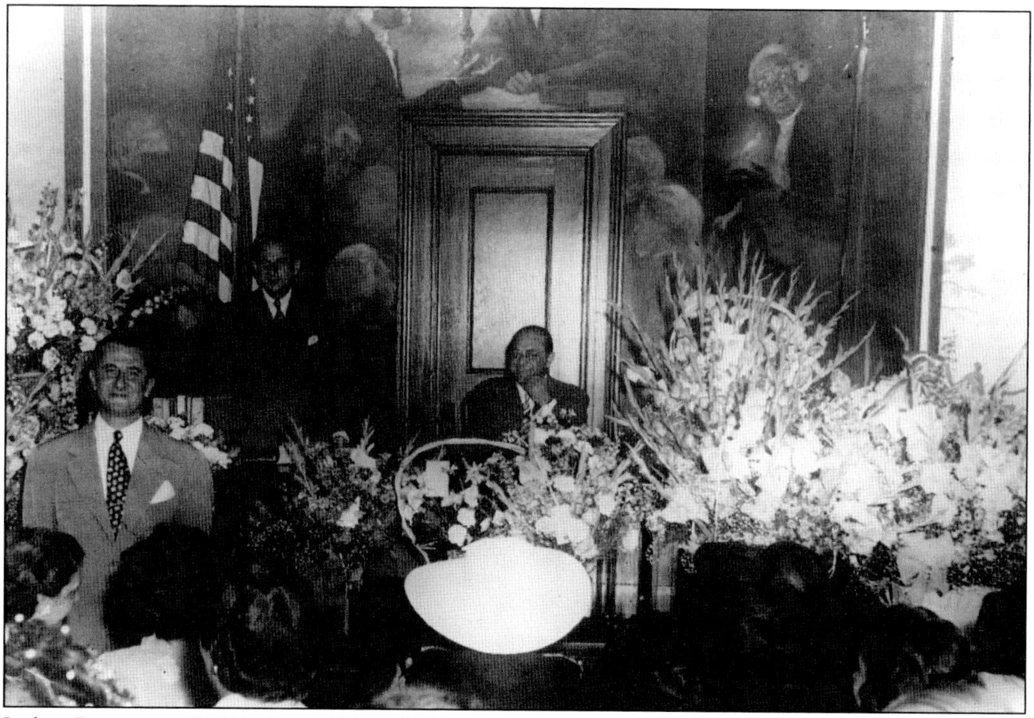

Judge Benjamin J. Weisberg (front left) stands at his installation in the old town hall in Stamford *c.* 1955.

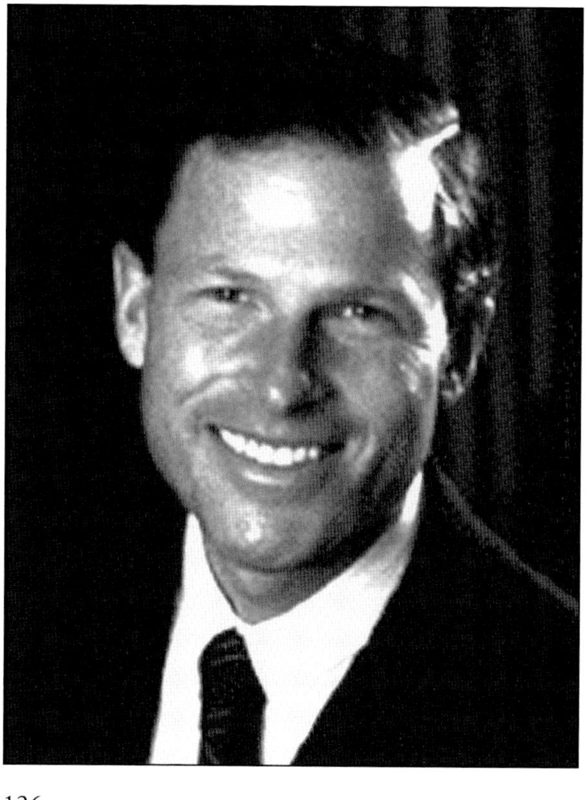

Connecticut Attorney General Richard Blumenthal lives in Greenwich with his wife, Cynthia, and their four children. Blumenthal is the 23rd attorney general of the state of Connecticut. He was elected to office in 1990 and reelected in 1994 and 1998.

Irwin Miller (left) accepts a contribution from Frances Brenner in 1987; with them is Morris Brenner (center). The gavel of the Hebrew Ladies Educational League became part of the collection at the archives of the Jewish Historical Society of Greater Stamford. The Hebrew Ladies Educational League was founded in 1906.

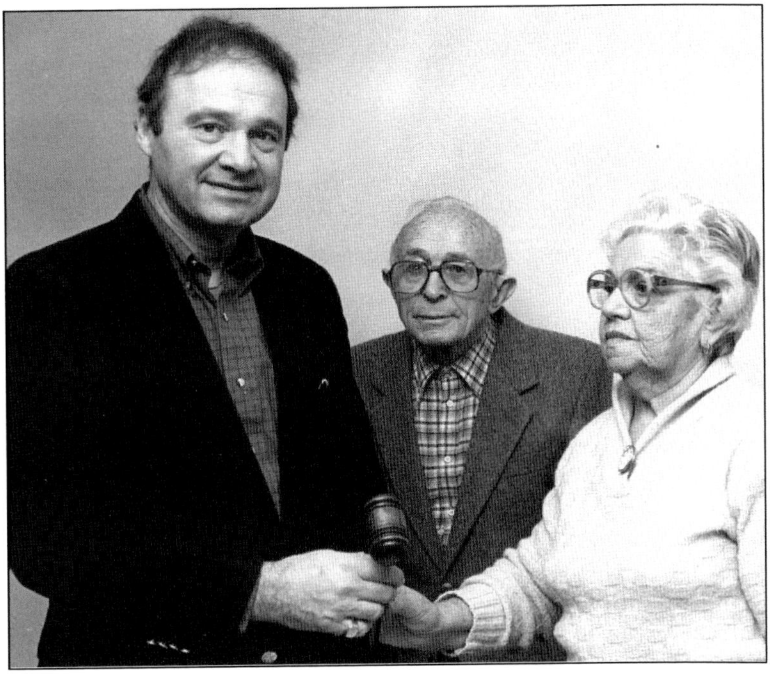

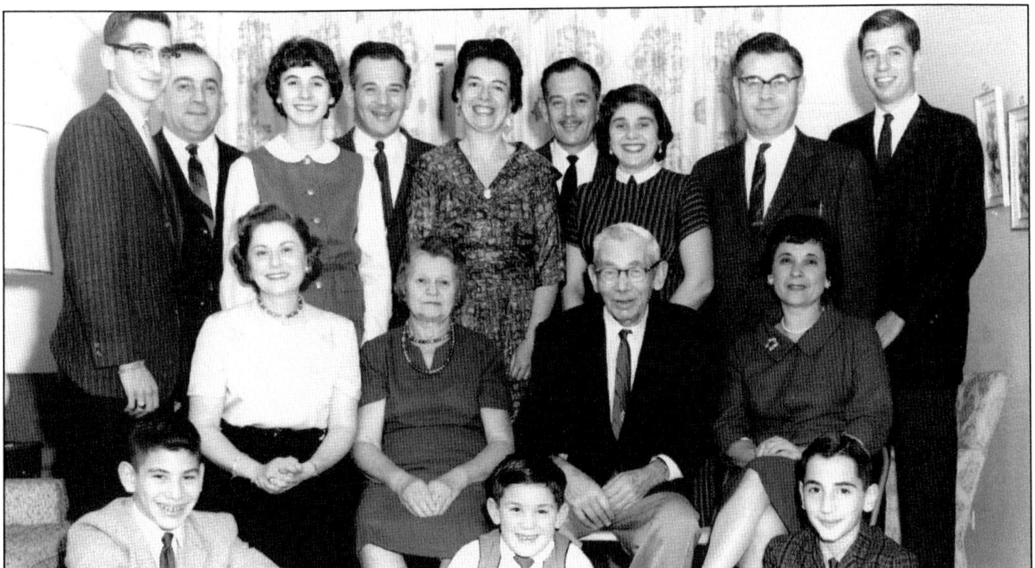

The Lang family is pictured in 1960. From left to right are the following: (front row) Ed, Richard, and Peter Strassberg; (middle row) Marjorie Strassberger, Elizabeth, Tony, and Ruth; (back row) Peter Strassberger, Jesse Strassberger, Sue, Fred, Ethel, Ira, Bernice, Josh, and Alan. Fred Lang was a national committeeman of the Jewish War Veterans. On May 12, 1965 he and his wife were given a private audience with His Holiness Pope Paul during a visit to the Vatican. The Pope said that the visit was a signal of friendship between peoples of all faiths. He expressed sympathy for Jewish people who do not have freedom and told of his hope for peace and justice throughout the world.

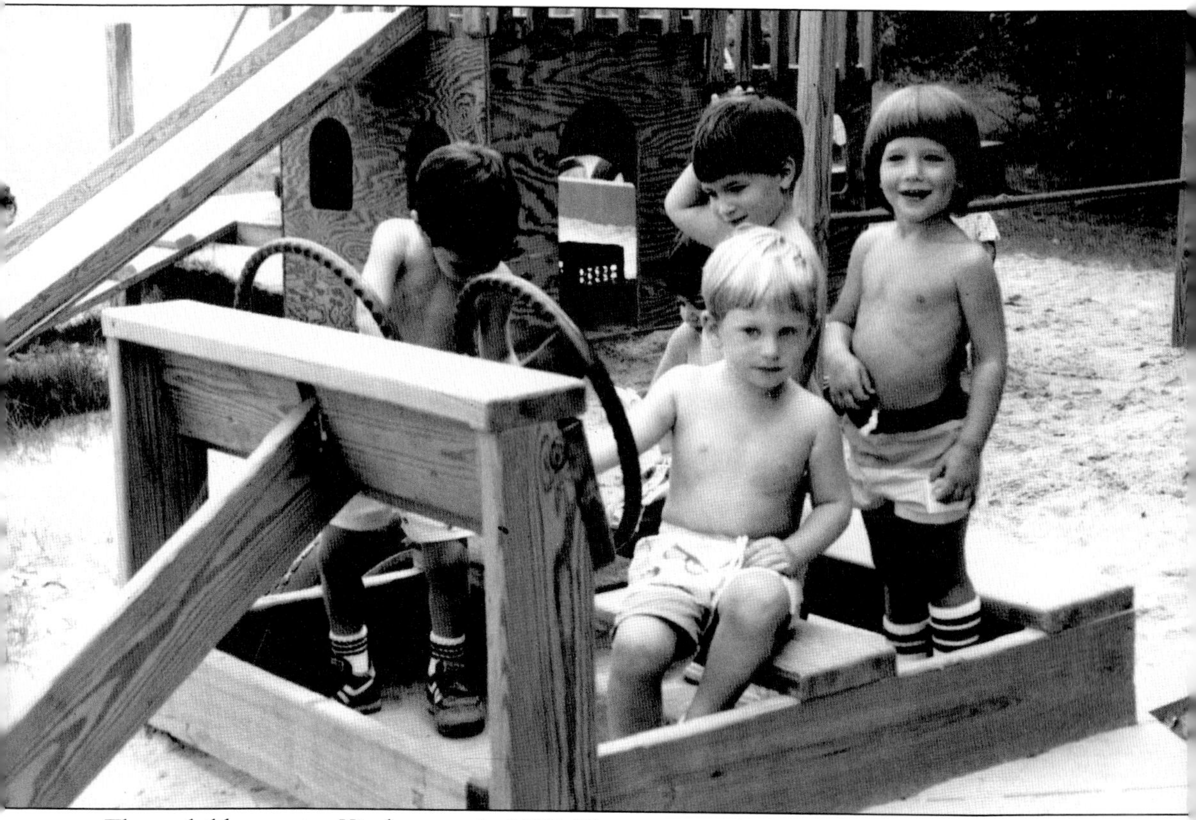

These children enjoy Kindercamp in 1988. The past is prologue; the children are the future in a world of righteousness and peace.